Global 2000:
Implications for Canada

This study was commissioned at the initiative of Environment
Canada and its publication sponsored by the Canadian
Association for the Club of Rome.

Other Pergamon Titles of Related Interest

Barney	The Global 2000 Report to the President of the U.S. — Volume II: The Technical Report
Barney	The Global 2000 Report to the President of the U.S. — Volume III: The Government's Global Model
Chou & Harmon, Jr.	Critical Food Issues of the Eighties
Dolman	Global Planning and Resource Management
Godet	The Crisis in Forecasting and the Emergence of the "Prospective" Approach
Stewart	Transitional Energy Policy: 1980-2030

Club of Rome Reports

Botkin et al.	No Limits to Learning
de Montbrial	Energy: The Countdown
Gabor et al.	Beyond the Age of Waste 2nd edition
Giarini	Dialogue of Health and Welfare
Hawrylyshyn	Road Maps to the Future
Laszlo & Bierman	Goals in a Global Community
Peccei	The Human Quality
Peccei	One Hundred Pages for the Future (IP)

Related Pergamon Journals

Conservation & Recycling
Futuribles
Materials and Society
Regional Studies
Socio-Economic Planning Sciences
Technology in Society
World Development

Global 2000:

Implications for Canada

By
G.O. Barney
P.H. Freeman
C.A. Ulinski

Gerald O. Barney and Associates, Inc.
1730 North Lynn Street
Suite 400
Arlington, VA 22209
U.S.A.

Pergamon Press
Toronto • Oxford • New York • Sydney • Paris • Frankfurt

Pergamon Press Offices:

Canada	Pergamon Press Canada Ltd., Suite 104, 150 Consumers Road, Willowdale, Ontario, Canada M2J 1P9
U.K.	Pergamon Press Ltd., Headington Hill Hall, Oxford, OX3 0BW, England
U.S.A.	Pergamon Press Inc., Maxwell House, Fairview Park, Elmsford, New York 10523, U.S.A.
Australia	Pergamon Press (Aust.) Pty. Ltd., P.O. Box 544, Potts Point, N.S.W. 2011, Australia
France	Pergamon Press SARL, 24 rue des Ecoles, 75240 Paris, Cedex 05, France
Federal Republic of Germany	Pergamon Press GmbH, Hammerweg 6, 6242 Kronberg-Taunus, Federal Republic of Germany

Canadian Cataloguing in Publication Data
Barney, Gerald O.
   Global 2000: Implications for Canada
Bibliography: p.
Includes index.
ISBN 0-08-025390-3 (bound). — ISBN 0-08-025389-X (pbk.)

1. Global 2000 Study (U.S.)   2. Environmental policy — Canada.   3. Natural resources — Canada.   4. Food supply — Canada.   5. Twenty-first century — Forecasts. 6. Twentieth century — Forecasts.   7. Economic forecasting — Canada.   8. Canada — Economic conditions — 1971 -   I. Freeman, P.H.   II. Ulinski, C.A.   III. Title.
HC120.E5B37   333.7   C81-095044-8

Typesetting by EGR Graphics Ltd., Toronto, Ontario, Canada

Printed and Bound in Canada

Contents

v

Appendices

Tables

Figures

Preface

In the past few years, Canadians have been thinking increasingly about their place and progress in the world. There have been conferences, reports and meetings on a wide range of futures oriented topics, such as the Canadian Conference on Global Modelling held in Ottawa in 1978 and the first Global Conference on the Future held in Toronto in 1980 on the theme of "Thinking Globally — Acting Locally." Canadian Government agencies have developed studies on trends in forestry, food production, population growth, economic activity, to name but only a few.

Growing Canadian interests in future developments stem from the realization that Canada, though richly endowed with wealth and natural resources, is set in a world that is faced with some enormous problems, such as global resource depletion, population growth and economic disparities that manifest themselves in poverty, inequity and injustice, social turmoil and widespread conflict. Canadian interest in the future also stems from a better understanding of how policy and technological decisions that are made today affect lives and conditions tomorrow. A full appreciation of the issues and opportunities ahead will require a more comprehensive perspective than has characterized planning in the past.

This report continues the Canadian consideration of these issues, in this case through an initial examination of the picture as seen from outside of Canada. The assessments presented in this document rely primarily upon *The Global 2000 Report to the President,* published in the United States in mid-1980.

The *Global 2000 Report* was prepared at the request of President Carter, who directed the Council on Environmental Quality and the Department of State to study the "probable changes in the world's population, natural resources and environment through the end of the century," in order to serve as "the foundation of longer term planning."

The study took some three years and approximately $1 million to complete. Fourteen U.S. Government agencies — ranging from the Department of Agriculture to the Central Intelligence Agency — participated in assembling the base data and in providing the projections that appear in this three-volume, 1,200 page report. It is a professional and technical report rather than a political one. So far, French, Spanish, German and Japanese translations have appeared.

The examination, in this study, of the *Global 2000 Report* and its implications for Canada has several purposes. First, the review provides Canadians with a summary overview of the thinking of some of the professional people in the United States. The Report displays their assumptions and projections for Canadian resources and the Canadian economy and compares these with such Canadian data and projections as are readily available. The Report provides a first glimpse of issues in a global context to which Canadians may wish to give further consideration.

Secondly, the Report is regarded as the first step in a process that is designed to focus closer attention upon the complex interlinkages in our socioeconomic system. Any attempt to clarify the issues and to display their intricate interactions should provide a better base for well informed public discussion of the nature of world problems and their relevance to day-to-day decisions in Canada. The material presented should enable Canadians to focus their attention upon the issues that have been identified and which clearly require some conscious and deliberate review and possibly some concrete policy or action.

The substance of the message is that Canada, with its rich resource endowment, faces a relatively bright future in a world that may become subject to some serious calamities. While Canada's resources appear to be fully adequate for her own needs, in a global context the supplies are merely a drop in the ocean. In these circumstances Canada will become subject to progressively increasing pressures for the development of her resources to meet external demands, whereas longer term national interest may suggest somewhat different, possibly more restrained resource development plans.

The report discussing Canada has been prepared by Dr. Gerald O. Barney and Associates, Inc., the same firm retained by the U.S. Government to manage and direct the preparation of *The Global 2000 Report to the President.* The study was commissioned at the initiative of Environment Canada with financial contributions from Agriculture Canada, the Canadian International Development Agency (CIDA), the Department of Industry, Trade and Commerce and Statistics Canada. It is, however, a report to the Canadian Government, and not a Canadian Government report. The views presented in this study are the authors' interpretations of a U.S. assessment of the future and its implications for Canada. Its findings and conclusions are thoughts generated by outside observers — with the strengths and limitations inherent in such an effort, but with ideas that Canadians may find useful. Some preliminary comments, observations and criticisms are included in the report in order to illustrate that many of the statements and conclusions appear contentious.

It is to be emphasized therefore that the purpose of this report is merely to provide a starting point for further dialogue and for action. Its contents or indeed overall conclusions are neither defended nor rejected. The simple intent of this initiative is merely to generate the professional groundwork which can focus attention upon the complexity of the strategic implications of any findings. Thus, a better informed dialogue can develop, leading to better policy development, appropriate action plans and indeed concrete recommendations. Since the issues discussed clearly reveal that no individual, no region or interest group, no country can remain isolated in our highly interdependent world, the starting material presented here, together with its progressive improvement and refinement, should provide the basis for better dialogue and interaction among all concerned and thus to true progress and socioeconomic development.

If this relatively modest initiative can be nurtured from its fragile start to a more robust exercise that encompasses both local and global interests, then the effort will prove to have been well worthwhile. The study is intended to provide a better basis for the consideration of a wide range of concrete issues such as Canada's resource management policies in a global context where food, energy, wood and forest product developments, to name only a few, may be forced upon the country from the outside, unless some firm guidelines are decided upon internally. The orientation of the structure of the economy, of the direction of capital formation and investment, of immigration policies, of social services and taxation, etc., all depend heavily upon the conditions that are discussed in this study.

The Report now provides perhaps no more than a broad guide to the issues of possible concern. However, it does constitute an invitation to all concerned to contribute their skills and expertise, to help improve, refine and develop our knowledge base and thus provide some concrete and practical support to policy development and to national and international dialogues and actions.

Canadian Association
for the Club of Rome

Introduction

The Canadian Association for the Club of Rome is privileged to sponsor the publication of *Global 2000: Implications for Canada*. The study in its entirety focuses on issues and policy implications vital to Canada's future and central to the concerns of the Association.

The Club of Rome grew out of an initiative of Dr. Aurelio Peccei which, in 1968, brought together in a Rome meeting a group of distinguished businessmen, officials and academics sharing a concern for the future well-being of a world threatened by global-scale problems of resources, environment, and population. Out of that meeting grew a program of activities which has had major impact on understandings and attitudes of men and women around the globe, as well as on our governments and our institutions.

The Canadian Association for the Club of Rome was formed in 1973. Like the Club of Rome itself, its membership includes some one hundred persons who share a keen concern for the ecological, resource and population future of this world and for sustainable economic growth. To that end, the Association has provided forums for interchange and dialogue through conferences and through dissemination of literature.

For the Canadian Association for the Club of Rome, a central focus has been always the special circumstances and resulting policy needs of Canada, well endowed as it is with space and resources (including large energy supply and food supply potentials). The present work addresses itself directly to such questions. It provides the basis for reasoned and balanced assessment of Canada's role in a world which may be increasingly constrained by population pressures, food and energy limitations, and an overstressed environment. In sponsoring its publication, the Association is carrying forward its own task.

Generous contributions from the following have enabled the Association to accept the responsibility for the publication of this report:

The Alberta Gas Trunk Line Company Ltd.
Dofasco Inc.
Domtar Inc.
The Royal Bank of Canada
The Seagram Co.
Thorne Riddell & Co.
Canadian Pacific Ltd.

Ronald S. Ritchie
Member, Club of Rome
Chairman, Canadian Association
for the Club of Rome

xiii

Executive Summary

Global 2000: Implications for Canada

There has been increasing concern in Canada about global resource depletion, population growth and economic disparities that bring in their wake grave social problems of poverty, unrest and conflict.

Due to similar concern, a study was developed in the United States in response to a Directive by President Carter to assess the "probable changes in the world's population, natural resources and environment through the end of the century," which could serve as "the foundation for longer term planning." The *Global 2000 Report to the President* took three years to complete, cost $1 million and was published in the United States in mid-1980. Since that time initiatives have been taken here in Canada to assess the implications for Canada of the findings in the Global 2000 Report.

Global 2000: Implications for Canada has now been prepared by Dr. Gerald O. Barney and Associates (the same firm that prepared the Global 2000 Report to the President). The document summarizes the major findings of the U.S. report and presents a view from the outside of Canada and its future in light of the U.S. report. Additional insight is provided by a comparison of the findings of certain Canadian studies with the projections of the *Global 2000 Report*.

Appendices include a Bibliography (with some annotation) of Canadian Studies of Canadian and World Futures; an Overview of Canadian Policy Models; and U.S. Models of Potential Interest to Canada.

The Global 2000 Report to the President

The *Global 2000 Report* is of interest to Canada because it provides a useful background to the thinking of professional people in the United States; it displays U.S. Government assumptions and projections on the economy of the world and on resources; it sets forth the major global issues of this and the next decade; and it focuses attention on the complex interdependencies in our global socioeconomic system.

The *Global 2000 Report* is generally more comprehensive than other global models insofar as it contains more details on sectors such as food and agriculture, forests, water, energy, etc. However, the linkages among the sectors are not as complete as in other models and this tends to give the *Global 2000 Report* an optimistic bias.

Principal Findings of the Global 2000 Report to the President

- Rapid world population growth will continue, mostly in the poorest countries. GNP per capita will remain low in most less-developed countries (LDCs) and the gap between rich and poor nations will widen.

- World food production will increase 90 percent from 1970 to 2000, but the bulk of the increase will go to countries with already high per capita food consumption. Real food prices will double.

xv

- Arable land will increase only 4 percent by 2000, and most of the increased food output will have to be from higher yields, which will mean increasingly heavy dependence on oil.

- World oil production will reach maximum estimated capacity, even with rapidly increasing prices. Many LDCs will have difficulties meeting energy needs. Fuel-wood demands will exceed supplies by 25 percent.

- Mineral resources will meet projected demands, but production costs will increase and the 25 percent of world population in industrial countries will continue to absorb 75 percent of world mineral production.

- Regional water shortages will become more severe. Population growth alone will double water requirements in nearly half the world and deforestation in many LDCs will make water supplies increasingly erratic.

- There will be significant losses of world forests as demand for forest products increases. Growing stocks of commercial-size timber are projected to decline 50 percent per capita. By 2000, 40 percent of the remaining forest cover in LDCs will be gone.

- There will be serious world-wide deterioration of agricultural soils. The spread of desert-like conditions is likely to accelerate.

- Atmospheric concentrations of carbon dioxide and ozone-depleting chemicals will increase at rates that could alter the world's climate and upper atmosphere significantly by 2050. Acid rain will continue to damage lakes, soils and crops.

- Extinction of plant and animal species will increase dramatically and 20 percent of all species on earth may be irretrievably lost as their habitats vanish, especially in tropical forests.

Thus, the *Global 2000 Report* concludes that vigorous, determined, new initiatives are needed if worsening poverty and human suffering, environmental degradation and international tension and conflicts are to be prevented. There are no quick fixes. The only solutions to the problems of population, resources and environment are complex and long-term. *These problems are inextricably linked to some of the most perplexing and persistent problems in the world — poverty, injustice and social conflict.* An era of unprecedented cooperation and commitment is essential. *The available evidence leaves no doubt that the world faces enormous, urgent and complex problems in the decades immediately ahead. Prompt and vigorous changes in public policy around the world are needed now.* Long lead times are required for effective action.

The Canadian Future: A View from the Outside

The analysis of the implications for Canada of the findings in the *Global 2000 Report* suggests that in the midst of gloomy global developments, Canada can be expected to face a relatively bright future: its resources are evidently ample to meet the needs of a population even in excess of 30 million, although it is to be realized that in comparison to global demands, the supplies are totally inadequate. Nevertheless *it is apparent that there will be increasing pressures upon Canada for ever greater supplies to the rest of the world of basic resources, such as food, energy, forest products, minerals, which in turn will place increasing stress upon land, air and water resources in the country.* In these circumstances *there is evident need for concerted attention to the wise use of resources in Canada that will ensure that the exploitation of natural wealth will be dictated by longer term national/global interests rather than short-term gains or political expedience.* Such prudence in the development and supply of resources to the rest of the world will inevitably demand some very hard choices and responsible stewardship as well as the careful protection of environmental resources and of sustainable resource yields.

Specifically, the *Global 2000: Implications for Canada* study concludes that relative to many other nations, Canada faces a promising future insofar as the nation has:

* a well-educated population and is not overpopulated.

* a large (albeit not wholly domestically owned) capital base and a high income and GNP per capita.

* abundant and relatively inexpensive food supplies.

* abundant and relatively stable forests.

* abundant mineral and energy resources to meet its own needs and is thus much less dependent on foreign energy supplies than many other nations.

* relatively few environmental problems compared with many other countries, even though there are severe problems with acid rain and some potentially difficult agricultural soil and water problems.

* is unlikely to be invaded or isolated from its largest trade partner.

* can expect increasing interest in its resources.

Notwithstanding these favourable conditions, Canada does face some vulnerabilities and comparative disadvantages:

* it is largely a resource exporting economy and therefore needs trading partners as a base for a strong economy.

* immigration pressures will increase.

* it may approach the limit of its grain export potential before the end of the century.

* it remains vulnerable to climatic changes.

* it may continue to experience some internal tensions that relate to resource development policies.

The biggest threat to Canada may be the disturbance of its economy because of dislocations in the global economy. As an open, resource exporting country, Canada is vulnerable to economic dislocations in the rest of the world that are likely to occur in the years ahead, e.g., balance of payments problems, protectionism, financial and other economic calamities. Also, a cooling of the world's climate (or even a few years of adverse weather in Canada) could seriously increase Canada's vulnerability to any economic disruptions taking place in other parts of the world.

Global economic problems resulting from population growth, resource (especially oil) depletion and environmental deterioration will thus be very large indeed over the coming decades. *Even with unprecedented cooperation among nations, it will be difficult for Canada to protect itself to any extent from excessive economic vulnerability while still playing a responsible role as a leading nation.*

- Among issues that already occupy Canadians are foreign ownership, the processing or manufacture of mineral commodities, dependence on foreign technology and capital, as well as pollution from U.S. sources.

- Canada seems weak in policies and resource management programs that ensure stable trade and continuing productivity of renewable resources, as well as value added by manufacture and processing.

- Canada's principal vulnerabilities as well as its principal opportunities lie in the primacy of its relationships with the United States. Some major potential developments are important for Canada to keep in mind. For example, the United States is becoming more interdependent with the rest of the world and therefore more vulnerable to world conditions in ways that could affect U.S.-Canadian relationships. The United States is committed to a hard path approach to energy, with coal development a problem for both countries.

- Canada would do well to broaden its trade (70 percent is with the United States) and to recognize that there could be continuing differences of perspective on energy, acid rain, water, fisheries and grain.

- The big trading opportunities for Canada are likely to be in the new industrializing countries — Brazil, Mexico, Indonesia, etc. Canada is also in a unique position to play an important role in world development. It is respected by the South as well as by the North and, like the LDCs, has pursued a foreign policy that emphasizes multilateral relations.

- It would be desirable for Canada, the United States and the rest of the world to have a clearer sense of how the North American food markets will operate in the future. The proposal for a Joint U.S.-Canadian Commission on Food Policy deserves further consideration.

- Resource-related internal tensions are likely to be easier to deal with now than they will be in 10 or 20 years since they will become more intense as time goes on. Canada also needs to plan how it will achieve balanced development of its energy resources, including oil, natural gas, coal, nuclear, solar and hydro power as well as biomass.

- Canada is second only to Japan in its dependence on a healthy world economy and active world trade. A major war, a disruption in the flow of Middle East oil or a serious disruption in the operation of the international monetary system would have a significant effect on this country.

- Canada is entering a unique moment in its history and is beginning to find itself in possession of considerable bargaining power. Actions need to be taken now to enable it to capitalize on its opportunities. There are a number of issues on which Canada might assemble and integrate studies. Many inconsistencies underlie the assumptions behind the *Global 2000 Report* which concluded by stating that the executive agencies of the U.S. Government "were not now capable of providing the President with internally consistent projections of world trends in population, resources and environment." In Canada, too, different agencies have been making different assumptions about growth rates, external demand, weather, fuel prices, capital availability, and so on.

• Many issues need to be addressed. Should Canada have an explicit population policy? How can Canada control its population? What vision does Canada have for the future cultural mix of her society? How will this affect her immigration policies? What role should Canada play regarding political refugees and future famine victims? What is the impact of immigration on housing? What are the implications of the increasing average age of the Canadian population? How can higher-than-average growth projected for the Canadian West be best managed? How can Canada's agricultural lands be protected from urban sprawl?

• Many benefits of Canadian resources are not accruing to Canadians. Canada may want to restructure its resource trade. Resource exportation is capital intensive and produces relatively few jobs.

• Are nuclear reactors, telecommunications and aeronautical manufacturing the technologies of the future? What technologies does Canada need in order to derive most benefit from its resources? What should be the Canadian criteria for selecting technologies?

• Climate presents a potential threat. Canada would be acutely affected by warming or cooling. What monitoring, educational and research steps could be undertaken now? How flexible is the response of Canadian producers to shifts in demand and weather changes? Should Canada actively encourage the development of an international food reserve system? Should possible increased climatic variability during the remainder of the century be taken into account in Canadian food and agriculture projections? What are the economic trade-offs of farmland losses to urban uses? What are the potential impacts of soil degradation?

• How can Canada build up stocks of oceanic species and maintain them at sustainable levels in the face of increasing demands on her fish from foreign countries? How can marine mammals, or their habitats, be managed so as to avoid costly conflicts between the fishermen and the mammals?

• Are policies in place to deal with accelerated demands for forest resources? What impact is acid rain having on forests? Have cost estimates been made on the protection of fragile Northern ecosystems?

• What are the impacts of irrigation and of energy development on water resources from hydropower development?

• How can Canada obtain maximum economic and social benefits from its energy resources?

• What will be the economic costs of environmental protection between now and 2000, and the ultimate costs of inadequate protection?

The objective of this Study concerning Canada is thus to provide a more comprehensive basis for consideration, in a global context, of a wide range of concrete issues.

Canada and Global Developments:
A View from the Outside

1. A Summary of The Global 2000 Report to the President

This report — *Global 2000: Implications for Canada* — finds its roots in a major U.S. Government study on currently observed trends in the world. The U.S. Study — *The Global 2000 Report to the President* — was undertaken at the direction of former President Carter. President Carter in 1977 wrote, " . . . I am directing the Council on Environmental Quality and the Department of State, working in cooperation with . . . other appropriate agencies, to make a . . . study of the probable changes in the world's population, natural resources, and environment through the end of the century. This study will serve as the foundation for our longer-term planning." This chapter presents an abridged text of volume 1 of the *Global 2000 Report to the President*. The discussion in this section makes only limited reference to Canada, but provides a global context for a review of the implications for Canada of the findings in the *Global 2000 Report*.

Major Findings and Conclusions

If present trends continue, the world in 2000 will be more crowded, more polluted, less stable ecologically, and more vulnerable to disruption than the world we live in now. Serious stresses involving population, resources, and environment are clearly visible ahead. Despite greater material output, the world's people will be poorer in many ways than they are today.

For hundreds of millions of the desperately poor, the outlook for food and other necessities of life will be no better. For many it will be worse. Barring revolutionary advances in technology, life for most people on earth will be more precarious in 2000 than it is now — unless the nations of the world act decisively to alter current trends.

This, in essence, is the picture emerging from the U.S. Government's projections of probable changes in world population, resources, and environment by the end of the century, as presented in the Global 2000 Study. They do not predict what will occur. Rather, they depict conditions that are likely to develop if there are no changes in public policies, institutions, or rates of technological advance, and if there are no wars or other major disruptions. A keener awareness of the nature of the current trends, however, may induce changes that will alter these trends and the projected outcome.

Principal Findings

Rapid growth in world population will hardly have altered by 2000. The world's population will grow from 4 billion in 1975 to 6.35 billion in 2000, an increase of more than 50 percent. The rate of growth will slow only marginally, from 1.8 percent a year to 1.7 percent. In terms of sheer numbers, population will be growing faster in 2000 than it is today, with 100 million people added each year compared with 75 million in 1975. Ninety percent of this growth will occur in the poorest countries.

While the economies of the less developed countries (LDCs) are expected to grow at faster rates than those of the industrialized nations, the gross national product per

3

capita in most LDCs remains low. The average gross national product per capita is projected to rise substantially in some LDCs (especially in Latin America), but in the great populous nations of South Asia it remains below $200 a year (in 1975 dollars). The large existing gap between the rich and poor nations widens.

World food production is projected to increase 90 percent over the 30 years from 1970 to 2000. This translates into a global per capita increase of less than 15 percent over the same period. The bulk of that increase goes to countries that already have relatively high per capita food consumption. Meanwhile per capita consumption in South Asia, the Middle East, and the LDCs of Africa will scarcely improve or will actually decline below present inadequate levels. At the same time, real prices for food are expected to double.

Arable land will increase only 4 percent by 2000, so that most of the increased output of food will have to come from higher yields. Most of the elements that now contribute to higher yields — fertilizer, pesticides, power for irrigation, and fuel for machinery — depend heavily on oil and gas.

During the 1990s world oil production will approach geological estimates of maximum production capacity, even with rapidly increasing petroleum prices. The Study projects that the richer industrialized nations will be able to command enough oil and other commercial energy supplies to meet rising demands through 1990. With the expected price increases, many LDCs will have increasing difficulties meeting energy needs. For the one-quarter of humankind that depends primarily on wood for fuel, the outlook is bleak. Needs for fuelwood will exceed available supplies by about 25 percent before the turn of the century.

While the world's finite fuel resources — coal, oil, gas, oil shale, tar sands, and uranium — are theoretically sufficient for centuries, they are not evenly distributed; they pose difficult economic and environmental problems; and they vary greatly in their amenability to exploitation and use.

Nonfuel mineral resources generally appear sufficient to meet projected demands through 2000, but further discoveries and investments will be needed to maintain reserves. In addition, production costs will increase with energy prices and may make some nonfuel mineral resources uneconomic. The quarter of the world's population that inhabits industrial countries will continue to absorb three-fourths of the world's mineral production.

Regional water shortages will become more severe. In the 1970-2000 period population growth alone will cause requirements for water to double in nearly half the world. Still greater increases would be needed to improve standards of living. In many LDCs, water supplies will become increasingly erratic by 2000 as a result of extensive deforestation. Development of new water supplies will become more costly virtually everywhere.

Significant losses of world forests will continue over the next 20 years as demand for forest products and fuelwood increases. Growing stocks of commercial-size timber are projected to decline 50 percent per capita. The world's forests are now disappearing at the rate of 18-20 million hectares a year (an area half the size of California), with most of the loss occurring in the humid tropical forests of Africa, Asia, and South America. The projections indicate that by 2000 some 40 percent of the remaining forest cover in LDCs will be gone.

Serious deterioration of agricultural soils will occur worldwide, due to erosion, loss of organic matter, desertification, salinization, alkalinization, and waterlogging.

Already, an area of cropland and grassland approximately the size of Maine is becoming barren wasteland each year, and the spread of desert-like conditions is likely to accelerate.

Atmospheric concentrations of carbon dioxide and ozone-depleting chemicals are expected to increase at rates that could alter the world's climate and upper atmosphere significantly by 2050. Acid rain from increased combustion of fossil fuels (especially coal) threatens damage to lakes, soils, and crops. Radioactive and other hazardous materials present health and safety problems in increasing numbers of countries.

Extinctions of plant and animal species will increase dramatically. Hundreds of thousands of species — perhaps as many as 20 percent of all species on earth — will be irretrievably lost as their habitats vanish, especially in tropical forests.

The future depicted by the U.S. Government projections, briefly outlined above, may actually understate the impending problems. The methods available for carrying out the Study led to certain gaps and inconsistencies that tend to impart an optimistic bias. For example, most of the individual projections for the various sectors studied — food, minerals, energy, and so on — assume that sufficient capital, energy, water, and land will be available in each of these sectors to meet their needs, regardless of the competing needs of the other sectors. More consistent, better integrated projections would produce a still more emphatic picture of intensifying stresses, as the world enters the twenty-first century.

Conclusions

At present and projected growth rates, the world's population would reach 10 billion by 2030 and would approach 30 billion by the end of the twenty-first century. These levels correspond closely to estimates by the U.S. National Academy of Sciences of the maximum carrying capacity of the entire earth. Already the populations in sub-Saharan Africa and in the Himalayan hills of Asia have exceeded the carrying capacity of the immediate area, triggering an erosion of the land's capacity to support life. The resulting poverty and ill health have further complicated efforts to reduce fertility. Unless this circle of interlinked problems is broken soon, population growth in such areas will unfortunately be slowed for reasons other than declining birth rates. Hunger and disease will claim more babies and young children, and more of those surviving will be mentally and physically handicapped by childhood malnutrition.

Indeed, the problems of preserving the carrying capacity of the earth and sustaining the possibility of a decent life for the human beings that inhabit it are enormous and close upon us. Yet there is reason for hope. It must be emphasized that the Global 2000 Study's projections are based on the assumption that national policies regarding population stabilization, resource conservation, and environmental protection will remain essentially unchanged through the end of the century. But in fact, policies are beginning to change. In some areas, forests are being replanted after cutting. Some nations are taking steps to reduce soil losses and desertification. Interest in energy conservation is growing, and large sums are being invested in exploring alternatives to petroleum dependence. The need for family planning is slowly becoming better understood. Water supplies are being improved and waste treatment systems built. High-yield seeds are widely available and seed banks are being expanded. Some wildlands with their genetic resources are being protected. Natural predators and selective pesticides are being substituted for persistent and destructive pesticides.

Encouraging as these developments are, they are far from adequate to meet the global challenges projected in this Study. Vigorous, determined new initiatives are needed if worsening poverty and human suffering, environmental degradation, and international tension and conflicts are to be prevented. There are no quick fixes. The only solutions to the problems of population, resources, and environment are complex and long-term. These problems are inextricably linked to some of the most perplexing and persistent problems in the world — poverty, injustice, and social conflict. New and imaginative ideas — and a willingness to act on them — are essential.

The needed changes go far beyond the capability and responsibility of the United States or any other single nation. An era of unprecedented cooperation and commitment is essential. A high priority for all nations must be a thorough assessment of policies relating to population, resources, and environment. *The Global 2000 Report to the President* recognizes that the United States, possessing the world's largest economy, can expect its policies to have a significant influence on global trends. An equally important priority identified for the United States is to cooperate generously and justly with other nations — particularly in the areas of trade, investment, and assistance — in seeking solutions to the many problems that extend beyond national boundaries. There are many unfulfilled opportunities for the United States to cooperate with other nations in efforts to relieve poverty and hunger, stabilize population, and enhance economic and environmental productivity. Further cooperation among other nations is also needed to strengthen international mechanisms for protecting and utilizing the "global commons" — the oceans and atmosphere.

To meet the challenges described in the Study, the United States is urged to improve its ability to identify emerging problems and assess alternative responses. In using and evaluating the U.S. Government's present capability for long-term global analysis, the Study found serious inconsistencies in the methods and assumptions employed by the various agencies in making their projections. The Global 2000 Study itself made a start toward resolving these inadequacies. It represents the U.S. Government's first attempt to produce an interrelated set of population, resource, and environmental projections, and it has brought forth the most consistent set of global projections yet achieved by U.S. agencies. Nevertheless, the projections still contain serious gaps and contradictions that must be corrected if the U.S. Government's analytic capability is to be improved. It is suggested in the Report that at present the Federal agencies are not always capable of providing projections of the quality needed for long-term policy decisions.

While limited resources may be a contributing factor in some instances, the primary problem is lack of coordination. The U.S. Government is said to need a mechanism for a continuous review of the assumptions and methods that the Federal agencies use in their projection models and for assurance that the agencies' models are sound, consistent, and well documented. The improved analyses that could result would provide not only a clearer sense of emerging problems and opportunities, but also a better means for evaluating alternative responses, and a better basis for decisions of worldwide significance.

With its limitations and rough approximations, the Global 2000 Study may be seen as no more than a reconnaissance of the future; nonetheless its conclusions are reinforced by similar findings of other recent global studies that were examined in the course of the Global 2000 Study (see p. 34). All these studies are in general agreement on the nature of the problems and on the threats they pose to the future welfare of humankind. The available evidence leaves no doubt that the world faces enormous, urgent, and complex problems in the decades immediately ahead. Prompt and vigorous changes in public policy around the world are needed to avoid or minimize these problems before they become unmanageable. Long lead times are required for effective action. If decisions are delayed until the problems become worse, options for effective action will be severely reduced.

The U.S. Global 2000 Study in Brief

The President's directive establishing the Global 2000 Study called for a "study of the probable changes in the world's population, natural resources, and environment through the end of the century" and indicated that the Study as a whole was to "serve as the foundation of our longer-term planning." The findings of the Study identify problems to which world attention must be directed. But because all study reports eventually become dated and less useful, the Study's findings alone cannot provide the foundation called for in the directive. The necessary foundation for longer term planning lies not in study findings per se, but in the U.S. Government's continuing institutional capabilities — skilled personnel, data, and analytical models — for developing studies and analyses. Therefore, to meet the objectives stated in the President's directive, the Global 2000 Study was designed not only to assess probable changes in the world's population, natural resources, and environment, but also, through the study process itself, to identify and strengthen the U.S. Government's capability for longer term planning and analysis.

Building the Study

The process chosen for the Global 2000 Study was to develop trend projections using, to the fullest extent possible, the long-term global data and models routinely employed by U.S. Federal agencies. The process also included a detailed analysis of the Government's global modeling capabilities as well as a comparison of the Government's findings with those of other global analyses.

Currently, the principal limitation in the Government's long-term global analytical capability is that the models for various sectors were not designed to be used together in a consistent and interactive manner. With the Government's current models, the individual sectors addressed in the Global 2000 Study could be interrelated only by developing projections sequentially, that is, by using the results of some of the projections as inputs to others.

The Global 2000 Study developed its projections in a way that furthered interactions, improved internal consistency, and generally strengthened the Government's global models. However, the effort to harmonize and integrate the Study's projections was only partially successful. Many internal contradictions and inconsistencies could not be resolved. Inconsistencies arose immediately from the fact that sequential projections are not as interactive as events in the real world, or as projections that could be achieved in an improved model.

Difficulties also arise from multiple allocation of resources. Most of the quantitative projections simply assume that resource needs in the sector they cover — needs for capital, energy, land, water, minerals — will be met. Since the needs for each sector are not clearly identified, they cannot be summed up and compared with estimates of what might be available. It is very likely that the same resources have been allocated to more than one sector.

Equally significant, some of the Study's resource projections implicitly assume that the goods and services provided in the past by the earth's land, air, and water will continue to be available in larger and larger amounts, with no maintenance problems and no increase in costs. The Global 2000 Study projections for the environment cast serious doubt on these assumptions.

Collectively, the inconsistencies and missing linkages that are unavoidable with the Government's current global models affect the Global 2000 projections in many ways. Analysis of the assumptions underlying the projections and comparisons with other global projections suggest that most of the Study's quantitative results understate the severity of potential problems the world will face as it prepares to enter the twenty-first century.

The question naturally arises as to whether circumstances have changed significantly since the earliest projections were made in 1977. The answer is no. What changes have occurred generally support the projections and highlight the problems identified. The brief summaries of the projections (beginning below) each conclude with comments on how the projections might be altered if redeveloped today.

The Global 2000 Study has three major underlying assumptions. First, the projections assume a general continuation around the world of present public policy relating to population stabilization, natural resource conservation, and environmental protection. The projections thus point to what is expected if policies continue without significant changes.

The second major assumption relates to the effects of technological developments and of the market mechanism. The Study assumes that rapid rates of technological development and adoption will continue, and that the rate of development will be spurred on by efforts to deal with problems identified by this Study. The projections all assume that price, operating through the market mechanism, will reduce demand whenever supply constraints are encountered.

Third, the Study assumes that there will be no major disruptions of international trade as a result of war, disturbance of the international monetary system, or political disruption. The findings of the Study do, however, point to increasing potential for international conflict and increasing stress on international financial arrangements. Should wars or a significant disturbance of the international monetary system occur, the projected trends would be altered in unpredictable ways.

Because of the limitations outlined above, the Global 2000 Study is not the definitive study of future population, resource, and environment conditions. Nor is it intended to be a prediction. The Study does provide the most internally consistent and interrelated set of global projections available so far from the U.S. Government. Furthermore, its major findings are supported by a variety of nongovernmental global studies based on more highly interactive models that project similar trends through the year 2000 or beyond.

Population and Income

Population and income projections provided the starting point for the Study. These projections were used wherever possible in the resource projections to estimate demand.

Population

One of the most important findings of the Global 2000 Study is that enormous growth in the world's population will occur by 2000 under any of the wide range of assumptions considered in the Study. The world's population increases 55 percent from 4.1 billion people in 1975 to 6.35 billion by 2000, under the Study's medium-growth projections.* While there is some uncertainty in these numbers, even the lowest-growth population projection shows a 46 percent increase — to 5.9 billion people by the end of the century. A population of around 6 billion is a virtual certainty for 2000 even if fertility rates were somehow to drop quickly to replacement levels (assuming there are no disastrous wars, famine, or pestilence).

Another important finding is that the rapid growth of the world's population will not slow appreciably. The rate of growth per year in 1975 was 1.8 percent; the projected rate for 2000 is 1.7 percent. Even under the lowest growth projected, the number of persons being added annually to the world's population will be significantly greater in 2000 than today.

Most of the population growth (92 percent) will occur in the less developed countries (LDCs) rather than in the industrialized countries. Of the 6.35 billion people in the world in 2000, 5 billion will live in LDCs. The LDCs' share of the world's population increased from 66 percent in 1950 to 72 percent in 1975, and is expected to reach 79 percent by 2000. LDC population growth rates will drop slightly, from 2.2 percent a year in 1975 to 2 percent in 2000, compared with 0.7 percent and 0.5 percent in developed countries. In some LDCs, growth rates will still be more than 3 percent a year in 2000. Table 1-1 summarizes the population projections.

In addition to rapid population growth, the LDCs will experience dramatic movements of rural populations to cities and adjacent settlements. If present trends continue, many LDC cities will become almost inconceivably large and crowded. By 2000, Mexico City is projected to have more than 30 million people — roughly three times the present population of the New York metropolitan area. Calcutta will approach 20 million. Greater Bombay, Greater Cairo, Jakarta, and Seoul are all expected to be in the 15-20 million range, and 400 cities will have passed the million mark.

Rapid urban growth will put extreme pressures on sanitation, water supplies, health care, food, shelter, and jobs. LDCs will have to increase urban services approximately two-thirds by 2000 just to stay even with 1975 levels of service per capita. The majority of people in large LDC cities are likely to live in "uncontrolled settlements" — slums and shantytowns where sanitation and other public services are minimal at best. In many large cities — for example, Bombay, Calcutta, Mexico City, Rio de Janeiro, Seoul, Taipei — a quarter or more of the population already lives in uncontrolled settlements, and the trend is sharply upward. It is not certain whether the trends projected for enormous increases in LDC urban populations will in fact continue for 20 years. In the years ahead, lack of food for the urban poor, lack of jobs, and increasing illness and misery may slow the growth of LDC cities and alter the trend.

Difficult as urban conditions are, conditions in rural areas of many LDCs are generally worse. Food, water, health, and income problems are often most severe in outlying agricultural and grazing areas. In some areas rural-urban migration and rapid urban growth are being accelerated by deteriorating rural conditions.

An updated medium-series population projection would show little change from the Global 2000 Study projections. World population in 2000 would be estimated at about 6.18 (as opposed to 6.35) billion, a reduction of less than 3 percent. The expectation

---

* Most of the projections in the Technical Report — including the population projections — provide a high, medium, and low series. Generally, only the medium series are discussed in this Summary Report.

TABLE 1-1
Population Projections for World, Major Regions, and Selected Countries

	1975	2000	Percent Increase by 2000	Average Annual Percent Increase	Percent of World Population in 2000
	millions				
World	4,090	6,351	55	1.8	100
More developed regions	1,131	1,323	17	0.6	21
Less developed regions	2,959	5,028	70	2.1	79
Major regions					
Africa	399	814	104	2.9	13
Asia and Oceania	2,274	3,630	60	1.9	57
Latin America	325	637	96	2.7	10
U.S.S.R. and Eastern Europe	384	460	20	0.7	7
North America, Western Europe, Japan, Australia and New Zealand	708	809	14	0.5	13

Source: Global 2000 Technical Report, Table 2-10.

would remain that, in absolute numbers, population will be growing more rapidly by the end of the century than today.

Income

Projected declines in fertility rates are based in part on anticipated social and economic progress, which is ultimately reflected in increased income. Income projections were not possible, and gross national product (GNP) projections were used as surrogates. GNP, a rough and inadequate measure of social and economic welfare, is projected to increase worldwide by 145 percent over 25 years from 1975 to 2000. But because of population growth, per capita GNP increases much more slowly, from $1,500 in 1975 to $2,300 in 2000 – an increase of 53 percent. For both the poorer and the richer countries, rates of growth in GNP are projected to decelerate after 1985.

The present income disparities between the wealthiest and poorest nations are projected to widen. Assuming that present trends continue, the groups of industrialized countries will have a per capita GNP of nearly $8,500 (in 1975 dollars) in 2000, and North America, Western Europe, Australia, New Zealand, and Japan will average more than $11,000. By contrast, per capita GNP in the LDCs will average less than $600. For every $1 increase in GNP per capita in the LDCs, a $20 increase is projected for the industrialized countries. Tables 1-2 and 1-3 summarize the GNP projections.

Updated GNP projections would indicate somewhat lower economic growth than shown in the Global 2000 projections. Projections for the member nations of the Organization for Economic Cooperation and Development (OECD) have been revised downward over the past several years because of the effects of increasing petroleum prices and because of anticipated measures to reduce inflation. In turn, depressed growth in the OECD economies is expected to lead to slowed growth in LDC economies.

Resources

The Global 2000 Study resource projections are based to the greatest extent possible on the population and GNP projections presented previously. The resource projections cover food, fisheries, forests, nonfuel minerals, water, and energy.

Food

The Global 2000 Study projects world food production to increase at an average annual rate of about 2.2 percent over the 1970-2000 period. This rate of increase is roughly equal to the record growth rates experienced during the 1950s, 1960s, and early 1970s, including the period of the so-called Green Revolution. Assuming no deterioration in climate or weather, food production is projected to be 90 percent higher in 2000 than in 1970.

The projections indicate that most of the increase in food production will come from more intensive use of yield-enhancing, energy-intensive inputs and technologies, such as fertilizers, pesticides, herbicides, and irrigation — in many cases with diminishing returns. Land under cultivation is projected to increase only 4 percent by 2000 because most good land is already being cultivated. In the early 1970s one hectare of arable land supported an average of 2.6 persons; by 2000 one hectare will have to support 4 persons.

Because of the tightening land constraint, food production is not likely to increase fast enough to meet rising demands unless world agriculture becomes significantly more dependent on petroleum and petroleum-related inputs. Increased petroleum dependence also has implications for the cost of food production. After decades of

TABLE 1-2

GNP Estimates (1975) and Projections and Growth Rates (1985, 2000) by Major Regions and Selected Countries and Regions

(Billions of constant 1975 U.S. $)

	1975 GNP	1975-85 Growth Rate	1985 Projections [a]	1985-2000 Growth Rate	2000 Projections [a]
		(percent)		*(percent)*	
World	6,025	4.1	8,991	3.3	14,677
More developed regions	4,892	3.9	7,150	3.1	11,224
Less developed regions	1,133	5.0	1,841	4.3	3,452
Major Regions					
Africa	162	5.2	268	4.3	505
Asia and Oceania	697	4.6	1,097	4.2	2,023
Latin America [b]	326	5.6	564	4.5	1,092
U.S.S.R. and Eastern Europe	996	3.3	1,371	2.8	2,060
North America, Western Europe, Japan, Australia and New Zealand	3,844	4.0	5,691	3.1	8,996

a. Projected growth rates of gross national product were developed using complex computer simulation techniques described in Chapter 16 of the Global 2000 Technical Report. These projections represent the result of applying those projected growth rates to the 1975 GNP data presented in the 1976 World Bank Atlas. Projections shown here are for medium-growth rates.

b. Includes Puerto Rico.

Source: Global 2000 Technical Report, Table 3-3.

TABLE 1-3

Per Capita GNP Estimates (1975) and Projections and Growth Rates (1985, 2000) by Major Regions and Selected Countries and Regions

(Constant 1975 U.S. $)

	1975	Average Annual Growth Rate 1975-85	1985 Projections	Average Annual Growth Rate 1985-2000	2000 Projections [a]
		(percent)		*(percent)*	
World	1,473	2.3	1,841	1.5	2,311
More developed countries	4,325	3.2	5,901	2.5	8,485
Less developed countries	382	2.8	501	2.1	587
Major regions					
Africa	405	2.2	505	1.4	620
Asia and Oceania	306	2.7	398	2.3	557
Latin America [b]	1,005	2.6	1,304	1.8	1,715
U.S.S.R. and Eastern Europe	2,591	2.4	3,279	2.1	4,472
North America, Western Europe, Japan, Australia and New Zealand	5,431	3.4	7,597	2.6	11,117

a. The medium-series projections of gross national product and population presented in Tables 3-3 and 3-4 of the Global 2000 Technical Report were used to calculate the 1975, 1985, and 2000 per capita gross national product figures presented in this table.

b. Includes Puerto Rico.

Source: Global 2000 Technical Report, Table 3-5.

generally falling prices, the real price of food is projected to increase 95 percent over the 1970-2000 period, in significant part as a result of increased petroleum dependence. If energy prices in fact rise more rapidly than the projections anticipate, then the effect on food prices could be still more marked. Moreover, as the year 2000 approaches and more marginal, weather-sensitive lands are brought into production around the world, weather-related swings in production and demand will widen.

On the average, world food production is projected to increase more rapidly than world population, with average per capita consumption increasing about 15 percent between 1970 and 2000. Per capita consumption in the industrialized nations is projected to rise 21 percent from 1970 levels, with increases of from 40 to more than 50 percent in Japan, Eastern Europe, and the U.S.S.R., and 28 percent in the United States.* In the LDCs, however, rising food output will barely keep ahead of population growth.

An increase of 9 percent in per capita food consumption is projected for the LDCs as a whole, but with enormous variations among regions and nations. The great populous countries of South Asia — expected to contain 1.3 billion people by 2000 — improve hardly at all, nor do large areas of low-income North Africa and the Middle East. Per capita consumption in the sub-Saharan African LDCs will actually decline, according to the projections. The LDCs showing the greatest per capita growth (increases of about 25 percent) are concentrated in Latin America and East Asia. Table 1-4 summarizes the projections for food production and consumption, and Table 1-5 shows per capita food consumption by regions.

The outlook for improved diets for the poorest people in the poorest LDCs is sobering. In the 1970s, consumption of calories in the LDCs averaged only 94 percent of the minimum requirements set by the U.N. Food and Agriculture Organization (FAO).** Moreover, income and food distribution within individual LDCs is so skewed that national average caloric consumption generally must be 10-20 percent above minimum levels before the poorest are likely to be able to afford a diet that meets the FAO minimum standard.

Latin America is the only major LDC region where average caloric consumption is projected to be 20 percent or more above the FAO minimum standard in the year 2000. In the other LDC regions — South, East, and Southeast Asia, poor areas of North Africa and the Middle East, and especially Central Africa, where a calamitous drop in food per capita is projected — the quantity of food available to the poorest groups of people will simply be insufficient to permit children to reach normal body weight and intelligence and to permit normal activity and good health in adults. Consumption in the LDCs of central Africa is projected to be more than 20 percent below the FAO minimum standard, assuming no recurrence of severe drought.

-----

* "Consumption" statistics are based on the amount of food that leaves the farms and does not leave the country and therefore include transportation and processing losses. Projected increases in per capita consumption in countries like the United States, where average consumption is already at least nutritionally adequate, reflect increasing losses of food during transportation and processing and might also be accounted for by increased industrial demand for grain, especially for fermentation into fuels.

** The FAO standard indicates the *minimum* consumption that will allow normal activity and good health in adults and will permit children to reach normal body weight and intelligence in the absence of disease.

TABLE 1-4
Grain Production, Consumption, and Trade, Actual and Projected, and Percentage Increase in Total Food Production and Consumption

	Grain (million metric tons)			Food (percentage increase over the 1970-2000 period)
	1969-71	1973-75	2000	
Industrialized countries				
Production	401.7	434.7	679.1	43.7
Consumption	374.3	374.6	610.8	47.4
Trade	+ 32.1	+ 61.6	+ 68.3	
United States				
Production	208.7	228.7	402.0	78.5
Consumption	169.0	158.5	272.4	51.3
Trade	+ 39.9	+ 72.9	+ 129.6	
Other developed exporters				
Production	58.6	61.2	106.1	55.6
Consumption	33.2	34.3	65.2	66.8
Trade	+ 28.4	+ 27.7	+ 40.9	
Western Europe				
Production	121.7	132.9	153.0	14.6
Consumption	144.2	151.7	213.1	31.6
Trade	- 21.8	- 19.7	- 60.1	
Japan				
Production	12.7	11.9	18.0	31.5
Consumption	27.9	30.1	60.1	92.8
Trade	- 14.4	- 19.3	- 42.1	
Centrally planned countries				
Production	401.0	439.4	722.0	74.0
Consumption	406.6	472.4	758.5	79.9
Trade	- 5.2	- 24.0	- 36.5	
Eastern Europe				
Production	72.1	89.4	140.0	83.2
Consumption	78.7	97.7	151.5	81.7
Trade	- 6.1	- 7.8	- 11.5	
U.S.S.R.				
Production	165.0	179.3	290.0	72.7
Consumption	161.0	200.7	305.0	85.9
Trade	+ 3.9	- 10.6	- 15.0	
People's Republic of China				
Production	163.9	176.9	292.0	69.0
Consumption	166.9	180.8	302.0	71.4
Trade	- 3.0	- 3.9	- 10.0	
Less developed countries				
Production	306.5	328.7	740.6	147.7
Consumption	326.6	355.0	772.4	142.8
Trade	- 18.5	- 29.5	- 31.8	

TABLE 1-4 (Cont.)

	Grain (million metric tons)			Food (percentage increase over the 1970-2000 period)
	1969-71	1973-75	2000	
Exporters [a]				
Production	30.1	34.5	84.0	125.0
Consumption	18.4	21.5	36.0	58.0
Trade	+ 11.3	+ 13.1	+ 48.0	
Importers [b]				
Production	276.4	294.2	656.6	149.3
Consumption	308.2	333.5	736.4	148.9
Trade	- 29.8	- 42.6	- 79.8	
Latin America				
Production	63.8	72.0	185.9	184.4
Consumption	61.2	71.2	166.0	165.3
Trade	+ 3.2	+ 0.2	+ 19.9	
North Africa / Middle East				
Production	38.9	42.4	89.0	157.8
Consumption	49.5	54.1	123.7	167.3
Trade	- 9.1	- 13.8	- 29.7	
Other African LDCs				
Production	32.0	31.3	63.7	104.9
Consumption	33.0	33.8	63.0	96.4
Trade	- 1.0	- 2.4	+ 0.7	
South Asia				
Production	119.1	127.7	259.0	116.8
Consumption	125.3	135.1	275.7	119.4
Trade	- 6.2	- 9.3	- 16.7	
Southeast Asia				
Production	22.8	21.4	65.0	210.0
Consumption	19.3	17.9	47.0	163.6
Trade	+ 3.4	+ 3.7	+ 18.0	
East Asia				
Production	29.9	34.0	73.0	155.3
Consumption	38.3	42.9	97.0	164.9
Trade	- 8.8	- 9.7	- 24.0	
World				
Production / Consumption	1,108.0	1,202.0	2,141.7	91.0

Note: In trade figures, plus sign indicates export, minus sign indicates import.
a. Argentina and Thailand.
b. All others, including several countries that export in some scenarios (e.g., Brazil, Indonesia and Colombia).
Source: Global 2000 Technical Report, Table 6-5.

TABLE 1-5

**Per Capita Grain Production, Consumption, and Trade, Actual and Projected,
and Percantage Increase in Per Capita Total Food Production and Consumption**

	Grain (kg per capita)			Food (percentage increase over the 1970-2000 period)
	1969-71	1973-75	2000	
Industrialized countries				
Production	573.6	592.6	769.8	18.4
Consumption	534.4	510.7	692.4	21.2
Trade	+ 45.8	+ 84.0	+ 77.4	
United States				
Production	1,018.6	1,079.3	1,640.3	51.1
Consumption	824.9	748.0	1,111.5	28.3
Trade	+ 194.7	+ 344.0	+ 528.8	
Other developed exporters				
Production	1,015.6	917.0	915.6	- 11.3
Consumption	575.4	514.0	562.6	- 5.7
Trade	+ 492.2	+ 415.0	+ 353.0	
Western Europe				
Production	364.9	388.4	394.0	1.0
Consumption	432.4	443.3	548.8	15.5
Trade	- 65.4	- 57.6	- 154.8	
Japan				
Production	121.7	108.5	135.4	6.1
Consumption	267.5	274.4	452.3	54.2
Trade	- 138.1	- 175.9	- 316.7	
Centrally planned countries				
Production	356.1	368.0	451.1	29.6
Consumption	361.0	395.6	473.9	35.8
Trade	- 4.6	- 20.1	- 22.8	
Eastern Europe				
Production	574.0	693.0	921.9	53.3
Consumption	626.6	757.4	997.6	52.1
Trade	- 48.6	- 60.5	- 75.8	
U.S.S.R.				
Production	697.6	711.2	903.2	28.1
Consumption	663.1	796.1	949.9	41.4
Trade	+ 16.1	- 42.0	- 46.7	
People's Republic of China				
Production	216.3	217.6	259.0	17.4
Consumption	220.2	222.4	267.8	19.1
Trade	- 4.0	- 4.8	- 8.8	
Less developed countries				
Production	176.7	168.7	197.1	10.8
Consumption	188.3	182.2	205.5	8.6
Trade	- 10.7	- 15.1	- 8.4	

TABLE 1-5 (Cont.)

	Grain (kg per capita)			Food (percentage increase over the
	1969-71	1973-75	2000	1970-2000 period)
Exporters [a]				
Production	491.0	521.9	671.7	10.4
Consumption	300.1	325.3	287.8	- 22.6
Trade	+ 184.3	+ 198.2	+ 383.9	
Importers [b]				
Production	159.4	173.8	180.7	10.8
Consumption	177.7	193.6	202.7	10.8
Trade	- 17.2	- 24.1	- 21.9	
Latin America				
Production	236.1	241.0	311.4	33.7
Consumption	226.5	238.3	278.1	25.1
Trade	+ 11.8	+ 2.7	+ 33.3	
North Africa / Middle East				
Production	217.1	214.6	222.5	- 1.8
Consumption	276.2	273.8	292.8	2.2
Trade	- 50.8	- 69.8	- 70.3	
Other African LDCs				
Production	134.9	118.3	113.2	- 15.5
Consumption	139.1	127.7	112.0	- 19.1
Trade	- 4.2	- 9.1	+ 1.2	
South Asia				
Production	161.6	162.4	170.0	4.6
Consumption	170.0	171.8	181.0	5.8
Trade	- 8.4	- 11.8	- 11.0	
Southeast Asia				
Production	244.7	214.5	316.5	35.9
Consumption	207.2	182.6	228.5	14.6
Trade	+ 37.5	+ 31.9	+ 87.5	
East Asia				
Production	137.3	136.0	163.5	22.8
Consumption	176.2	171.5	217.3	27.3
Trade	- 40.4	- 38.8	- 53.8	
World				
Production / Consumption	311.5	313.6	343.2	14.5

Note: In trade figures, plus sign indicates export, minus sign indicates import.
a. Argentina and Thailand.
b. All others, including several countries that export in some scenarios (e.g., Brazil, Indonesia and Colombia).
Source: Global 2000 Technical Report, Table 6-6.

The projected food situation has many implications for food assistance and trade. In the developing world, the need for imported food is expected to grow. The most prosperous LDCs will turn increasingly to the world commercial markets. In the poorest countries, which lack the wherewithal to buy food, requirements for international food assistance will expand. LDC exporters (especially Argentina and Thailand) are expected to enlarge food production for export because of their cost advantage over countries dependent on energy-intensive inputs. LDC grain-exporting countries, which accounted for only a little more than 10 percent of the world grain market in 1975, are expected to capture more than 20 percent of the market by 2000.

Revised and updated food projections would reflect reduced estimates of future yields, increased pressure on the agricultural resource base, and several changes in national food policies.

Farmers' costs of raising — and even maintaining — yields have increased rapidly in recent years. The costs of energy-intensive, yield-enhancing inputs — fertilizers, pesticides, and fuels — have risen very rapidly throughout the world, and where these inputs are heavily used, increased applications are bringing diminishing returns. In the United States, the real cost of producing food increased roughly 10 percent in both 1978 and 1979. Other industrialized countries have experienced comparable production cost increases. Cost increases in the LDCs appear to be lower, but are still 2-3 times the annual increases of the 1960s and early 1970s. While there have been significant improvements recently in the yields of selected crops, the diminishing returns and rapidly rising costs of yield-enhancing inputs suggest that yields overall will increase more slowly than projected.

Worldwide, the use of yield-enhancing inputs is likely to be less, and soil deterioration greater, than expected. As a result, revised food projections would show a tighter food future — somewhat less production and somewhat higher prices — than indicated in the Global 2000 projections.

Fisheries

Fish is an important component of the world's diet and has sometimes been put forth as a possible partial solution to world food shortages. Unfortunately, the world harvest of fish is expected to rise little, if at all, by the year 2000.* The world catch of naturally produced fish leveled off in the 1970s at about 70 million metric tons a year (60 million metric tons for marine fisheries, 10 million metric tons for freshwater species). Harvests of traditional fisheries are not likely to increase on a sustained basis, and indeed to maintain them will take good management and improved protection of the marine environment. Some potential for greater harvests comes from aquaculture and from nontraditional marine species, such as Antarctic krill, that are little used at present for direct human consumption.

Traditional freshwater and marine species might be augmented in some areas by means of aquaculture. The 1976 FAO World Conference on Aquaculture concluded that a five to tenfold increase in production from aquaculture would be possible by 2000, given adequate financial and technical support. (Aquaculture contributed an

---

*   The food projections assumed that the world fish catch would increase at essentially the same rate as population and are therefore likely to prove too optimistic on this point. (See Chapters 6, 14, and 18 of the Global 2000 Technical Report for further discussion of this point.)

estimated 6 million metric tons to the world's total catch in 1975.) However, limited investment and technical support, as well as increasing pollution of freshwater ponds and coastal water, are likely to be a serious impediment to such growth.

Updated fisheries projections would show little change from the Global 2000 Study projections. FAO fisheries statistics for 1978 show a world catch of 72.4 million metric tons. Perhaps the biggest change would stem from a careful analysis of the effects of the large increase in oil prices that occurred in 1979. Scattered observations suggest that fishing fleets throughout the world are being adversely affected except where governments are keeping oil prices to fishing boats artificially low.

Forests

If present trends continue, both forest cover and growing stocks of commercial-size wood in the less developed regions (Latin America, Africa, Asia, and Oceania) will decline 40 percent by 2000. In the industrialized regions (Europe, the U.S.S.R., North America, Japan, Australia, New Zealand) forests will decline only 0.5 percent and growing stock about 5 percent. Growing stock per capita is expected to decline 47 percent worldwide and 63 percent in LDCs. Table 1-6 shows projected forest cover and growing stocks by region for 1978 and 2000.

TABLE 1-6
Estimates of World Forest Resources,
1978 and 2000

	Closed Forest [a] (millions of hectares)		Growing Stock (billions cu m overbark)	
	1978	2000	1978	2000
U.S.S.R.	785	775	79	77
Europe	140	150	15	13
North America	470	464	58	55
Japan, Australia, New Zealand	69	68	4	4
Subtotal	1,464	1,457	156	149
Latin America	550	329	94	54
Africa	188	150	39	31
Asia and Pacific LDCs	361	181	38	19
Subtotal (LDCs)	1,099	660	171	104
Total (world)	2,563	2,117	327	253
			Growing Stock per Capita (cu m biomass)	
Industrial countries			142	114
LDCs			57	21
Global			76	40

a. Closed forests are relatively dense and productive forests. They are defined variously in different parts of the world. For further details, see Global 2000 Technical Report, footnote, p. 117.

Source: Global 2000 Technical Report, Table 13-29.

Deforestation is projected to continue until about 2020, when the total world forest area will stabilize at about 1.8 billion hectares. Most of the loss will occur in the tropical forests of the developing world. About 1.45 billion hectares of forest in the industrialized nations has already stabilized and about 0.37 billion hectares of forest in the LDCs is physically or economically inaccessible. By 2020, virtually all of the physically accessible forest in the LDCs is expected to have been cut.

The real prices of wood products — fuelwood, sawn lumber, wood panels, paper, wood-based chemicals, and so on — are expected to rise considerably as GNP (and thus also demand) rises and world supplies tighten. In the industrialized nations, the effects may be disruptive, but not catastrophic. In the less developed countries, however, 90 percent of wood consumption goes for cooking and heating, and wood is a necessity of life. Loss of woodlands will force people in many LDCs to pay steeply rising prices for fuelwood and charcoal or to spend much more effort collecting wood — or else to do without.

Updated forest projections would present much the same picture as the Global 2000 Study projections. The rapid increase in the price of crude oil will probably limit the penetration of kerosene sales into areas now depending on fuelwood and dung and, as a result, demand for fuelwood may be somewhat higher than expected. Some replanting of cut tropical areas is occurring, but only at low rates similar to those assumed in the Global 2000 Study projections. Perhaps the most encouraging developments are those associated with heightened international awareness of the seriousness of current trends in world forests.

Water

The Global 2000 Study population, GNP, and resource projections all imply rapidly increasing demands for fresh water. Increases of at least 200-300 percent in world water withdrawals are expected over the 1975-2000 period. By far the largest part of the increase is for irrigation. The United Nations has estimated that water needed for irrigation, which accounted for 70 percent of human uses of water in 1967, would double by 2000. Moreover, irrigation is a highly consumptive use, that is, much of the water withdrawn for this purpose is not available for immediate reuse because it evaporates, is transpired by plants, or becomes salinated.

Regional water shortages and deterioration of water quality, already serious in many parts of the world, are likely to become worse by 2000. Estimates of per capita water availability for 1971 and 2000 show demands for water at least doubling (relative to 1971) in nearly half of the countries of the world as a result of population growth alone, *without allowance for other causes of increased demand.* Still greater increases would be needed to improve standards of living.

Much of the increased demand for water will be in the LDCs of Africa, South Asia, the Middle East, and Latin America, where in many areas fresh water for human consumption and irrigation is already in short supply. Although the data are sketchy, it is known that several nations in these areas will be approaching their maximum developable water supply by 2000, and that it will be quite expensive to develop the water remaining. Moreover, many LDCs will also suffer destabilization of water supplies following extensive loss of forests. In the industrialized countries competition among different uses of water — for increasing food production, new energy systems (such as production of synthetic fuels from coal and shale), increasing power generation, expanding food production, and increasing needs of other industries — will aggravate water shortages in many areas.

Updated water projections would present essentially the same picture. The only significant change that has occurred since the projections were developed is that the price of energy (especially oil) has increased markedly. Increased energy costs will adversely affect the economics of many water development projects, and may reduce the amount of water available for a variety of uses. Irrigation, which usually requires large amounts of energy for pumping, may be particularly affected.

Nonfuel Minerals

The trends for nonfuel minerals, like those for the other resources considered in the Global 2000 Study, show steady increases in demand and consumption. The global demand for and consumption of most major nonfuel mineral commodities is projected to increase 3-5 percent annually, slightly more than doubling by 2000. Consumption of all major steelmaking mineral commodities is projected to increase at least 3 percent annually. Consumption of all mineral commodities for fertilizer production is projected to grow at more than 3 percent annually, with consumption of phosphate rock growing at 5.2 percent per year — the highest growth rate projected for any of the major nonfuel mineral commodities. The nonferrous metals show widely varying projected growth rates; the growth rate for aluminum, 4.3 percent per year, is the largest.

The projections suggest that the LDCs' share of nonfuel mineral use will increase only modestly. Over the 1971-75 period, Latin America, Africa, and Asia used 7 percent of the world's aluminum production, 9 percent of the copper, and 12 percent of the iron ore. The three-quarters of the world's population living in these regions in 2000 are projected to use only 8 percent of aluminum production, 13 percent of copper production, and 17 percent of iron ore production. The one-quarter of the world's population that inhabits industrial countries is projected to continue absorbing more than three-fourths of the world's nonfuel minerals production.

The projections point to no mineral exhaustion problems but further discoveries and investments will be needed to maintain reserves and production of several mineral commodities at desirable levels. In most cases, however, the resource potential is still large, especially for low grade ores.

Updated nonfuel minerals projections would need to give further attention to two factors affecting investment in mining. One is the shift over the past decade in investment in extraction and processing away from the developing countries toward industrialized countries (although this trend may now be reversing). The other factor is the rapid increase in energy prices. Production of many nonfuel minerals is highly energy-intensive, and the recent and projected increases in oil prices can be expected to slow the expansion of these mineral supplies.

Energy

The Global 2000 Study's energy projections show no early relief from the world's energy problems. The projections point out that petroleum production capacity is not increasing as rapidly as demand. Furthermore, the rate at which petroleum reserves are being added per unit of exploratory effort appears to be falling. Engineering and geological considerations suggest that world petroleum production will peak before the end of the century. Political and economic decisions in the OPEC countries could cause oil production to level off even before technological constraints come into play. A world transition away from petroleum dependence must take place, but there is still much uncertainty as to how this transition will occur. In the face of this uncertainty, it was not possible at the time the Global 2000 energy projections were made — late

1977 — for the Department of Energy to develop meaningful energy projections beyond 1990. Updated Energy Dept. analyses, discussed at the end of this section, extend the global energy projections available from the U.S. Government to 1995.

Energy Dept. projections prepared for the Study show large increases in demand for all commercial sources over the 1975-90 period (see Table 1-7). World energy demand is projected to increase 58 percent, reaching 384 quads (quadrillion British thermal units) by 1990. Nuclear and hydro sources (primarily nuclear) increase most rapidly (226 percent by 1990), followed by oil (58 percent), natural gas (43 percent), and coal (13 percent). Oil is projected to remain the world's leading energy source, providing 46-47 percent of the world's total energy through 1990, assuming that the real price of oil on the international market increases 65 percent over the 1975-90 period. The energy projections indicate that there is considerable potential for reductions in energy consumption.

Per capita energy consumption is projected to increase everywhere. The largest increase — 72 percent over the 1975-90 period — is in industrialized countries other than the United States. The smallest increase, 12 percent, is in the centrally planned economies of Eastern Europe. The percentage increases for the United States and for the LDCs are the same — 27 percent — but actual per capita energy consumption is very different. By 2000, U.S. per capita energy consumption is projected to be about 422 million Btu (British thermal units) annually. In the LDCs, it will be only 14 million Btu, up from 11 million in 1975 (see Table 1-8).

While prices for oil and other commercial energy sources are rising, fuelwood — the poor person's oil — is expected to become far less available than it is today. The FAO has estimated that the demand for fuelwood in LDCs will increase at 2.2 percent per year, leading to local fuelwood shortages in 1994 totaling 650 million cubic meters — approximately 25 percent of the projected need. Scarcities are now local but expanding. In the arid Sahel of Africa, fuelwood gathering has become a full-time job requiring in some places 360 person-days of work per household per year. When demand is concentrated in cities, surrounding areas have already become barren for considerable distances — 50 to 100 kilometers in some places. Urban families, too far from collectible wood, spend 20 to 30 percent of their income on wood in some West African cities.

The projected shortfall of fuelwood implies that fuel consumption for essential uses will be reduced, deforestation expanded, wood prices increased, and growing amounts of dung and crop residues shifted from the field to the cooking fire. No explicit projections of dung and crop residue combustion could be made for the Study, but it is known that a shift toward burning these organic materials is already well advanced in the Himalayan hills, in the treeless Ganges plain of India, in other parts of Asia, and in the Andean region of South America. The FAO reports that in 1970 India burned 68 million tons of cow dung and 39 million tons of vegetable waste, accounting for roughly a third of the nation's total noncommercial energy consumption that year. Worldwide, an estimated 150-400 million tons of dung are burned annually for fuel.

Updated energy projections have been developed by the Department of Energy based on new price scenarios that include the rapid 1979 increase in the price of crude oil. The new price scenarios are not markedly different from the earlier estimates for the 1990s. The new medium-scenario price for 1995 is $40 per barrel (in 1979 dollars), which is about 10 percent higher than the $36 price (1979 dollars) implied by the earlier scenario. However, the prices for the early 1980s are almost 100 percent higher than

TABLE 1-7

Global Primary[a] Energy Use, 1975 and 1990, by Energy Type

	1975		1990		Percentage Increase (1975-90)	Average Annual Percentage Increase
	10^{15} Btu	Percentage of Total	10^{15} Btu[b]	Percentage of Total		
Oil	113	46	179	47	58	3.1
Coal	68	28	77	20	13	0.8
Natural gas	46	19	66	17	43	2.4
Nuclear and hydro	19	8[c]	62	16[c]	226	7.9
Solar (other than conservation / and hydro)[d]						
Total	246	100	384	100	56	3.0

a. All of the nuclear and much of the coal primary (i.e., input) energy is used thermally to generate electricity. In the process, approximately two-thirds of the primary energy is lost as waste heat. The figures given here are primary energy.

b. The conversions from the Energy Dept. projections in Table 10-8 of the Global 2000 Technical Report were made as follows: *Oil* 84.8 x 10⁶ bbl/day x 365 days x 5.8 x 10⁶ Btu/bbl = 179 x 10⁶ Btu. *Coal:* 5,424 x 10⁶ short tons/yr x 14.1 x 10⁴ Btu/short ton [Energy Dept. figure for world average grade coal] = 77 x 10¹⁵ Btu. *Natural gas:* 64.4 x 10¹² ft³/yr x 1,032 Btu/ft³ = 66 x 10¹⁵ Btu. *Nuclear and Hydro:* 6,009 x 10¹² Wh [output]/yr x 3,412 Btu/Wh x 3 input Btu/output Btu = 62 x 10¹² Btu.

c. After deductions for lost (waste) heat (see note a), the corresponding figures for output energy are 2.7 percent in 1975 and 6.0 in 1990.

d. The IIES projection model is able to include solar only as a conservation or hydro.

Source: Global 2000 Technical Report, Table 13-32.

TABLE 1-8
Per Capita Global Primary Energy Use, Annually, 1975 and 1990

	1975		1990			
	10^6 Btu	Percentage of World Average	10^6 Btu	Percentage of World Average	Percentage Increase (1975-90)	Average Annual Percentage Increase
United States	332	553	442	586	27	1.6
Other industrialized countries	136	227	234	325	72	3.6
Less developed countries [a]	11	18	14	19	27	1.6
Centrally planned economies	58	97	65	90	12	0.8
World	60	100	72	100	20	1.2

a. Since population projections were not made separately for the OPEC countries, those countries have been included here in the LDC category.

Source: Global 2000 Technical Report, Table 13-34.

those in the projections made by the Energy Dept. in late 1977 for the Study. The sudden large increase in oil prices of 1979 is likely to have a more disruptive effect on other sectors than would the gradual increase assumed in the Global 2000 Study projections.

The Energy Dept.'s new projections differ in several ways from those reported in this Study. Demand is projected to be lower because of the higher prices and also because of reduced estimates of economic growth. Coal is projected to provide a somewhat larger share of the total energy supply. The nuclear projections for the OECD countries are lower, reflecting revised estimates of the speed at which new nuclear plants will be built. Updated estimates of OPEC maximum production are lower than earlier estimates, reflecting trends toward resource conservation by the OPEC nations. The higher oil prices will encourage the adoption of alternative fuels and technologies, including solar technology and conservation measures.

Environmental Consequences

The population, income, and resource projections all imply significant consequences for the quality of the world environment. Virtually every aspect of the earth's ecosystems and resource base will be affected.

Impacts on Agriculture

Perhaps the most serious environmental development will be an accelerating deterioration and loss of the resources essential for agriculture. This overall development includes soil erosion; loss of nutrients and compaction of soils; increasing salinization of both irrigated land and water used for irrigation; loss of high-quality cropland to urban development; crop damage due to increasing air and water pollution; extinction of local and wild crop strains needed by plant breeders for improving cultivated varities; and more frequent and more severe regional water shortages — especially where energy and industrial developments compete for water supplies, or where forest losses are heavy and the earth can no longer absorb, store, and regulate the discharge of water.

Deterioration of soils is occurring rapidly in LDCs, with the spread of desert-like conditions in drier regions, and heavy erosion in more humid areas. Present global losses to desertification are estimated at around 6 million hectares a year (an area about the size of Maine), including 3.2 million hectares of rangeland, 2.5 million hectares of rainfed cropland, and 125 thousand hectares of irrigated farmland. Principal direct causes are overgrazing, destructive cropping practices, and use of woody plants for fuel.

At present estimated rates of desertification, the world's desert areas (now some 800 million hectares) would expand almost 20 percent by 2000. But there is reason to expect that losses to desertification will accelerate, as increasing numbers of people in the world's drier regions put more pressures on the land to meet their needs for livestock range, cropland, and fuelwood.

Although soil loss and deterioration are especially serious in many LDCs, they are also affecting agricultural prospects in industrialized nations. Present rates of soil loss in many industrialized nations cannot be sustained without serious implications for crop production. In the United States, for example, the Soil Conservation Service, looking at wind and water erosion of U.S. soils, has concluded that to sustain crop production indefinitely at even present levels, soil losses must be cut in half.

The outlook for making such gains in the United States and elsewhere is not good. The food and forestry projections imply increasing pressures on soils throughout the world. Losses due to improper irrigation, reduced fallow periods, cultivation of steep and marginal lands, and reduced vegetative cover can be expected to accelerate, especially in North and Central Africa, the humid and high-altitude portions of Latin America, and much of South Asia. In the industrialized regions, increasing use of chemical fertilizers, high-yield plant varieties, irrigation water, and herbicides and pesticides have so far compensated for basic declines in soil conditions. However, heavy dependence on chemical fertilizers also leads to losses of soil organic matter, reducing the capacity of the soil to retain moisture.

Damage and loss of irrigated lands are especially significant because these lands have yields far above average. About half of the world's irrigated land has already been damaged to some degree by salinity, alkalinity, and waterlogging, and much of the additional land expected to be irrigated by 1990 is highly vulnerable to irrigation-related damage.

Loss of good cropland to urban encroachment is another problem affecting all countries. Cities and industries are often located on a nation's best agricultural land — rich, well-watered alluvial soils in gently sloping river valleys. In the industrialized countries that are members of the OECD, the amount of land devoted to urban uses has been increasing twice as fast as population. The limited data available for LDCs point to similar trends.

The rising yields assumed by the Global 2000 food projections depend on wider adoption of existing high-yield agricultural technology and on accelerating use of fertilizers, irrigation, pesticides, and herbicides. These yield-enhancing inputs, projected to more than double in use world-wide and to quadruple in LDCs, are heavily dependent on fossil fuels. Even now, a rapid escalation of fossil fuel prices or a sudden interruption of supply could severely disturb world agricultural production, raise food prices, and deprive larger numbers of people of adequate food. As agriculture becomes still more dependent on energy-intensive inputs, the potential for disruption will be even greater.

Accelerating use of pesticides is expected to raise crop yields quickly and substantially, especially in LDCs. Yet, many of these chemicals produce a wide range of serious consequences, some of which adversely affect agricultural production. Destruction of pest predator populations and the increasing resistance of pests to heavily used pesticides have already proved to be significant agricultural problems. On California farms, for example, 17 of 25 major agricultural pests are now resistant to one or more types of pesticides, and the populations of pest predators have been severely reduced. Many millions of dollars in crop damage are now caused annually in California by resistant pests whose natural predators have been destroyed.

Crop yields are expected to be increased significantly by much wider use of high-yield strains of grains. Unfortunately, large monocultures of genetically identical crops pose increased risks of catastrophic loss from insect attacks or crop epidemics. The corn blight that struck the U.S. corn belt in 1970 provided a clear illustration of the vulnerability of genetically identical monocultures.

Impacts on Water Resources

The quality of the world's water resources is virtually certain to suffer from the changes taking place between now and the year 2000. Water pollution from heavy application of pesticides will cause increasing difficulties. In the industrialized countries, shifts from widespread use of long-lived chemicals such as DDT are now underway, but in the LDCs — where the largest increases in agricultural chemical use is projected

— it is likely that the persistent pesticides will continue to be used. Pesticide use in LDCs is expected to at least quadruple over the 1975-2000 period (a sixfold increase is possible if recent rates of increase continue). Pollution from the persistent pesticides in irrigation canals, ponds, and rice paddies is already a worrisome problem. Farmers in some parts of Asia are reluctant to stock paddies and ponds because fish are being killed by pesticides. This means a serious loss of high-quality protein for the diets of rural families.

In addition to the potential impacts on soils discussed above, irrigation adversely affects water quality by adding salt to the water returning to streams and rivers. Downstream from extensive irrigation projects the water may become too saline for further use, unless expensive desalinization measures are undertaken. As the use of water for irrigation increases, water salinity problems are certain to increase as well.

Water pollution in LDCs is likely to worsen as the urban population soars and industry expands. Already the waters below many LDC cities are heavily polluted with sewage and wastes from pulp and paper mills, tanneries, slaughterhouses, oil refineries, and chemical plants.

River basin development that combines flood control, generation of electricity, and irrigation is likely to increase in many less developed regions, where most of the world's untapped hydropower potential lies. While providing many benefits, large-scale dams and irrigation projects can also cause highly adverse changes in both freshwater and coastal ecosystems, creating health problems (including schistosomiasis, river blindness, malaria), inundating valuable lands, and displacing populations. In addition, if erosion in the watersheds of these projects is not controlled, siltation and buildup of sediments may greatly reduce the useful life of the projects.

Virtually all of the Global 2000 Study's projections point to increasing destruction or pollution of coastal ecosystems, a resource on which the commercially important fisheries of the world depend heavily. It is estimated that 60-80 percent of commercially valuable marine fishery species use estuaries, salt marshes, or mangrove swamps for habitat at some point in their life cycle. Reef habitats also provide food and shelter for large numbers of fish and invertebrate species. Rapidly expanding cities and industry are likely to claim coastal wetland areas for development; and increasing coastal pollution from agriculture, industry, logging, water resources development, energy systems, and coastal communities is anticipated in many areas.

Impacts of Forest Losses

The projected rapid, widespread loss of tropical forests will have severe adverse effects on water and other resources. Deforestation — especially in South Asia, the Amazon basin, and central Africa — will destabilize water flows, leading to siltation of streams, reservoirs behind hydroelectric dams, and irrigation works, to depletion of groundwater, to intensified flooding, and to aggravated water shortages during dry periods. In South and Southeast Asia approximately one billion people live in heavily farmed alluvial basins and valleys that depend on forested mountain watersheds for their water. If present trends continue, forests in these regions will be reduced by about half in 2000, and erosion, siltation, and erratic streamflows will seriously affect food production.

In many tropical forests, the soils, land forms, temperatures, patterns of rainfall, and distribution of nutrients are in precarious balance. When these forests are disturbed by extensive cutting, neither trees nor productive grasses will grow again.

Even in less fragile tropical forests, the great diversity of species is lost after extensive cutting.

Impacts on the World's Atmosphere and Climate

Among the emerging environmental stresses are some that affect the chemical and physical nature of the atmosphere. Several are recognized as problems; others are more conjectural but nevertheless of concern.

Quantitative projections of urban air quality around the world are not possible with the data and models now available, but further pollution in LDCs and some industrial nations is virtually certain to occur under present policies and practices. In LDC cities, industrial growth projected for the next 20 years is likely to worsen air quality. Even now, observations in scattered LDC cities show levels of sulfur dioxide, particulates, nitrogen dioxide, and carbon monoxide far above levels considered safe by the World Health Organization. In some cities, such as Bombay and Caracas, recent rapid changes in the numbers of cars and trucks have aggravated air pollution.

Despite recent progress in reducing various types of air pollution in many industrialized countries, air quality there is likely to worsen as increased amounts of fossil fuels, especially coal, are burned. Emissions of sulfur and nitrogen oxides are particularly troubling because they combine with water vapor in the atmosphere to form acid rain or produce other acid deposition. In large areas of Norway, Sweden, southern Canada, and the eastern United States, the pH value of rainfall has dropped from 5.7 to below 4.5, well into the acidic range. Also, rainfall has almost certainly become more acid in parts of Germany, Eastern Europe, and the U.S.S.R., although available data are incomplete.

The effects of acid rain are not yet fully understood, but damage has already been observed in lakes, forests, soils, crops, nitrogen-fixing plants, and building materials. Damage to lakes has been studied most extensively. For example, of 1,500 lakes in southern Norway with a pH below 4.3, 70 percent had no fish. Similar damage has been observed in the Adirondack Mountains of New York and in parts of Canada. River fish are also severely affected. In the last 20 years, first salmon and then trout disappeared in many Norwegian rivers as acidity increased.

Another environmental problem related to the combustion of fossil fuels (and perhaps also to the global loss of forests and soil humus) is the increasing concentration of carbon dioxide in the earth's atmosphere. Rising CO_2 concentrations are of concern because of their potential for causing a warming of the earth. Scientific opinion differs on the possible consequences, but a widely held view is that highly disruptive effects on world agriculture would occur before the middle of the twenty-first century. The CO_2 content of the world's atmosphere has increased about 15 percent in the last century and by 2000 is expected to be nearly a third higher than preindustrial levels. If the projected rates of increase in fossil fuel combustion (about 2 percent per year) were to continue, a doubling of the CO_2 content of the atmosphere could be expected after the middle of the next century; and if deforestation substantially reduces tropical forests (as projected), a doubling of atmospheric CO_2 could occur sooner. The result could be significant alterations of precipitation patterns around the world, and a $2°$-$3°C$ rise in temperatures in the middle latitudes of the earth. Agriculture and other human endeavors would have great difficulty in adapting to such large, rapid changes in climate. Even a $1°C$ increase in average global temperatures would make the earth's climate warmer than it has been any time in the last 1,000 years.

A carbon dioxide-induced temperature rise is expected to be 3 or 4 times greater at the poles than in the middle latitudes. An increase of 5°-10°C in polar temperatures could eventually lead to the melting of the Greenland and Antarctic ice caps and a gradual rise in sea level, forcing abandonment of many coastal cities.

Ozone is another major concern. The stratospheric ozone layer protects the earth from damaging ultraviolet light. However, the ozone layer is being threatened by chlorofluorocarbon emissions from aerosol cans and refrigeration equipment, by nitrous oxide (N_2O) emissions from the denitrification of both organic and inorganic nitrogen fertilizers, and possibly by the effects of high-altitude aircraft flights. Only the United States and a few other countries have made serious efforts to date to control the use of aerosol cans. Refrigerants and nitrogen fertilizers present even more difficult challenges. The most widely discussed effect of ozone depletion and the resulting increase in ultraviolet light is an increased incidence of skin cancer, but damage to food crops would also be significant and might actually prove to be the most serious ozone related problem.

Impacts of Nuclear Energy

The problems presented by the projected production of increasing amounts of nuclear power are different from but no less serious than those related to fossil fuel combustion. The risk of radioactive contamination of the environment due to nuclear power reactor accidents will be increased, as will the potential for proliferation of nuclear weapons. No nation has yet conducted a demonstration program for the satisfactory disposal of radioactive wastes, and the amount of wastes is increasing rapidly. Several hundred thousand tons of highly radioactive spent nuclear fuel will be generated over the lifetimes of the nuclear plants likely to be constructed through the year 2000. In addition, nuclear power production will create millions of cubic meters of low-level radioactive wastes, and uranium mining and processing will lead to the production of hundreds of millions of tons of low-level radioactive tailings. It has not yet been demonstrated that all of these high- and low-level wastes from nuclear power production can be safely stored and disposed of without incident. Some of the by-products of reactors, it should be noted, have half-lives approximately five times as long as the period of recorded history.

Species Extinctions

Finally, the world faces an urgent problem of loss of plant and animal genetic resources. An estimate prepared for the Global 2000 Study suggests that between half a million and 2 million species — 15 to 20 percent of all species on earth — could be extinguished by 2000, mainly because of loss of wild habitat but also in part because of pollution. Extinction of species on this scale is without precedent in human history.

One-half to two-thirds of the extinctions projected to occur by 2000 will result from the clearing or degradation of tropical forests. Insect, other invertebrate, and plant species — many of them unclassified and unexamined by scientists — will account for most of the losses. The potential value of this genetic reservoir is immense. If preserved and carefully managed, tropical forest species could be a sustainable source of new foods (especially nuts and fruits), pharmaceutical chemicals, natural predators of pests, building materials, speciality woods, fuel, and so on. Even careful husbandry of the remaining biotic resources of the tropics cannot compensate for the swift, massive losses that are to be expected if present trends continue.

Current trends also threaten freshwater and marine species. Physical alterations — damming, channelization, siltation — and pollution by salts, acid rain, pesticides, and other toxic chemicals are profoundly affecting freshwater ecosystems throughout the world. At present 274 freshwater vertebrate taxa are threatened with extinction, and by the year 2000 many may have been lost.

Some of the most important genetic losses will involve the extinction not of species but of subspecies and varieties of cereal grains. Four-fifths of the world's food supplies are derived from less than two dozen plant and animal species. Wild and local domestic strains are needed for breeding resistance to pests and pathogens into the high-yield varieties now widely used. These varietal stocks are rapidly diminishing as marginal wild lands are brought into cultivation. Local domesticated varieties, often uniquely suited to local conditions, are also being lost as higher yield varieties displace them. And the increasing practice of monoculture of a few strains — which makes crops more vulnerable to disease epidemics or plagues of pests — is occurring at the same time that the genetic resources to resist such disasters are being lost.

Entering the Twenty-First Century

The preceding sections have presented individually the many projections made by U.S. Government agencies for the Global 2000 Study. How are these projections to be interpreted collectively? What do they imply about the world's entry into the twenty-first century?

The world in 2000 will be different from the world today in important ways. There will be more people. For every two persons on the earth in 1975 there will be three in 2000. The number of poor will have increased. Four-fifths of the world's population will live in less developed countries. Furthermore, in terms of persons per year added to the world, population growth will be 40 percent *higher* in 2000 than in 1975.

The gap between the richest and the poorest will have increased. By every measure of material welfare the study provides — per capita GNP and consumption of food, energy, and minerals — the gap will widen. For example, the gap between the GNP per capita in the LDCs and the industrialized countries is projected to grow from about $4,000 in 1975 to about $7,900 in 2000. Great disparities within countries are also expected to continue.

There will be fewer resources to go around. While on a world-wide average there was about four-tenths of a hectare of arable land per person in 1975, there will be only about one-quarter hectare per person in 2000. By 2000 nearly 1,000 billion barrels of the world's total original petroleum resource of approximately 2,000 billion barrels will have been consumed. Over just the 1975-2000 period, the world's remaining petroleum resources per capita can be expected to decline by at least 50 percent. Over the same period world per capita water supplies will decline by 35 percent because of greater population alone; increasing competing demands will put further pressure on available water supplies. The world's per capita growing stock of wood is projected to be 47 percent lower in 2000 than in 1978.

The environment will have lost important life-supporting capabilities. By 2000, 40 percent of the forests still remaining in the LDCs in 1978 will have been razed. The atmospheric concentration of carbon dioxide will be nearly one-third higher than pre-industrial levels. Soil erosion will have removed, on the average, several inches of soil from croplands all over the world. Desertification (including salinization) may have claimed a significant fraction of the world's rangeland and cropland. Over little more than two decades, 15-20 percent of the earth's total species of plants and animals will have become extinct — a loss of at least 500,000 species.

Prices will be higher. The price of many of the most vital resources is projected to rise in real terms — that is, over and above inflation. In order to meet projected demand, a 100 percent increase in the real price of food will be required. To keep energy demand in line with anticipated supplies, the real price of energy is assumed to rise more than 150 percent over the 1975-2000 period. Supplies of water, agricultural land, forest products, and many traditional marine fish species are projected to decline relative to growing demand at current prices, which suggests that real price rises will occur in these sectors too. Collectively, the projections suggest that resource-based inflationary pressures will continue and intensify, especially in nations that are poor in resources or are rapidly depleting their resources.

The world will be more vulnerable both to natural disaster and to disruptions from human causes. Most nations are likely to be still more dependent on foreign sources of energy in 2000 than they are today. Food production will be more vulnerable to disruptions of fossil fuel energy supplies and to weather fluctuations as cultivation expands to more marginal areas. The loss of diverse germ plasm in local strains and wild progenitors of food crops, together with the increase of monoculture, could lead to greater risks of massive crop failures. Larger numbers of people will be vulnerable to higher food prices or even famine when adverse weather occurs. The world will be more vulnerable to the disruptive effects of war. The tensions that could lead to war will have multiplied. The potential for conflict over fresh water alone is underscored by the fact that out of 200 of the world's major river basins, 148 are shared by two countries and 52 are shared by three to ten countries. Long-standing conflicts over shared rivers such as the Plata (Brazil, Argentina), Euphrates (Syria, Iraq), or Ganges (Bangladesh, India) could easily intensify.

Finally, it must be emphasized that if public policy continues generally unchanged the world will be different as a result of lost opportunities. The adverse effects of many of the trends discussed in this Study will not be fully evident until 2000 or later; yet the actions that are necessary to change the trends cannot be postponed without foreclosing important options. The opportunity to stabilize the world's population below 10 billion, for example, is slipping away; Robert McNamara, President of the World Bank, has noted that for every decade of delay in reaching replacement fertility, the world's ultimately stabilized population will be about 11 percent greater. Similar losses of opportunity accompany delayed perceptions or action in other areas. If energy policies and decisions are based on yesterday's (or even today's) oil prices, the opportunity to wisely invest scarce capital resources will be lost as a consequence of undervaluing conservation and efficiency. If agricultural research continues to focus on increasing yields through practices that are highly energy-intensive, both energy resources and the time needed to develop alternative practices will be lost.

The full effects of rising concentrations of carbon dioxide, depletion of stratospheric ozone, deterioration of soils, increasing introduction of complex persistent toxic chemicals into the environment, and massive extinction of species may not occur until well after 2000. Yet once such global environmental problems are in motion they are very difficult to reverse. In fact, few if any of the problems addressed in the Global 2000 Study are amenable to quick technological or policy fixes; rather, they are inextricably mixed with the world's most perplexing social and economic problems.

Perhaps the most troubling problems are those in which population growth and poverty lead to serious long-term declines in the productivity of renewable natural resource systems. In some areas the capacity of renewable resource systems to support human populations is already being seriously damaged by efforts of present populations to meet desperate immediate needs, and the damage threatens to become worse.

Examples of serious deterioration of the earth's most basic resources can already be found today in scattered places in all nations, including the industrialized countries and the better endowed LDCs. For instance, erosion of agricultural soil and salinization of highly productive irrigated farmland is increasingly evident in the United States, and extensive deforestation, with more or less permanent soil degradation, has occurred in Brazil, Venezuela, and Colombia. But problems related to the decline of the earth's carrying capacity are most immediate, severe, and tragic in those regions of the earth containing the poorest LDCs.

Sub-Saharan Africa faces the problem of exhaustion of its resource base in an acute form. Many causes and effects have come together there to produce excessive demands on the environment, leading to expansion of the desert. Over-grazing, fuel-wood gathering, and destructive cropping practices are the principal immediate causes of a series of transitions from open woodland, to scrub, to fragile semiarid range, to worthless weeds and bare earth. Matters are made worse when people are forced by scarcity of fuelwood to burn animal dung and crop wastes. The soil, deprived of organic matter, loses fertility and the ability to hold water — and the desert expands. In Bangladesh, Pakistan, and large parts of India, efforts by growing numbers of people to meet their basic needs are damaging the very cropland, pasture, forests, and water supplies on which they must depend for a livelihood. To restore the lands and soils would require decades — if not centuries — *after* the existing pressures on the land have diminished. But the pressures are growing, not diminishing.

There are no quick or easy solutions, particularly in those regions where population pressure is already leading to a reduction of the carrying capacity of the land. In such regions a complex of social and economic factors (including very low incomes, in-equitable land tenure, limited or no educational opportunities, a lack of non-agricultural jobs, and economic pressures toward higher fertility) underlies the decline in the land's carrying capacity. Furthermore, it is generally believed that social and economic conditions must improve before fertility levels will decline to replacement levels. Thus a vicious circle of causality may be at work. Environmental deterioration caused by large populations creates living conditions that make reductions in fertility difficult to achieve; all the while, continuing population growth increases further the pressures on the environment and land.

The declines in carrying capacity already being observed in scattered areas around the world point to a phenomenon that could easily be much more widespread by 2000. In fact, the best evidence now available — even allowing for the many beneficial effects of technological developments and adoptions — suggests that by 2000 the world's human population may be within only a few generations of reaching the entire planet's carrying capacity.

The Global 2000 Study does not estimate the earth's carrying capacity, but it does provide a basis for evaluating an earlier estimate published in the U.S. National Academy of Sciences' report, *Resources and Man.* In this 1969 report, the Academy concluded that a world population of 10 billion "is close to (if not above) the maximum that an *intensively managed* world might hope to support with some degree of comfort and individual choice." The Academy also concluded that even with the sacrifice of individual freedom and choice, and even with chronic near starvation for the great majority, the human population of the world is unlikely to ever exceed 30 billion.

Nothing in the Global 2000 Study counters the Academy's conclusions. If anything, data gathered over the past decade suggest the Academy may have underestimated the extent of some problems, especially deforestation and the loss and deterioration of soils.

At present and projected growth rates, the world's population would rapidly approach the Academy's figures. If the fertility and mortality rates projected for 2000 were to continue unchanged into the twenty-first century, the world's population would reach 10 billion by 2030. Thus anyone with a present life expectancy of an additional 50 years could expect to see the world population reach 10 billion. This same rate of growth would produce a population of nearly 30 billion before the end of the twenty-first century.

Here it must be emphasized that, unlike most of the Global 2000 Study projections, the population projections assume extensive policy changes and developments to reduce fertility rates. Without the assumed policy changes, the projected rate of population growth would be still more rapid.

Unfortunately population growth may be slowed for reasons other than declining birth rates. As the world's populations exceed and reduce the land's carrying capacity in widening areas, the trends of the last century or two toward improved health and longer life may come to a halt. Hunger and disease may claim more lives — especially lives of babies and young children. More of those surviving infancy may be mentally and physically handicapped by childhood malnutrition.

The time for action to prevent this outcome is running out. Unless nations collectively and individually take bold and imaginative steps toward improved social and economic conditions, reduced fertility, better management of resources, and protection of the environment, the world must expect a troubled entry into the twenty-first century.

The U.S. Global 2000 Study Compared with Other Global Studies

In the course of the Global 2000 Study, the U.S. Government's several models (here referred to collectively as the "Government's global model") and their projections were compared with those of five other global studies — the Latin American World Model, the World 2 and World 3 models (which were the basis for the 1972 *Limits to Growth* report to the Club of Rome), the United Nations World Model, and the Model of International Relations in Agriculture. The purpose was not only to compare the results of different projections, but also to see whether and how different assumptions and model structures may have led to different projections and findings.

The Global 2000 Study's principal findings are generally consistent with those of the five other global studies despite considerable differences in models and assumptions. On the whole, the other studies and their models lack the richness of detail that the Government's global model provides for the various individual sectors — food and agriculture, forests, water, energy, and so on. However, the linkages among the sectors in the other models are much more complete. Many apparent inconsistencies and contradictions in the Global 2000 projections arc due to the weakness of the linkages among sectors of the Government's global model.

Another important difference is that the U.S. Government's projections stop at the year 2000 or before, while the other global studies project well into the twenty-first century. The most dramatic developments projected in the other studies — serious re-source scarcities, population declines due to rising death rates, severe environmental deterioration — generally occur in the first half of the twenty-first century and thus cannot be compared with the Government's projections. Up to the turn of the century, all of the analyses, including the Government's, indicate more or less similar trends: continued economic growth in most areas, continued population growth everywhere, reduced energy growth, an increasingly tight and expensive food situation, increasing water problems, and growing environmental stress.

The Global 2000 Study conducted an experiment with two of the more integrated nongovernment models to answer the question: "How would projections from the Government's global model be different if the model were more integrated and included more linkages and feedback?" The linkages in the two nongovernment models were severed so that they bore some resemblance to the unconnected and inconsistent structure of the Government's global model. Chosen for the experiment were the World 3 model and the World Integrated Model.

In both models, severing the linkages led to distinctly more favorable outcomes. On the basis of results with World 3, the Global 2000 Study concluded that a more integrated Government model would project that:

- Increasing competition among agriculture, industry, and energy development for capital would lead to even higher resource cost inflation and significant decreases in real GNP growth (this assumes no major technological advances).

- The rising food prices and regional declines in food consumption per capita that are currently projected would be intensified by competition for capital and by de-gradation of the land.

- Slower GNP and agricultural growth would lead to higher death rates from wide-spread hunger — or from outright starvation — and to higher birth rates, with greater numbers of people trapped in absolute poverty.

- A decisive global downturn in incomes and food per capita would probably not take place until a decade or two after 2000 (this assumes no political disruptions).

When links in the World Integrated Model (WIM) were cut, outcomes again were more favorable. The results of the unlinked version were comparable to the Global 2000 quantitative projections for global GNP, population, grain production, fertilizer use, and energy use. But in the original integrated version of WIM, gross world product was 21 percent lower than in the unlinked version — $11.7 trillion instead of $14.8 trillion in 2000. In the linked version, world agricultural production rose 85 percent instead of 107 percent; grain available for human consumption rose less than 85 percent because some of the grain was fed to animals for increased meat production. Popula-tion rose only to 5.9 billion rather than 6.2 billion, in part because of widespread starvation (158 million deaths cumulatively by 2000) and in part because of lower birth rates in the industrialized countries. The effects of severing the linkages are much less in lightly populated regions with a wealth of natural resources, such as North America, than in regions under stress, where great numbers of people are living at the margin of existence. In North America, the difference in GNP per capita was about 5 percent; in South Asia, about 30 percent.

The inescapable conclusion is that the omission of linkages imparts an optimistic bias to the Global 2000 Study's (and the U.S. Government's) quantitative projections.

This appears to be particularly true of the GNP projections. The experiments with the World Integrated Model suggest that the Study's figure for gross world product in 2000 may be 15-20 percent too high.

2. The Canadian Future: A View from the Outside

The Global 2000 Report to the President makes it clear that the nations of the world have become intricately interdependent and that if present policies continue, major changes of an undesirable nature can be expected throughout the world, changes that will affect every nation, including Canada.

Compared with most of the world, Canada faces a relatively promising future. Canada is in the fortunate position of having abundant resources, including minerals, water, energy, forests, fisheries, and agricultural lands. Canada is not overpopulated. Canada can also feed itself (despite its reliance on imported food during the winter months), which is a degree of security few nations have today. Canada's population is well educated. While Canada is somewhat dependent on foreign technology to develop its resources, even in this regard Canada is better positioned than many other nations. Canada has a large capital base (albeit not wholly Canadian owned) and a high per capita income. Canada does have some environmental problems (especially acid rain and agricultural water and soil problems), but compared to desertification in Africa, deforestation in the tropics and erosion in South Asia, Canada's environmental problems are of modest proportions. Although the country would be highly exposed in a nuclear exchange between the United States and the Soviet Union, Canada is not likely to face a direct military threat. Overall Canada has many comparative advantages — a nation of abundance in a world of increasing need.

This is not to say that Canada has no problems or vulnerabilities. Canada, seen from the outside, has not implemented an energy policy adequate for the 1980s and 1990s. Canada also appears to be ill prepared for the immigration pressures that will no doubt increase. Canada will remain highly vulnerable to climatic shifts and may approach the limit of its grain exporting potential before the end of the century. Canada is expected by outsiders to continue to experience internal, regional tensions relating to resource development policies.

Canada's greatest vulnerability — its resource exporting economy — also constitutes its most fundamental strength. The world will need Canadian resources increasingly in the coming decades; however, *major* dislocations in the world economy are virtually certain and these dislocations can be expected to feed back to and adversely affect the Canadian economy. As the world's population swells toward 6 billion or more, small local conflicts will have increasing potential for expansion into regional conflicts with disruptive effects on the world's economy and for financial institutions. Fluctuating demands for resources will create many difficulties in the management of the Canadian economy. In the case of food, for example, Canada (with the United States) will be forced in bad crop years to decide who eats and who does not.

As an open, resource-exporting economy, Canada clearly can not isolate itself from conditions in the rest of the world. This fact was demonstrated in the Canadian experience with the first oil shock in 1973 when the OPEC nations quadrupled the price of petroleum. There were at that time more than a few Canadians saying to each other, "We're all right. Canada, you know, is a resource *exporter*. World oil problems don't affect us."* By late 1974, however, the world economy had been depressed by the oil shock and Canadians were beginning to feel the effects in their own economy of reduced world demand for their resources.

This experience of what some Canadians now refer to as "the 1974 effect" has demonstrated that the economic well-being of Canada is highly dependent on economic conditions in the rest of the world. To develop and capitalize on its resources, Canada must be able to export them. This situation, of course, makes Canada — like the resource-exporting less developed countries (LDCs) — very vulnerable to even normal economic fluctuations in the world economy let alone major dislocations.

What can Canada do to protect itself at least partially from excessive economic vulnerability while still playing a responsible role as a leading nation in our global society? Isolation is evidently not feasible. Throughout the coming decades, the world developments described in *The Global 2000 Report to the President* will have a major impact on the Canadian economy no matter what Canada does. However, by staying involved and working to minimize any global disruptions, Canada has a good opportunity to reduce the impacts on itself and indeed on the world as a whole. Nonetheless, there will still be costs and pressures. One can visualize developments in which Canada, as one Canadian put it recently, becomes "the hewer of wood and drawer of potash" for its major trading partners. That need not be the case, however, if Canada carefully plans its future economic and political thrusts and relations with the rest of the world (especially with the United States) and if the country's resources are suitably husbanded.

The assessment of the issues to be faced by Canada are discussed herein from the point of view of an outsider, with the limitations and perspective that such a viewpoint provides. The observations make few judgments, and raise many more questions than they answer. It is hoped that the issues raised will be of assistance to Canadians in shaping their future.

Canada's Evolving Relations: Beyond the 1980s

In the early 1980s Canada's fortunes will be closely tied to those of her OECD trading partners, especially the United States. After the mid-1980s, however, Canada could be in a position to determine its own future, rather than having it shaped by external factors alone. Canada could, if it wished, make (rather than be shaped by) world economic events. This opportunity stems principally from Canada's situation as a resource-wealthy nation in a world in which per capita availability of many resources is declining.

Canada's greatest opportunity in the decades ahead rests upon its relative wealth of resources and abundance of space. Present and projected world trends, as depicted by the Global 2000 and other studies, show Canada with a combination of emerging opportunities. These opportunities rest upon increasing bargaining power by Canada as demands for resources intensify.

Canada basically presents a paradox. On the one hand Canada is a developed

---

* There was a similar, but somewhat different, experience in the United States, where the majority of the public did not know the United States imported oil.

nation with a per capita GNP of approximately \$7,000 and a diversified industrial base. On the other hand Canada's economy is structurally similar to that of many resource-exporting LDCs. Canada is a major exporter of minerals, metals, natural gas, wheat, lumber, pulp, paper and fish, which altogether constitute more than half of Canada's total exports.[1]

Foreign markets for Canada's various commodities are virtually certain to expand in the coming decades. In fact, the demand for many commodities such as certain minerals, wheat and lumber, will probably increase at a rate faster than the average rates of economic growth, due (in the case of minerals and lumber) to the contraction of supplies elsewhere and (in the case of wheat) to the higher than average growth in demand combined with a relative flattening of the supply curve as production potentials are reached and the supply of unused arable land diminishes around the world.

Increasing foreign demand for its export commodities places Canada in the position of being able to choose from among a number of options for exploiting this situation to the greatest advantage. It also raises a number of important issues which have begun to occupy Canadians, such as the extent of foreign ownership of Canadian resources and industry (a carefully monitored aspect of the Canadian economy), the extent of processing or manufacture of commodities (value added questions), the role of foreign technology and capital, and the "importation of pollution" from the United States.

In the international arena, Canada will find its political power enhanced by its resource surpluses. This should in turn enhance Canada's unique role as a small, Western bloc developed nation that does not represent a military threat to the world. Canada can influence world events through political and commercial ties with the United States in particular, as well as the rest of the world. Thus, if grain is to be used as an instrument of peace (or war, according to one's outlook), for example, Canada could be reckoned as a world power, able to export grain and decide who may be given access to the supplies.

However, with increased international political influence also comes a number of questions. If, as is likely, Canada's international political leverage is enhanced in proportion with the greater demand for her resource surpluses, how will Canada exercise this leverage? To what extent would this leverage be influenced by foreign ownership or other foreign participation in the Canadian economy? To what extent does Canada's dependency on resource exports to the United States, Japan and Europe put it in league with (or at least in sympathetic standing with) LDC nations whose economies are dependent upon exports of basic resources?

The opportunity for increased Canadian exports seems to be fully understood and appreciated at high levels of government policymaking, but, looked at from the outside, Canada seems very weak in its ability to put into place foreign policies and resource management programs that will ensure stable trade, continuing productivity of renewable resources and maximum value added from renewable and non-renewable resources. Canada is not expected to be able to take full advantage of its opportunities until it makes some significant changes in its trade arrangements and domestic economy. With regard to trade, Canada may need to obtain greater control over its resource wealth and development by renegotiating terms of trade and other agreements with foreign capital sources and by broadening the base of Canadian trade. Domestically, Canada must deal effectively with its energy economy (which is now a liability and vulnerability) and with the future of its population growth (especially immigration).

Relations with the United States

Canada's relations with the United States are extensive and complex and it is not possible here to project the future evolution of these relations in any detail.* From the perspective of the Global 2000 Study, however, a few major developments seem likely.

It must be recognized from the outset that United States and Canadian influences on each other in the decades ahead are taken as granted. Such influences are not only unavoidable, but in fact beneficial in many ways to both Canada and the United States. The U.S. economy provides a large market close to Canada. Trade is easy and convenient. About 70 percent of Canada's trade is with the United States, and about half of the foreign investment in Canada is of U.S. origin.

The Global 2000 Study describes several trends in the United States that are likely to have significant implications for U.S.-Canadian relations. The primary change is that the United States, like most nations, is becoming more interdependent with — or perhaps even more dependent upon — the rest of the world for resources. As a result, the United States may in time become less able to determine and shape its future and in fact may become more vulnerable to conditions in the rest of the world.

Probably the single most important fact about the future of the United States is this: *The United States has already burned half of its ultimately recoverable conventional crude oil.* As can be seen in Figure 2-1, no other area of the world has burned so much of this resource.

The United States must develop a new energy economy. It might be possible — on a crash basis — to make a major shift in the U.S. energy economy over a period as short as 15 years. In the interim, the United States will remain critically dependent on oil from the Middle East. What are the chances of a complete interruption in the flow of oil from the Middle East sometime in that period? Assuming that 15 years are available for the development of a new U.S. energy economy, does the United States have a clear policy, plan and commitment?

The United States has adopted and abandoned several energy plans since 1973 — Project Independence, the National Energy Plan (NEP), NEP II, etc. To the extent that these various plans have addressed the long term, they have assumed that nuclear fission and coal would fill in for oil until nuclear fusion was developed and on-line, providing energy "too cheap to meter." While progress has been made on fusion energy, this technology is still decades away at best and it is expected to be at least as expensive as fission energy.[2]

Recently, the role of fission energy in filling the oil gap has come under further question. There have long been public concerns over reactor safety, nuclear waste disposal and the proliferation of nuclear weapons facilitated by fission power and the nuclear accident at Three Mile Island (TMI) did nothing to reassure the public on these points. Nevertheless, until recently, the financial community has continued to regard nuclear energy as a good investment. Since the TMI accident, the risks of insurance

---

*	For an excellent and exhaustive analysis of resources in Canadian-U.S. relations, see C.E. Beigie and A.D. Hero, Jr., *Natural Resources in United States-Canadian Relations*, Boulder: Westview Press, 1980. This three-volume work will be required reading for many years for everyone seriously interested in U.S.-Canadian relations and in resource issues.

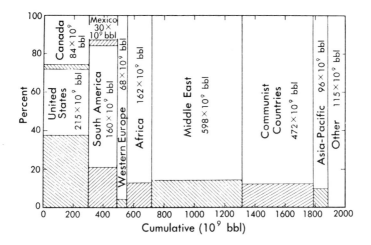

Figure 2-1. Distribution and present production of ultimately recoverable conventional crude oil resources of the world. Shaded areas represent cumulative production to date. *Source: Global 2000,* vol. 2, Washington: Government Printing Office, 1980, p. 352.

have been reevaluated and new safety procedures and equipment considered. As a result, the economics of nuclear power are looking much less favorable to the financial community. The most recent economic study of nuclear power found that the cost of constructing nuclear power plants in the United States will continue to increase rapidly and as a result, by the late 1980s, electricity from new nuclear plants will be at least 25 percent more expensive than electricity from coal plants.[3]

The TMI accident also raises questions about the wisdom of allowing a significant portion of any nation's energy to come from nuclear reactors. The TMI accident greatly increased public concern about the safety of fission reactors. If a somewhat more serious accident should occur — one involving a death or significant release of radioactive materials into the environment — there would likely be a strong and immediate demand to close all plants. If the United States had a heavy dependence on nuclear energy, a serious accident could be as disruptive as the loss of Middle Eastern oil would be now.

Coal development is also a problem for the United States — and for Canada. The United States has large coal deposits, but burning coal on a scale that would permit a significant reduction in the use of oil would release large amounts of sulfur and nitrogen oxides (even with pollution control efforts) and increase problems with acid rain in both the United States and Canada. In analyzing the environmental implications of U.S. energy plans, the Department of Energy concluded in 1978 that there would be little or no improvement in sulfur oxide (SOx) emissions. The few improvements that might occur would take place by 1985 when it is assumed that standards for existing sources will have been met. The Energy Department found that if SO_x emissions are to be reduced by 1990, the retirement of old plants must be accelerated or the standards tightened.[4] It is unlikely that air pollution standards in the United States will be tightened in the near future; if anything, the standards may be relaxed.

Over and above the sulfur oxide problems, a massive shift to coal use in the United States would accelerate the rate at which carbon dioxide is accumulating in the atmosphere, bringing nearer the time when a significant human-induced effect on the world's climate will occur. Also, labor disputes in the U.S. coal industry have a long history of violence and death and a shift to coal would also increase the vulnerability of the U.S. economy to violent and highly disruptive strikes.

In 1979, the U.S. Congress decided to make a major effort to develop a synthetic fuels market in the United States. Out of this effort the U.S. Synfuels Corporation was created. This initiative is now encountering difficulty in the face of a desire to reduce the U.S. Government's budget.

The current approach emphasizes deregulation of oil and gas prices. Deregulation will increase prices, spur domestic production and encourage conservation, but will do little to provide a satisfactory long-term replacement for oil.

The United States may succeed in resolving its energy problems before there is a major disruption in supplies, but progress to date is not wholly encouraging.

Energy is not the only long-term problem facing the United States. Another is the major shift occurring in the ethnic and linguistic composition of the U.S. population. Spanish speaking people of Latin American origin already make up a substantial fraction of the population in the Southwest and the Hispanic fraction of the population is expected to continue growing. The annual number of illegal immigrants (most of whom are from Latin America) has been estimated to be approximately equal now to the natural increase in the United States. If current demographic trends continue over the next century, about 40 percent of the U.S. population will be made up of post-1980 immigrants and their descendants.[5]

Canada has experience already with the tensions that different languages and cultures can introduce into a society, and the Canadian experience may soon be repeated in the United States. Throughout the Southwest there are heated debates over whether voting information should (or must) be available in Spanish. Spanish language education is even a hotter issue. Bilingual education was a significant issue in recent U.S. elections. Senator S.I. Hayakawa has introduced a Constitutional amendment declaring that "the English language shall be the official language of the United States." Senator Hayakawa told the Senate that he was introducing this amendment "to clarify the confusing signals we have given in recent years to immigrant groups," and because "we are being dishonest with linguistic minority groups if we tell them they can take full part in American life without learning the English language."[6]

Passing constitutional amendments, defeating members of Congress and other protests will do little to alter the tide of change. The fact is that the United States shares a border of approximately 1,500 miles with Mexico, and the disparities of conditions on either side of the border are too large to permit easy or peaceful control of immigration from Mexico and other Latin American countries into the United States.

The importance for Mexicans of access to the United States labor market can be seen through a brief examination of the Mexican income base. The Mexican labor force was approximately 20.2 million* in 1980.[7] It is estimated that 40-50 percent of the

---

* In terms of the labor activity rate, this represents 29 percent of the Mexican population. This rate is very low and reflects the fact that roughly half of the Mexican population is under the age of 18 and that only a small percentage of Mexican women are traditionally found in the labor force.

Mexican labor force are effectively unemployed, which means that the total employed is at most 12 million. It is conservatively estimated that there are 5 million Mexicans illegally resident in the United States today. Assuming that 4 million of these are working and that they, on the average, are earning three times what their fellow workers are earning in Mexico, the earnings of the 4 million in the United States are similar to those of the 12 million in Mexico. Since much of the earnings of Mexicans in the United States is sent back to Mexico, the value of the United States as something more than a "safety valve" is apparent.

Mexico City is only 500 miles south of the United States border. United Nations medium variant projections show Mexico City growing from 10.9 million in 1975 to more than 30 million by 2000.[8] Mexico City, already the largest city in the world, would then contain more than three times the current population of the metropolitan New York area with the additional problems of inadequate supplies of food, housing, transportation and sanitation and with severe air pollution. The severity of the water problems are illustrated by the fact that the city is gradually sinking as the level of water in the aquifer under the city is reduced.

Mexico also faces serious food problems. Mexico's population is growing at more than three percent per year and in 1974 Mexico imported 9.4 million metric tons of grain — comparable to the amount India imported during its worst famine. Mexico has plans to use its oil wealth to revitalize its agriculture, to spur growth centers away from Mexico City, and to improve its infrastructure generally, but the political challenges in the decades ahead will be enormous. Income disparities are wide and growing. The average Mexican never expected to become wealthy from Mexican oil, but he certainly did not expect to become *poorer*. Yet this is exactly what has happened as wages have remained low and double-digit inflation has eroded purchasing power. While now regarded as a stable nation, Mexico (and several other Central American countries) has a high potential for political and economic instability over the next few decades. The United States will certainly be affected by migration and perhaps by much more.

A changing population and serious, unresolved energy problems are some of the difficulties that the United States — Canada's largest trading partner — will face in the coming decades. The United States may succeed in coping with these issues without serious disruptions of its economy and without complicating its relations with Canada, but it would probably be prudent for Canada to broaden its trade somewhat. Seventy percent is a very large fraction of trade for any nation to have with another single economy.

It would also be prudent for Canada to recognize that there will be continuing differences of perspective with the United States on resource matters, especially energy, water, fisheries and environmental matters, especially acid rain. As the United States continues to deplete its oil resource, U.S. and Canadian perceptions of the Canadian energy resources are likely to differ. The U.S. Department of Energy expects Canada to be in a position to export some energy; Canada, by contrast, sees itself as needing to import energy. While there is some difference of opinion, Canada, from either perspective, is relatively well off with regard to energy.

U.S. interest in Canadian (and Mexican) energy resources is likely to increase in the years ahead. U.S. officials have come to understand that there is not likely to be much oil available from Canada, but there is likely to be growing interest in Canadian natural gas, possibly to the advantage of Canada. Canada has large reserves of natural gas, but it would be more difficult to export gas to Europe or Japan, than the United States, which provides a close, convenient market. There is, however, potential for tension in U.S.-Canada relations over Canadian gas: Canada is likely to want to use more — perhaps most — of its gas itself, especially as its efforts to reduce oil consumption increase.

Acid rain will continue to be a point of issue. Even with existing pollution control technologies, U.S. energy development plans are likely to result in increased release of oxides of sulfur and nitrogen and thus increase the problems caused by acid rain. Acid rain is not as important an issue in the United States as it is in Canada because only a few states are severely affected and so far these pollutants have not had a major impact on U.S. crops. In 1980 the United States and Canada signed a Memorandum of Intent on transboundary air pollution and if both countries abide by this agreement, acid rain problems should be reduced significantly in both countries.

Fish is another resource on which there has been some U.S.-Canada discussion already and on which there is potential for continued tension in the future. The issue will be difficult because of the strong political constituencies involved in both countries. In the United States, fishermen — especially in the Northeast, but also to some degree in the South — have put considerable pressure on Congress not to ratify the pending fishing treaty with Canada. To complicate matters, Mexico has unilaterally reduced the amount of fishing that U.S. fleets can do in Mexican waters. The Mexican action has put the U.S. fishing industry in a difficult situation and as a result the political pressure on Congress is likely to increase. It may be some time before the U.S.-Canada fishing treaty is signed and it is possible that further negotiations may be required. The fishing issue is being complicated by the perception in the United States that Canada is subsidizing its fishermen with low-priced fuel.

Water is likely to be an increasing issue in U.S.-Canada relations. The United States has already expressed interest in obtaining water from Canada or diverting waters in the United States in ways that would affect Canada. The Global 2000 Study, in addition to other work, suggests that the United States will likely be even more interested in water in the future than it has been in the past. Parts of the United States are quite short of water already and the need for water will continue to increase in the years ahead. The United States has asked Canada occasionally in the past whether it was interested in selling some of its water and Canada should not be surprised if in the future the United States asks again, perhaps even a bit more persistently than in the past. There is no question that Canada has large water resources and at least in the United States there is a view that Canada is rather wasteful in the way in which it manages its water.

At some point Canada may find it useful to make an overall assessment with the United States of U.S.-Canada water needs and resources. A careful analysis of options would demonstrate a Canadian sensitivity to water problems in the United States and could also be a useful mechanism for describing to the United States the full range of Canadian concerns — reducing Canada's water availability or water quality, effects on Canada's climate, etc. — in undertaking massive transfers of water.

International grain sales is another topic on which there is likely to be continued discussion between the United States and Canada. The Global 2000 projections suggest that increasingly large areas of marginal lands throughout the world will be planted with grain. This development will mean increased weather-related variation in world grain supplies: most years there will be little or no production from the marginal acres, but in one year out of five there will be a bumper crop and a flood of grain on the market. All this means that weather-related fluctuations in grain supply are almost certain to increase in the years ahead.

Weather-related fluctuations in demand are a problem for both U.S. and Canadian farmers and are likely to become even more of a problem as North America becomes increasingly the dominant supplier of grain for the international market. The problem for both the United States and Canada is that it is the farmer who is being asked to cope with the weather-related fluctuations, creating problems in farm policy and balance of payments. One year there may be tremendous demand for everything farmers can produce, while within a few years there is likely to be a glut.

To complicate matters further, production costs in the United States are among the highest in the world because U.S. farmers use so much energy directly and indirectly. As a result, grain buyers try to buy elsewhere and come to the United States only when they have bought as much as possible elsewhere. It also means that in years when crops around the world are reasonably good, Canada, Australia and other grain exporters have an edge on the market and can sell their grain first. When the other grain is gone, buyers come to the United States. As a result, the United States farmer is both the primary supplier and the residual supplier. The United States is likely to want to discuss with Canada means for distributing the responsibility for covering weather-related fluctuations.

In summary, Canada will continue to have good relations with the United States, but a number of issues — especially water diversion schemes, acid rain, natural gas exports and control of fluctuations in demand for grain — will continue to bring out differences of perspective. Canada will continue to trade extensively with the United States throughout the 1980s, but beyond that Canada should be able to broaden its trade and reduce current overreliance on U.S. markets. To restructure its trade, however, Canada must decide how to develop its relations with a number of other nations.

Relations with the Other OECD Nations

Can Canada broaden its trade by doing more business with the European members of the OECD? If the Global 2000 projections are even roughly accurate, Europe may be headed for some difficult decades and the opportunities for increased trade with Europe may be limited. The economic growth rate in Europe has already slowed substantially and continuing energy problems are likely to give Europe further economic troubles. Overall, the European market for Canadian resources is not likely to increase rapidly in the decades immediately ahead.

Japan is another possibility. The Global 2000 projections show the Japanese economy increasing at a steady rate, averaging 2.7 percent, nearly doubling over the 1975-2000 period. Japan will need resources and trading partners to sustain this growth. Canada has a number of resources Japan needs — lumber, pulp, paper, grain and nuclear technology. But the Japanese economy — despite its apparent strength — will remain highly vulnerable because of its large population and limited resources. Canada may wish to increase its trade with Japan to some degree, but Canada needs to broaden its trade well beyond the United States and Japan.

Relations with the Less Developed Countries

There are major opportunities for Canada to strengthen relations with and increase trade with the LDCs. The prospects for economic growth in the poorest LDCs are limited and in a few countries, per capita income and food consumption may actually decline. Major growth is expected in the newly industrializing countries — Mexico, Brazil, Venezuela, Indonesia, etc. — and major trading opportunities should develop.

Venezuela is now the third largest purchaser of Canadian exports and Canadian trade with the Philippines is significant and growing.

The opportunities for Canada to expand trade relations with the LDCs is likely to increase in the decades ahead. Canada's situation as a "have" nation will become increasingly evident, but being a "middle power" and having a small population with relative self-sufficiency in most resources, Canada is not vulnerable to accusations of exploitation.

Canada has a number of concerns in common with the LDCs. The Canadian economy is somewhat similar to a resource-rich, capital-limited LDC economy, except that Canada has a small, well educated, technologically competent population. Thus, although it is a Western industrialized nation, Canada can relate to many aspects of the development process. Canada, like the LDC resource-exporting economies, is vulnerable to major fluctuations in world demand and price for resource commodities.* As a result Canada has many concerns in common with the LDCs who desire fairer terms of trade for their resource exports. Canada therefore could and probably should seek a mediator and political role in relations between the industrialized nations of the North and the LDCs of the South.

Canada is in a unique position to be of assistance in the North-South dialogue. Because of a long history of thoughtful and sensitive foreign policy, Canada is respected and trusted by the South as well as the North. Canada has excellent ties to the Commonwealth, Francophone and Western Hemisphere nations, to the nations with centrally planned economies, as well as to the NATO and OECD nations. Canada, like the LDCs, has pursued a foreign policy that emphasizes multilateral relations, investing much time, effort, and financial support in developing ties to the United Nations agencies, the International Monetary Fund, other multilateral organizations and the GATT (General Agreement on Tariffs and Trade) process. As a result of these ties, Canada probably has more diplomatic channels open to it than virtually any other nation in the world.

Canada is also in a special position with regard to the world resource market. While Canada is and will remain a resource-rich country, it does not have nearly enough resources to solve the world's resource problems. There will, however, be growing interest in Canadian resources, and Canadian resource management policies can have a major impact on other nations' resource management and development policies.

Canada has at least two major resource management options: it can sell to the highest bidder, or it can demand disciplined action on the part of resource and food importing nations as a condition for access to Canadian resource supplies. By demanding a thoughtful and responsible approach to sustainable economic development, Canada could exert considerable pressure and influence with only marginal amounts of resources (on a world scale) if it demonstrates that its own resource management policies meet these goals. An approach to agriculture that recognizes and restricts the "export" of topsoils would be one very constructive such example.

---

* It must also be acknowledged that in some ways Canada competes with LDC resource exporters. One of Canada's competitive advantages is its political stability. Political instabilities in African and Latin American resource exporting countries help Canada's economy.

The most immediate and pressing opportunity facing Canadians is to develop policies for orderly world access to its grain markets. The world is approaching a period of several decades when pressure on the world's food production resources — especially soils, and groundwater — will be very high. Prices for grain are projected to increase more rapidly than general inflation and there will be temptation around the world to exploit agricultural resources heavily, resulting in long-term damage to the resource base.

Resolution of the world's food problems is a complex task that will require the cooperative efforts of all nations not just on food production, but also in limiting population growth. While it would be impossible to impose U.S. and Canadian food and population policies on other nations, it should be possible for the United States and Canada to insist that other nations follow internationally agreed upon programs to address the world's food problems. The World Plan of Action on population agreed upon at Bucharest and the International Food Strategy agreed upon at Rome are not perfect, but together they would accomplish much.

With these internationally agreed upon plans in mind, Lester R. Brown, President of the Worldwatch Institute, proposed in 1975 a Joint United States-Canadian Commission on Food Policy. This Joint Commission would have the following purposes:

• to formulate a North American food policy specifically designed to support a global food strategy that included the World Plan of Action on population and the International Food Strategy.

• to establish explicit guidelines for responsible, cooperative behavior in a world of food scarcity, ensuring ready access to the North American food markets for countries that are following internationally agreed upon strategies in food and population, and when supplies are low, restricting access for those that are not.

• to assess carefully North America's productive and export capacities as they relate to present and future needs of importing countries.

• to increase significantly North America's capacity to analyze and anticipate future changes in the world food economy by pooling the information-gathering and analytical resources of the two countries.

• to address a number of difficult analytical questions, e.g.: Will the food deficit in Asia continue to grow? Are the Soviets in fact planning to de-emphasize agricultural development and depend on North American farmers to meet an even greater share of their needs? Is the combination of uncontrolled population growth and ecological deterioration in Africa going to lead that region toward massive imports of grain? Will Mexico require major grain imports in the near future? Will North America be able to supply all the food the world will want at anything resembling historic price levels?

• to assure that farmers in both countries make the needed production and investment decisions by providing adequate incentives.

• to make a contribution to the resolution of the world's food problems by keeping all North American cropland in production until stocks can be built up in an international food reserve system.[9]

If the world projected in the Global 2000 Study is to be avoided, innovative new policies must be initiated very soon. Lester Brown's proposal for a Joint U.S.-Canada

Commission on Food Policy offers many useful possibilities and deserves much further attention by both countries.

Canada's Future Internal Relations

Canada's internal relations are perplexing to Americans. Sometimes we look with envy at Canada, thinking that it must be wonderful to have the luxury to argue so long and stridently about some of the things that Canadians argue over. Other times we become concerned, thinking that perhaps the biggest threat to Canada's future is not from an invasion or another Ice Age, but rather from internal tensions.

While it is risky for people so far removed to comment on Canada's internal tensions, it does seem that perhaps some of the tension in Canada is related to the issues discussed in the Global 2000 Study. More specifically, some of the tensions in Canada seem to be related to (1) differences in resource endowments among the Canadian provinces, and (2) differences in benefits (or perceived benefits) that accrue from the development of Canadian resources. To put it differently, there seem to be individual regional economies within the overall Canadian economy and these economies may be linked better to external markets than to the Canadian economy as a whole.

The individual regional economies in Canada have differing needs for resources, requirements for skilled and unskilled labor and needs for housing. Skilled manpower is needed in the resource-rich West and at the same time there are pockets of unemployed people in the resource-needy East. High priced natural resources would be an advantage to several provinces, but may work to the disadvantage of Central Canada.

On a globe, Canada appears large in every direction, but this geographic representation of Canada misses the essential political and economic reality of Canada. Politically and economically Canada is not large in every direction, but long and thin, stretched from Atlantic to Pacific along the border with the United States. Transportation, communication and economic linkages along the length of Canada are more difficult in some places than linkages across the border to the United States. The long, narrow nature of Canadian political and economic geography and the ever close proximity of the United States are factors that are not subject to change and if Canada is to remain a united people, it must manage its overall resource development (including the associated transportation, communication and economic linkages) in such a way that the political and economic fabric of Canada is strengthened, not weakened.

The issues of Canadian internal relations are too complex for detailed discussion here, but the Global 2000 Study is relevant to these issues in two general ways. First, to the extent that internal tensions in Canada are resource-related, these tensions are likely to be easier politically to deal with now than they will be in ten or twenty years when disparities and inequities that exist now are likely to have increased. Thus, it would seem prudent for Canadians to make every effort to find ways to deal with these tensions sooner rather than later.

The second way in which the Global 2000 Study relates domestically to Canada concerns energy. Canada's greatest vulnerability in an otherwise bright future is seen from the United States to stem from its domestic energy pricing. Canada urgently needs to begin the transition to energy-efficient technologies and capital stocks and this transition will be very slow in coming as long as domestic energy prices are kept artificially low. Artificially low domestic energy prices continue to encourage investment in energy-inefficient technologies, capital plant and product designs. Canada cannot afford to accumulate energy inefficient technologies and capital stocks that will require 20-50 years to depreciate and replace. The era of inexpensive energy is gone, and the sooner Canada makes the adjustment to world price levels the easier the adjustment will be. As in the United States, the biggest political issue will not be the increased price per se, but the questions of who is to receive the profit from the increased prices and how that profit is to be used.

Canada also needs to plan how it will achieve a balanced development of its energy resources, including oil, natural gas, coal, solar, nuclear, hydro as well as biomass. Continuing along the path on which petroleum provides a large share of total energy will lead to a number of complications. The petroleum would need to come from tar sands, and since difficulties exist in terms of the capital or the technology required for the rapid development of tar sands, Canada's energy development could become very dependent on foreign capital and technology. In addition, it is suggested that Canada would be wise to re-examine carefully the energy requirements of tar sands development. Like the U.S. energy economy, the Canadian energy economy is probably becoming more energy-intensive, requiring increasing amounts of primary energy to produce a unit of secondary energy for final demand.

The technologies and economics of tar sands exploitation have many similarities with the technologies and economics of oil shale exploitation and synthetic fuels generally. All of these technologies and resources are energy-intensive, requiring a large input of oil (or equivalent energy) to produce a barrel of oil. In the United States there has been a long debate over the price to which oil must rise before various synfuels become profitable. The most recent answer has come from the Congressional Research Service. The CRS concludes that *synfuels require so much oil and equivalent energy that they are not profitable at any price of oil:*

> [It] concludes that given the assumptions specified below, as oil price rises, projected cost of producing synfuel from a new planned plant using currently foreseeable technology increases proportionately. No matter how high the price of oil rises — even to $100 per barrel — a new plant built subsequent to arrival of oil at that price will not be economic as an investment prospect.
>
> For example, under present conditions, a new coal hydrogenation plant could produce synthetic liquid fuel for about $70 per barrel under this analysis, which would appear patently "uneconomical", compared with oil, now about $40 per barrel. However, to have this plant operating at the time when the present oil price doubles would be an attractive commercial venture. In fact, had such a plant been built about 6 years ago, when oil was $9 per barrel, its product cost of $28 per barrel would be "economical" today.
>
> This analysis assumes that the structure of the U.S. economy will remain essentially unchanged, and that design and construction of a new synfuel plant will take longer than the time required for the effects of oil price rises to ripple through the economy. As the dominant source of our energy, oil price "drives" the cost of all modern industry, including synfuels. Firm correlation is shown in the study between oil price and prices of other forms of energy and key commodities such as steel and cement. As manufacturing plants become more expensive to build and operate, the costs of their products rise, including the cost of synfuels.
>
> Plant operating costs, however, will increase more slowly than rising oil prices. Consequently, a synfuel plant built at any oil price, with the required

capital investment committed, will become progressively more economic with increasing oil prices; its product cost over time will attain parity with oil price. Thus, the sooner a plant is built, the better, assuming continuing oil price escalation.

However, even with continuously increasing oil prices, a synfuels plant would not necessarily appear to be a sound investment from the private sector investor point of view at a given point in time. Without subsidies and assuming any reasonable rate of oil price increase, the length of time between expenditure of the capital investment and recovery of capital from future higher prices may be unattractive, given the current and expected interest rates and the associated "time value of money." If oil prices should stop rising permanently, then no new synthetic fuels venture could be justified economically now or in the foreseeable future.

Realistic evaluation of synfuels, therefore, must always look ahead. Today's decision needs to be made in terms of its effect several years hence. The full economic benefit of building a plant now may not be realized for several years in a smoothly-running, fully depreciated facility selling synfuel very competitively with the then-current price of oil.[10]

Are synfuel plants (and perhaps tar sands plants) economically justifiable only when energy and other prices are inflating rapidly? Do depreciation schedules and tax incentives obscure the fact that synfuel plants — and perhaps also tar sands plants — do not in fact generate any profits? Does more energy go into the construction and operation of a synthetic fuel or a tar sands plant than is produced by the plant? Has net energy analysis demonstrated that tar sands plants are energy producers rather than energy consumers? These are questions that Canadians need to ask themselves as they plan the development of their energy resources.

Implicit in the balanced development of Canadian energy resources is a need for greater integration of the Canadian economy. Canada's major decision of the early 1980s is how to develop its energy. This decision should take into account how Canada will use its energy to further shape and evolve its economic and social future. Therefore, it is a decision that should be preceded by the screening of some of the possible alternatives for economic growth and development. It is imperative, therefore, that Canada look well into the future now in order to find the basis for making the most advantageous and beneficial decisions on the development of its energy and other resources.

Conclusions

The Global 2000 Report to the President concludes that if present policies continue, a number of world problems will have become more severe and more intertwined by the turn of the century than they are today. In this circumstance a number of developments can be anticipated in the world economy that would have significant implications for the future of Canada. Of all the industrialized nations, Canada is probably second only to Japan in the degree to which its economy depends on a healthy world economy and active world trade. A major war, a disruption in the flow of Middle East oil, a breakdown in the operation of the international monetary system . . . , any of a large number of possible events would have quite a significant effect on Canada.

How seriously should one take the Global 2000 Study's findings? The Study is not the work of a group of academics but rather is based on the best professional analysis and data that were available within the U.S. Government. Although the analysis has many limitations and weaknesses, the preponderance of the deficiencies bias the Study's findings in an optimistic direction.

Furthermore, the Study's conclusions are generally supported by every major analytical study of world problems now available. The Brandt Commission, for example, noted that:

> Current trends point to a sombre future for the world economy and international relations. A painful outlook for the poorer countries with no end to poverty and hunger; continuing world stagnation combined with inflation; international monetary disorder; mounting debts and deficits; protectionism; major tensions between countries competing for energy, food and raw materials; growing world population and more unemployment in North and South; increasing threats to the environment and the international commons through deforestation and desertification, overfishing and overgrazing, the pollution of air and water, and overshadowing everything the menacing arms race.
>
> For these trends to continue is dangerous enough, but they can easily worsen. A number of poor countries are threatened with the irreversible destruction of their ecological systems; many more face growing food deficits and possible mass starvation. In the international economy there is the possibility of competitive trade restrictions or devaluations; a collapse of credit with defaults by major debtors, or bank failures, a deepening recession under possible energy shortages or further failures of international cooperation; and intensified struggle for spheres of interest and influence or for control over resources, leading to military conflicts. The 1980s could witness even greater catastrophes than the 1930s.[11]

Both this passage from the Brandt Commission's report and the conclusions of the Global 2000 Study are based on an assumption of a continuation of present policies around the world. Policies, of course, must change. How should Canada's policies change? How can actions be taken now that will have maximum benefit to Canada's growth as a people and a nation among the family of nations?

While several Canadian reports[12] begin to address these questions, our conclusion is that Canadians do not have an adequately clear image of their nation or of the evolving world of which they are a part. Canadians need to awaken to and address a number of matters that are pressing fast upon them. Only by addressing these matters promptly can Canada hope to avoid some very serious problems with capital investments, industry and technology in the years not far ahead.

It is suggested therefore that Canadians confront more deliberately the issues concerning Canada's future. Canada needs to undertake a careful examination of its strengths in a dynamically evolving world. Such an examination goes far beyond what would be possible or appropriate for a report such as this, but a number of domestic and international issues can be raised here, which should be considered by Canadians in the examination of their options for shaping their future.

The Domestic Issues

As a first step toward developing a clearer sense of Canada's options, Canada might decide to assemble and integrate any existing studies regarding its various sectors in an effort to confront a number of questions that do not seem to have been fully answered. The issues that need to be addressed in an integrated Canadian study cover everything included in the Global 2000 Study and more. Canadians will have their own perceptions and priorities, but the following list should provide at least a starting point.

Clarifying Assumptions

In the process of assembling and integrating the existing Canadian studies, it would be useful to examine carefully the assumptions underlying the various studies and projections. Studies are never any better than their assumptions and unless the assumptions are clearly identified and carefully examined, important issues may simply be assumed away.

In the course of preparing the U.S. Global 2000 Study, the assumptions underlying the U.S. projections were examined and many inconsistencies and contradictions were found. The inconsistencies and contradictions were so extensive that the U.S. Study concluded: "the executive agencies of the United States Government are not now capable of providing the President with internally consistent projections of world trends in population, resources and environment for the next two decades." The U.S. Government agencies desperately need to improve the analytical quality of their policy analysis.

In preparing this report for Canada, a number of Canadian studies of world trends and Canada's own future were reviewed. In this brief review it was not possible to perform the detailed analysis of assumptions that was made in the U.S. Global 2000 Study, but a preliminary impression is that some of the inconsistencies that exist in the U.S. analyses also exist in Canadian studies. Different Canadian agencies are also making different assumptions about growth rates, external demand, weather, fuel prices, capital availability, etc., some of which may provide a somewhat distorted or even unrealistically optimistic picture of what lies ahead for Canada.

One of the most important contributions that an integration of existing Canadian studies could make would be the initiation of procedures for the development of more consistent assumptions for future studies. If assumptions are not clear and consistent, important issues are easily passed over and lost in the cracks between areas covered by different responsibility centres.

Population Issues

One of Canada's major national advantages for the future is that is has a relatively small population. Should Canada have an explicit population policy? If so, roughly how large should Canada's population be? Ten times its present size? Twice? Half?

How can Canada control its population? Birth rates are always difficult to influence, and immigration will be a continuing important factor for Canada's population. Could (or should) immigration from Commonwealth Nations ever be reduced? Could immigration from the United States ever be controlled if there were significantly different standards of living in the two countries? Could there ever be significant differences in standard of living in the two countries?

The world's experience with the Vietnamese boat people and the U.S. experience with Cuba's policy to allow large numbers of particular groups of people to emigrate to the United States illustrates the need for each nation to decide what number of refugees it can accept. What role can and could Canada play in resolving the plight of political refugees and future victims of famine?

Limited financial opportunities in slow-growing economies of poorer LDCs will lead many of the more educated people to the industrialized nations, including Canada. Should Canada selectively admit well educated, professional people to Canada? If immigration pressures continue or even increase, will the Canadian job market be able to supply the needed jobs?

Since immigrants are generally adults often with families, they create a demand on housing that is disproportionately high relative to their overall addition to the population. The resulting additional demand on the housing market may be salutary, but more extensive low income housing may be needed initially. How will the Canadian housing industry respond?

Immigrants will make Canadian society even more pluralistic, more like the ethnic and racial composition of the United States. Definition of what is "Canadian" may become confused; intercultural tensions may emerge. What are the implications of the present balance between immigration and emigration? What vision does Canada have for the future mix of its society? Should this matter be discussed before immigration policies simply respond to pressures that will no doubt increase further?

Another change is that the average age of the Canadian population is increasing, which means: (1) a slower growth in the labor force will occur, (2) a change in the ratio of income earners to total population will develop, and (3) special services for older people will be needed. What implications do these trends have for the Canadian economy?

The World War II baby boom will pass through its peak impact on the labor market in 1981. Does this mean that unemployment problems should lessen, if other conditions remain equal?

Higher-than-average growth is projected for the Canadian West. City growth may become disorderly around resource development areas, resulting in a decline in quality of life. How can rapid urban growth in the West best be managed?

Economic Issues

Canada may want to restructure its resource trade insofar as it exports resources with relatively low value-added, while importing machinery and other products with higher levels of value-added. Resource exportation is generally capital-intensive and produces relatively few jobs. Resource exportation produces rewards for the people who supply the equipment and make the investments. Are the rewards equitably distributed? Many Canadian resources have been developed by investments from outside of the country and efforts are being made to repatriate some of that investment. In the decades ahead Canada will probably find itself focusing much more on the distinction between trade balances — which are always very positive for Canada — and the very adverse balance of payments situation. The balance of payments problem is essentially due to dividend and interest payments sent out of the country. Canadians want money in their pockets, not just balanced trade. Canada will also want to find ways to increase manufacturing and other activities that add value to the resource base used.

Many benefits of Canadian resources do not at this time accrue to Canada or to Canadians. For both political and economic reasons, Canada will probably want to pay more attention to the recipients of benefits that accrue from Canadian resource exploitation in the future. How can Canada use her resource wealth to the greatest benefit?

Can Canada use the proceeds from resource commodity trade to develop an internally self-sustaining form of industrially oriented economic activity that would be relatively less vulnerable to world events, particularly to fluctuations in U.S. demand and supply? Or must Canada cast its fortunes unconditionally with those of the United States, seeking further integration of trade and communications?

A weighty body of opinion supports the theory that domestic supplies of capital are inadequate for rapid development of Canadian resources. It is now a seller's market for investment capital needed for Canada's energy development. Can Canada control investment capital sufficiently to ensure protection of environmental resources, e.g., adequate pollution controls on industry, adequate management of renewable resources?

Canada's comparative advantage based upon hydropower, for example, for manufacturing energy-intensive products (e.g., aluminum) includes definite costs to the renewable resource base. Are the impacts on the renewable resource base resulting from hydropower development being considered adequately in projections and planning?

Technological Issues

Canada has unique economic advantages in terms of its particular mix of natural resources. Canada prides itself in being strong in nuclear reactor technology, telecommunications and aeronautical equipment. Are these the technologies of Canada's future? What technologies does Canada *need* to derive the most benefit from its unique endowment of resources?

In order to maintain a measure of equity in technical relations with Japan and other OECD nations, Canada will have to place special emphasis on technological innovation and productivity advances to avoid becoming overly dependent on U.S. technological leadership. With a relatively small population and research base, can Canada hope to compete with Japan, the United States, and Europe in all technologies? If not, what criteria should be employed in selecting technologies for Canadian developments? What policy levers can be used to provide the requisite focus for particular areas of technology?

Is Canada, with all its resource wealth, too "relaxed" to compete with Japan in technological innovation?

Climate Issues

Climate presents a possible threat to Canada. The world has enjoyed a warmer than average period for the past four decades. Over hundreds of thousands of years, the earth has periodically experienced such warm periods, but many of these periods lasted no more than a few decades.

Climatologists are now about equally divided between the prospects for global warming and global cooling. If volcanic ash or some other factor causes the world's climate to return to more average temperatures — or even move to a period of below average temperatures — Canada would be severely affected. Large areas now in productive agriculture would become unproductive. Trees would grow more slowly. Precipitation would decrease and become more variable. Further global warming, if it occurs, would have equally large but possibly more beneficial implications for Canada.

Whether it is warming or cooling, Canada would be acutely affected by climatic change, and the world's climatic record clearly indicates that changes are to be expected.

What monitoring, education, and research steps could be undertaken now to anticipate climatic changes and prepare for future needs? Given Canada's vulnerability to climatic change, what political role could or should Canada play in international efforts to reduce CO_2 emissions?

Food Issues

Demand in OECD trading partners for grain may be near saturation and unlikely to increase significantly as populations and incomes level off. Middle income LDCs could however exert strong demand. The poorest LDCs will have the largest needs, but limited ability to pay. How can (or should) Canada keep the price of its grain at a level that the markets most in need will be able to afford?

Expansion of cereal production worldwide onto drier marginal lands enhances the potential for wide swings in world food production from year to year. How flexible is the Canadian grain production system to shifts in demand and the vicissitudes of weather?

Until there is an effective international food reserve, Canada will be in a position of deciding on the fate of human lives during times of famine in poor LDCs. How can Canada avoid the political pitfalls of being a major food surplus nation in the coming years of food insecurities and potentially disastrous shortages? Should Canada actively encourage the development of an international food reserve system?

Weather variability during the rest of the century may be an important issue for Canada. The coefficient of variability of wheat yields during the period 1927-77 was 25 percent in the Canadian wheat-growing Prairie Provinces. Because this variability showed a tendency to decrease in the end of the observation period (that is, during the 1953-73 optimum climatic period) and because of "improved technology" that buffers variability of yields, Agriculture Canada has assumed for planning purposes "a continuing variability of approximately 20 percent in Canadian wheat production."[13] To what extent does the "improved technology" involve the abandonment of moisture-conserving practices? Will substitute measures for moisture conservation (no-till practices, for instance) be equally effective? Will irrigation development be impelled by the probability of an increase in number of low-rainfall years? Considering the likelihood of a return to weather variability greater than in the 1950s and 1960s, is an estimate of a mere 20 percent coefficient of weather-related variability in production realistic? Should the possibility of increased weather variability during the remainder of the century be taken more adequately into account in Canadian food and agriculture projections? Should an analysis be made in terms of the synergisms of the potentially dry years and loss of organic matter in soils, especially in the Prairie Provinces?

Brazil, Argentina and Thailand have the agricultural resources necessary to produce large amounts of grain with relatively small applications of energy-intensive inputs. As a result, grain production costs in these countries could be significantly lower than in Canada and the United States. What will be the long-term implications of high-cost energy for the competitive position of Canadian agricultural commodities? To what degree is Canada's competitive position in the production of corn and other grains dependent on low energy prices? What would be the impact of energy price parity on the production of energy-intensive Canadian crops? Should Canada seek to better exploit the comparative advantage of barley production, rather than replace barley with wheat?

Canada's expansion of agricultural exports to the European Economic Community, Japan and developing countries and a shift away from the United States as its major trading partner in agricultural commodities makes Canada more dependent on global economic growth and stability of world trade patterns. To quote an OECD study: "Because so much of the pattern of Canadian [agricultural commodity] trade depends on the development of world markets, the stability of the emerging [Canadian] trading pattern remains uncertain."[14] What effect will the emergence of other nations as low-cost producers of grains have on Canadian grain trade? What long-term impact will high energy prices have on developing countries' (and Europe's) ability to buy energy-intensive grain produced in Canada (and the United States)?

The projected demand for grain suggests that there will be temptations to over-exploit the Canadian (and U.S.) agricultural resource base, leading to soil deterioration and lowered water tables. Estimates of Canada's (and the United States') food production and export capacity in the year 2000 vary widely. Would a rigorous reexamination of these estimates be useful in defining more accurately future Canadian grain export capabilities under varying degrees of soil and groundwater depletion? How serious are problems of land degradation? Is land degradation adequately reflected in the projections of food production and the costs of production? Has Canada planned adequately for the increasing demand for potash fertilizers for soybeans?

What significance will changes in Canadian dietary preferences have for Canadian food production patterns? Trends toward more fruits and vegetables in diets, for example, would increase demand for horticultural products and farmlands, many of which are threatened by urban sprawl.

Fisheries Issues

How can Canada responsibly build up stocks of oceanic species and maintain them at sustainable levels in the coming years of increasing demands for fish from foreign countries? How will decisions be made on allowable catch in times of abundance and in times of great demand from foreign fleets for access to Canadian fish stocks? How can marine mammals or their habitats be managed so as to avoid costly conflicts with fishermen?

Multiple species management of marine stocks is needed. How can such management be achieved technically and politically?

What impact is artificial salmon spawning having on the populations?

What impact is acid rain having on recreational and other inland fisheries?

Forestry Issues

A major decline in the growing stock of the world's forest, especially in the LDCs, could have a major impact in the forest products industries in Canada. There may be increasing demand for Canadian forest products with much higher prices. If this happens, it will take restraint and wisdom on the part of the Canadians to resist the temptation to overexploit their forest resources.

The major forestry issue will be to accurately forecast demands and to plan supplies accordingly. Are demands for the forest resources — for lumber, pulp, and perhaps biomass — increasing faster than projected? Are policies in place to deal with an accelerated demand on forest resources?

As demand increases the feasibility of cutting lower grade forests in the North, is silvicultural intensification on better forest sites in the South more appropriate than expanding exploitation into lower-grade Northern forests?

What is the long-term impact on forest site productivity of more complete utilization of trees by the forest products industry and by the energy industry (for methanol production)?

Water Issues

As a nation, Canada has abundant fresh water resources. The issues here concern how these resources will be developed. Will Canada undertake major diversion projects to provide more irrigation in the agricultural provinces? How will Canada respond to continuing efforts by the United States (and perhaps even Mexico) to obtain water from Canada or to alter flows in the United States that would affect Canadian ground and surface waters?

Energy Issues

Canada is richly endowed with energy resources, coal, uranium, natural gas, tar sands and biomass. How can Canada obtain maximum economic and social benefits from its energy development?

Are Canada's domestic energy pricing policies consistent with conservation and self-sufficiency goals?

Canada's energy demand has not increased as rapidly as expected. Are new, realistic demand projections needed?

What are the implications of Canada's National Energy Policy (NEP) on Canada's future energy development and self-sufficiency? One objective of the Canadian NEP is to increase Canadian ownership in the petroleum industry from the present 30 percent to 50 percent. In response, the oil industry (especially that part of the industry controlled by U.S. interests) has significantly reduced its rate of capital investments in Canada. At the same time, worldwide inflationary pressures caused by OPEC pricing policies and depleting oil reserves are tending to concentrate the available investment capital in the OPEC countries and in the major oil companies. How can Canada deal with the power that is concentrating in OPEC and the oil companies in order to obtain the capital and technology needed for Canadian energy development? What price must Canada pay for 50 percent ownership and energy self-sufficiency?

What trade policy will Canada adopt for its nonrenewable energy resources? Should Canada produce more energy than it needs and export the surplus? If so, to whom?

Does uranium have the potential of once again becoming a large export commodity and a significant source of new jobs?

How much *net* energy is produced by a tar sands plant over the lifetime of the plant?

One objective of Canada's NEP is to reduce demand for oil by, among other things, promoting gas substitution. Will this policy preclude further exports of natural gas to the United States beyond existing commitments?

Would Canada derive more benefits from exporting energy-intensive products rather than energy resources *per se?*

Nonfuel Minerals Issues

How vulnerable is Canada because of its dependency on overseas suppliers for tungsten and tin? Is Canada's 25-year needs base realistic?

Canada absorbs environmental costs of producing metal products for export. Do the prices reflect these costs? Would Canada be better off exporting finished products (rather than semi-finished products) and absorbing the additional pollution (or pollution control) costs? How much vertical integration is desirable in the Canadian economy?

Environmental Issues

What will be the economic cost of environmental protection between now and 2000, or the noneconomic costs of inadequate environmental protection? Are noneconomic costs of development being adequately taken into account? How will Canada control and manage the environmental problems associated with energy development?

To what extent does pollution control or resource conservation contribute to inflation, to productivity, and to employment, as well as to environmental and human health?

What are the impacts on water resources to be expected from irrigation and energy development in the Prairie Provinces?

What impacts on biological resources can be expected from hydropower development?

What impact is acid rain having on forests?

Increasing demand for forest products and minerals will increase feasibility of exploiting low grade resources in the northern territories. How much will it cost to protect the fragile northern ecosystems? Have cost estimates been made? Have the governments (federal and provincial) taken steps to protect these ecosystems adequately?

Urbanization of Canada's population is expected to continue. The growth of cities will cause continuing pressures for conversion of agricultural lands to urban uses. Much good cropland is likely to be lost and production of fruits and vegetables may be limited as a result. How can Canada's agricultural lands be protected from urban sprawl?

Should people be encouraged to settle more sparsely populated regions to avoid additional build-up in the Montreal-Toronto corridor?

The International Issues

If the future projected in the Global 2000 Study is to be avoided, each and every nation must contribute to the needed initiatives and policy changes. The previous section outlined a series of questions that relate to Canadian domestic policy. Attention to domestic issues, however, is not enough for Canada. Because of its open economy, traditions and history, Canada has both a vested interest in and a responsibility for leadership in resolving world problems.

The magnitude of the challenge facing the world is difficult to describe. Mark MacGuigan, Secretary of State for External Affairs, provided some perspective recently in a speech to the Royal Institute of International Affairs in London:

> It is important that we grasp the scale of the most recent [1979] oil shock. It is estimated that it will mean an income loss by the OECD [Organization for Economic Cooperation and Development] countries to Organization of Petroleum Exporting Countries (OPEC) of around $150 billion or 2 percent of gross national product. What is more, this drain will slow the OECD's economic activity by an estimated $250 billion below what it would otherwise have been by early 1981, for a total loss in one year of $400 billion. But it is not just the developed countries that will pay. The price rise will mean an income loss by the oil-importing developing countries of $30 billion, reduced export earnings of some $20 billion for them because of lower OECD growth, and other lost economic activity of roughly $25 billion, for a total loss of $75 billion by early 1981. We can see something of the relative scale of this shock by looking at its relation to aid. Aid this year is expected to total around $32 billion, *or roughly the same as the direct income loss to developing countries from the oil-price rise.*[15] [Emphasis added.]

Reflection on MacGuigan's speech brings to mind a number of questions: Can the developing countries ever expect to develop into petroleum-intensive economies? Can they develop into energy-intensive societies? Could the world's population be fed without the fertilizers and irrigation provided by petroleum and natural gas? Could major flows of petroleum be interrupted in the next decade or two? Can population growth be stopped? Why do people want large families? Would providing family planning to everyone reduce the average family size to two children? Where will the capital, the human resources, and the natural resources come from to rear, educate, house, and employ the approximately 2.5 billion babies that will be born during the last two decades of this century? How can economic progress in the poorest countries be financed? How will the debts of the poorest nations be paid? What happens if nations cannot pay their debts? Are the world's financial institutions capable of maintaining economic order? Will protectionism and tariff barriers help? What can technology contribute? Would space colonies contribute to solving the world's problems? Do nuclear weapons provide security? Would world security be increased by shifting significant amounts of weapons expenditures to economic assistance? How would the arms exporting industrialized nations manage the economic dislocations and unemployment that would follow a significant shift away from arms expenditures? Can terrorism be eliminated while large numbers of people feel they have nothing to lose? Can world security be achieved without solving the population, food, and poverty problems?

The Global 2000 Study does not answer these questions. The Study concludes only that to continue current policies around the world leads to a future in which a number of already serious world problems are still worse, not better. Since it examines only one policy option — continuation of present policies — the Global 2000 Study does not even provide a basis for recommending specific alternative policies. More work is needed before specific policy recommendations can be convincingly presented.

The next step that is needed is to assemble and evaluate the various proposed solutions to the world's interrelated problems. The Brandt Commission's report is one widely known set of recommendations. *The World Conservation Strategy,* the United Nations' Development Decade documents, the World Bank annual reports, and the *Report from Havana* issued by the Group of 77 are others. The Carter Administration published its recommendations days before leaving office and the Reagan Administration has expressed interest in preparing alternative recommendations. All of these recommendations need to be evaluated in comparison with the U.S. Government's global model and other global models to see if they lead to a future that is preferable to the future implied by a continuation of present policies. Only by carefully testing all of the proposed solutions with the best available models will it be possible to develop the necessary international consensus, cooperation and commitment to action.

The Brandt Commission's report is one of the most complete and highly regarded sets of recommendations now available and it provides an example of the testing and examination that needs to occur. The Brandt Commission's report[16] — even including the large volume of supporting papers[17] — does not provide convincing evidence that its recommendations would solve the world's problems. The analysis is too fragmented. The recommendations of the Commission need to be analyzed and tested on the best available world models. Such analysis with the U.S. Government's global model, for example, might point to a future very different than that depicted in the Global 2000 Study, but such an analysis might also show that changes well beyond those recommended by the Brandt Commission would be required to alter significantly the present course of human history.* On the basis of the analyses now available, there is simply no convincing report available on how the nations of the world should address the problems discussed in the Global 2000 Study — let alone the wide range of inter-related world security problems. A thoughtful plan for world development and security is urgently needed.

The world is not only groping for a set of convincing recommendations as to what to do next, it is groping for an entirely new model of development. For several decades world leaders have thought that they knew how to develop the world to look like, for example, Canada. Then came 1973, and the first oil shock. Thoughtful people around the world are now doubting that Canada — or the United States, or the Soviet Union, or Western Europe, or Japan — provides a useful model for world development. These economies are all too energy-intensive to serve as models — and probably cannot themselves continue many decades under their present economic structures.

Where are the new models? How are the nations of the world to develop in an era of expensive energy? Who will think through the new concept of development? The new concept is most likely to emerge from a society that has sufficient resource security to devote time and money to rethinking development; that has a self-interest in seeing increased economic stability and reduced tension in the world; that does not have the ideological obsessions of the superpowers; that has a tradition of scholarship, innovation and pragmatism; that is respected and not threatening to most nations of the world; and that has a fundamental concern for the well-being of future generations. While many nations fit several of these criteria, few if any are better suited than Canada.

If the future projected in the Global 2000 Study is to be avoided, truely major changes in public policies around the world must be made soon. To accomplish these changes the world desperately needs intellectual, political and diplomatic leadership. It is hoped that Canadians will recognize the nearly unique opportunity that their nation has to provide this leadership.

---

* The Brandt Commission's recommendations, combined with those of *The World Conservation Strategy* would probably have a more significant effect on the world's future, but neither of these reports addresses adequately the long-term financial effects of oil depletion or the financial (and other) implications of another few decades of the arms race.

References

1. Based on the latest *Canada Handbook* available at this writing: Statistics Canada, *Canada Handbook,* Ottawa: Supply and Services Canada, 1979, p. 232.

2. *The Global 2000 Report to the President,* vol. 2, Washington: Government Printing Office, 1980, p. 361.

3. *Power Plant Cost Escalation,* available from Komanoff Energy Associates, 333 West End Avenue, New York, N.Y. 10023.

4. *Global 2000,* vol. 2, p. 427.

5. Leon Bouvier, Testimony before the Joint Hearing of the House and Senate Subcommittee on Immigration and Refugee Policy, May 7, 1981, forthcoming in the report of the Subcommittees' hearings of May 5-7, 1981.

6. S.I. Hayakawa, "Proposed Constitutional Amendment with Respect to Proceedings and Documents in the English Language," *Congressional Record,* April 27, 1981.

7. International Labor Organization, *Labor Force Estimates and Projections,* vol. 3, *Latin America.* Geneva: United Nations, ILO, 1977, p. 52.

8. *Global 2000,* vol. 2, p. 242.

9. Lester R. Brown, *The Politics and Responsibility of The North American Breadbasket,* Washington: Worldwatch Institute, 1975, pp. 38-43.

10. Congressional Research Service, *Costs of Synthetic Fuels in Relation to Oil Prices,* Washington: Government Printing Office, March 1981, pp. 1-2.

11. The Independent Commission on International Development Issues, *North-South: A Program for Survival,* Cambridge, Mass.: The MIT Press, 1980, pp. 46-47.

12. See for example: Science Council of Canada, *Canada as a Conserver Society: Resource Uncertainties and the Need for New Technologies,* Ottawa: Supply and Services Canada, 1977; C. Starrs, *Canadians in Conversation About the Future,* Ottawa: Environment Canada, 1976; W. R. D. Sewell and H. D. Foster, *Images of Canadian Futures: The Role of Conservation and Renewable Resources,* Ottawa: Environment Canada, 1976.

13. Agriculture Canada, *Orientation of Canadian Agriculture,* vol. 3, Ottawa: Supply and Services Canada, 1977, p. 21.

14. Organization for Economic Co-operation and Development, *Recent Developments in Canadian Agricultural Policy,* Paris: Organization for Economic Co-operation and Development, 1978, p. 25.

15. From "New Dimensions in North-South Relations: A Canadian Perspective," an address by the Honorable Mark MacGuigan, Secretary of State for External Affairs, to the Royal Institute of International Affairs, London, England, July 7, 1980.

16. Independent Commission on International Development Issues, *North-South,* pp. 46-47.

17. Independent Commission on International Development Issues, *The Brandt Commission Papers,* The Hague: Independent Bureau for International Development Issues, 1981.

Canada's View of Global and Domestic Developments

3. Canadian Studies Compared with the U.S. Global 2000 Study's Projections for Canada

The Global 2000 Report to the President contains projections about the future of every nation, including Canada. The Global 2000 projections about the Canadian future provide some sense of what professional analysts in the U.S. Government are thinking about the future of the Canadian economy and the country's resources.

Several agencies and organizations participated in seminars and informal discussions during the preparation of the Canadian Report. In response to invitations to review the *Global 2000 Report to the President,* a number of comments have been received. The Global 2000 Study's major findings have been found to be generally consistent with those of other global models[1] despite some differences in methodology and assumptions.

All of the global studies indicate similar trends, namely, continued economic growth in most areas, continued population growth everywhere, reduced energy growth, tighter food supply situation with doubled food prices, increasing water problems and growing environmental degradation.

In the midst of these rather gloomy global developments, Canada can be expected to face a relatively bright future: her resources are evidently ample to meet the needs of a population even in excess of 30 million, although it is to be realized that in comparison with global demands, the supplies are totally inadequate. It is apparent that there will be increasing pressures upon Canada for ever greater supplies to the rest of the world of basic resources, such as food, energy, forest products, minerals, which in turn will place increasing stress upon land, air and water resources within the country. In these circumstances there is evident need for concerted attention to the wise use of resources in Canada that will ensure that the exploitation of natural wealth will be dictated by longer term national/global interests rather than short-term gains or political expediency. Such prudence in the development and supply of resources to the rest of the world will inevitably demand some very hard choices and responsible stewardship as well as the careful protection of environmental resources and of sustainable resource yields.

This chapter reviews what the Global 2000 Study projects for the future of Canada and, whenever possible, compares the Global 2000 projections with Canadian studies. It is often not possible to make full comparisons between the Global 2000 and the Canadian projections. In some cases, the Global 2000 Report has no explicit assessments for Canada, while in other cases, there are no corresponding Canadian data. Comparisons are also often difficult because the projections have been developed with different assumptions and using different models.

The Global 2000 Study could present country-specific data for only a limited number of countries. In most of the projections, Canada was included in a "North

American" total. In some cases it has been possible to locate the computer runs that were used for the Global 2000 projections and to obtain specific information for Canada. In other cases, only a North American total is available.

In spite of the difficulties, it has been possible to make many comparisons. While the U.S. and Canadian projections are generally close, there are a number of differences that are worth examining further.

Population

The U.S. Bureau of the Census (Census) population projections for Canada[2] — included in the Global 2000 Report are in close agreement with Canadian projections.[3] Information in the base documents used is, however, not sufficiently detailed for in-depth comparisons.

The U.S. Census and Canadian projections of Canada's population are presented in Table 3-1. The Canadian projection of 28.3 million by 2000 is within less than 2 percent of the U.S. medium projection of 27.9 million. This means that Canada can expect a continued population growth of about 0.6 percent per year, a growth rate that is well below the world average and certainly manageable in the Canadian economic and resource situation.

The assumptions underlying the U.S. Census projections, however, should be noted at least briefly. All population projections start with assumptions about population in the base year (1975 in this case)[4] and about future developments in fertility, mortality and migration. The U.S. assumptions about future demographic developments in Canada may be of interest to Canadians.

The total fertility rate for 1975 was estimated by considering the provisional 1975 official Canadian estimate of total births and the latest available official fertility rates for Canada for 1972 through 1974, as reported by the United Nations in 1976 and 1977. The age pattern of fertility for 1975 was the average pattern of the 1972 through 1974 reported age-specific fertility rates.

TABLE 3-1
Population Projections for Canada, 1975-2000
(Millions)

	1975	1980	1985	1990	1995	2000
U.S. Bureau of the Census Projection[a]						
Low	22.9	23.8	24.6	25.3	25.8	26.1
Medium	22.9	23.9	25.1	26.3	27.2	27.9
High	23.0	24.0	25.6	27.2	28.5	29.6
Canadian Projection[b]						
	N.A.	23.9	25.1	26.3	27.4	28.3

a. Includes the populations of Bermuda, Greenland and St. Pierre and Miquelon. In 1975, these populations totaled about 115,000, about 0.5 percent of the Canadian population. *Source:* U.S. Bureau of the Census, Detailed Population Projections. Prepared for the Global 2000 Study, unpublished data, October 13, 1977.

b. *Source:* Infometrica, Ltd., unpublished document, Canada, June 12, 1980.

Life tables for 1975 were estimated based on life expectancies at birth and age-sex patterns of mortality for 1975 as shown in official Canadian population projections as reported by Statistics Canada in 1974.

The U.S. assumption is that the Canadian total fertility rate (a measure of the total number of children the average woman will have during her lifetime), which has been declining since 1960, will not decline much further or may increase over the next two decades, as shown in Figure 3-1. The U.S. Census assumption for the high series is that Canadian couples will increase their family size from an average of less than 2 in 1975 to 2.5 in 2000. In the medium series, the total fertility rate (TFR) was assumed to increase to 2.1. In the low series the TFR was assumed to decline slightly to 1.7.[5]

In all U.S. Census projections, mortality assumptions were identical to those used in official Canadian projections. Life expectancy at birth was assumed to increase from 69.6 years to 70.2 years for males through the 1975-86 period and then to remain

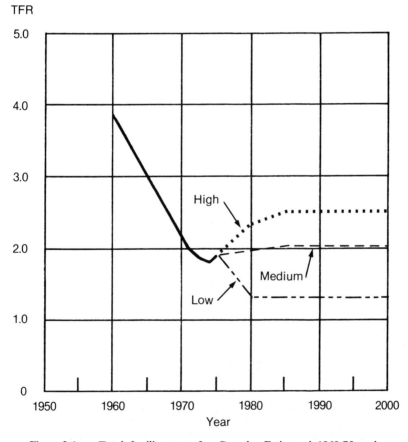

Figure 3-1.   Total fertility rates for Canada: Estimated 1960-75 and projected 1975-2000. *Source:* U.S. Bureau of the Census, *Illustrative Projections of World Population to the 21st Century,* Washington: Government Printing Office, 1979, p. 110.

constant at the 1986 level through 2000. For females, life expectancy at birth was assumed to increase from 76.7 years to 78.4 years through the 1975-86 period and then to remain constant at the 1986 level through 2000.[6]

It is noteworthy that the U.S. Bureau of the Census projections assume no net increase in total population attributable to migration.[7] The Global 2000 Study, on the other hand, cites a 1976 United Nations "Report on Monitoring Population Trends" in which net immigration to Canada of 2.2 million during 1950-74 was reported.[8] A recent increase in the number of migrants to Canada and the United States from the former British West Indies is also noted.[9] These figures suggest that immigration was contributing about 0.4 percent per year to the Canadian population, compared with a "natural increase" of about 0.6 percent. Recent trends and projected world conditions generally suggest that immigration may contribute even more to Canadian population growth in the decades ahead.

Gross National Product

There are significant differences between the gross national product (GNP) projections developed for the Global 2000 Study and those developed in Canada. There are also significant differences between both the Canadian and U.S. projections and what has actually occurred. All of the differences follow in significant part from the rapid increases since 1973 in the world price of petroleum, but to understand the differences, it is necessary to examine briefly how the Global 2000 and Canadian projections of Canada's GNP were developed.

Long-term economic projections are difficult and uncertain, and as a result GNP projections are rarely extended as much as 20-25 years even for a single nation. It was no surprise, therefore, that the U.S. Government agencies do not have a capacity to make 25-year regionally disaggregated GNP projections for all nations of the world. When needing long-term GNP projections, most U.S. Government agencies turn to the World Bank, which is the source the Global 2000 Study team turned to as well.

Even the World Bank does not routinely develop GNP projections for all nations of the world, or for periods as long as 25 years for the selected nations whose economies it does project. In 1975, however, the Bank did assist the Workshop on Alternative Energy Strategies (WAES)[10] at the Massachusetts Institute of Technology in developing a set of GNP projections for the industrialized and less industrialized countries. The Bank staff recommended that WAES projections[11] of GNP be used in the Global 2000 Study. The WAES projections were used for the industrialized and less industrialized nations; for the centrally planned economies (which were not included in the WAES Study), growth rate estimates were provided by the Central Intelligence Agency.

The WAES projections of GNP are somewhat difficult to interpret.[12] The WAES group started with projections provided by the Organization for Economic Co-operation and Development (OECD). The OECD figures were adjusted downward by the WAES group to reflect the fact that the OECD member states were basing their economic projections on assumed oil imports that in total exceeded the production capacity of the oil-exporting nations. The projections take account of the oil price increases in 1973, but not the increases of 1979. Analysis was also performed with the World Bank's SIMLINK (Simulated Trade Linkages)[13] model. Unfortunately, the WAES group did not record their work completely and the World Bank has destroyed the SIMLINK runs. Consequently, it is impossible to know exactly how these projections were developed.

The Global 2000/WAES projections suggest that in the decades ahead the Canadian economy will expand more slowly than during the 1960-72 period and more rapidly than during the 1972-76 period when increasing oil prices slowed economic growth significantly over much of the world. Canadian economic growth was relatively high over the 1960-72 period, averaging about 4.9 percent growth per year. During the 1972-76 period, Canadian economic growth slowed to an average of about 2.0 percent. The economic growth projected in the Global 2000 and WAES studies is about 4 percent per year in the early 1980s, slowing to about 3 percent by the end of the century, as shown in Tables 3-2 and 3-3. Per capita GNP projections are shown in Table 3-4.

TABLE 3-2
Growth Rates for Canadian GNP Assumed in the Global 2000 Study
(Percent)

		1975-85 Growth Rate			1985-2000 Growth Rate		
1960 72	1972- 76	High	Med.	Low	High	Med.	Low
4.9	2.0	4.9	4.0	3.1	3.7	3.1	2.5

Source: Global 2000 Report, vol. 2, Washington: Government Printing Office, 1980, pp. 43, 46.

TABLE 3-3
The Global 2000 Study's Projections of Canadian Gross National Product
(Millions of constant 1975 U.S. $)

	1985			2000		
1975	High	Med.	Low	High	Med.	Low
151,730	244,808	224,597	205,901	422,189	355,045	298,206

Source: Global 2000 Report, vol. 2, Washington: Government Printing Office, 1980, p. 46.

TABLE 3-4
Global 2000 Estimate (1975) and Projections (1985, 2000) of Canadian Per Capita GNP
(Constant 1975 U.S. $ per capita)

Range	1975	1985	2000
High [a]	6,626	9,952	16,175
Medium [b]	6,626	8,948	12,726
Low [c]	6,626	8,043	10,075

a High GNP and low population growth rates.
b. Medium GNP and medium population growth rates.
c. Low GNP and high population growth rates.

Source: The GNP figures (from p. 46, vol. 2 of *Global 2000*) are divided by the population figures given in Table 4-1 of this work.

The Canadian Government uses an advanced econometric model (CANDIDE) of its economy to develop GNP projections, but has apparently not made any projections that extend beyond 1985.[14] The CANDIDE projections of Canadian GNP were developed in 1978-79 and take into account more experience with increased petroleum prices than was included in the Global 2000 projections.

The CANDIDE model has been used to investigate a number of scenarios,[15] the most relevant of which is based on a weighted world market oil price of $20.78 ($ Cdn) in 1979, increasing 8.5 percent in 1980 and 7 percent per year thereafter to reach $36.41 in 1985 when the projection terminates. The CANDIDE projection assumes the domestic Canadian price will reach parity with the world price by the end of 1985. Actually, of course, the Organization of Petroleum Exporting Countries has already priced oil at about the price assumed for 1985.

The CANDIDE assumptions (see box for further details) include U.S. inflation, U.S. deregulation of oil by September 1981, and economic growth in the European OECD nations. U.S. inflation is assumed to peak at 9.3 percent in 1980 and decline to 7.6 percent in 1981. Real growth in the United States during 1981-85 was assumed to average 2.9 percent, during which it was expected that inflation rates would fall between 7.7 percent and 6.4 percent.[16]

All of the long-term GNP projections now available seem to have seriously underestimated the decelerating effects of the changing international energy economy and other factors in the economies of the industrialized nations.[17] The doubling in the world price of petroleum during 1979 and 1980 has drastically affected economic growth in the industrial nations. GNP growth in the industrialized nations has fallen from an average of 3.8 percent per year during 1968-78 to an average of 1 percent in 1980. The Global 2000 and WAES studies projected that GNP of the industrialized nations would grow between 3.1 and 4.9 percent over the entire 1976-1985 period. These projections were made in about 1975 and were therefore not influenced by the price hike of 1979. The CANDIDE projections of GNP were made in 1978-79 when the price of a barrel of oil on the world market had increased to about $20 U.S./bbl but subsequent price hikes have made these projections obsolete too.

Economic growth in the industrialized — and also the less industrialized — nations has proven to be quite vulnerable to world petroleum supplies and prices and events have overtaken both the Global 2000 and the CANDIDE projections. OPEC supply and price decisions continue to be highly uncertain, and as a result GNP projections will also continue to be quite uncertain. The long-term trend in world energy prices, virtually certain to continue upward,* results in economic growth that is likely to be substantially less than suggested in either the Global 2000 or the CANDIDE projections. For 1981, the OECD has projected a 1.25 percent GNP growth rate for Canada and the United States, and negative growth rates for Germany, England, and   Italy.[18] Figure 3-2 compares Global 2000, the CANDIDE and OECD projections.

---

*   The recent "glut" of oil demonstrates that Saudi Arabia still has production capacity adequate to flood the world oil market and impose price discipline on the OPEC members. It also demonstrates that Saudi Arabia has the capability to unilaterally increase OPEC's oil prices by cutting Saudi production. The "glut" does not in any way suggest that the world's long-term energy problems have been solved.

Assumptions in the CANDIDE Model*

External economic conditions:

	1980	1981	1981-1985
• U.S. Economy			
GNP (real growth)	—	2.9	2.9
Inflation	9.3	7.6	not specified
• OECD industrial growth	1.3	not specified	not specified

International trade flows:

• Volumes:

Uranium: continued high rates of export.

Electric power: 20 percent per year growth in exports.

Coal: weakening of exports initially; 5.0 percent per year growth in 1979 increasing to 7.5 percent per year growth by 1985.

Grains: strong rate of growth.

• Prices:

Uranium and electricity: remain high, reflecting the "general environment of 'high-priced' energy."

Minerals: continue present recovery (especially for iron and copper) and increase at "well over 6 percent per year range."
(Same for aluminum imports.)

Pulp: price declines reverse.

Wood and lumber: prices to continue dramatic increase of 12 percent per year, but fall to 6 percent per year by 1986.

Population:

Not described in the document. However, since growth in labor force is analyzed, demographic variables must be used. Different rates of growth are apparently not used.

Immigration:

Net immigration of 35,000 per year in 1979-80; 50,000 per year thereafter to 1986.

Other:

Domestic spending, federal, provincial and local; interest on public debt, government revenues (personal direct taxes, corporate direct taxes, indirect taxes, investment income); monetary policy.

Variables in the Different Scenarios

Domestic crude petroleum prices:

The model analyzes the consequences of three alternative pricing policies designed to bring the price of Canadian crude to parity with world oil prices.

• Parity by 1986

Assumes world prices increase by an average of 40 percent in 1979, 25 percent in 1980 and 7 percent thereafter, starting at a base in 1979 of

(cont'd. on p. 72)

(cont'd. from p. 71)

about $20/bbl and ending at $36.41 in 1985. *The world market price has already attained this level.*

- Parity by January 1982
  The same assumptions are used as in the preceding alternative, but parity would be attained earlier when the international price had attained $27.56, and requiring an increase in Canada of $3.50/bbl every 6 months.

- No parity
  No real rise in international oil prices; 8 percent per annum inflation.

Assumptions common to all scenarios:

- increased natural gas exports (over 1979 level) of 0.3 Tcf in 1980 and 1981, and 0.1 Tcf from 1982 to 1985.
- 35 million bbl/year "swap" of crude oil with the United States (represents about 13 percent of Canada's imports in 1979).
- 1.5 percent per annum increase in energy demand.
- substitution of natural gas for oil wherever possible.
- import 40 percent of domestically consumed crude petroleum in 1985.
- investment of $25 billion (1971 dollars) in electric utilities during 1979-85 period.
- investment of $2.5 billion (1971 $) in the pipeline system.
- investment through 1975 of $4.7 billion (1971 $) in oil sands development; no production until 1986.

Postulated responses to the oil pricing alternatives:

- personal saving rate declines from 10 percent to 9 percent.
- high participation rate in the labor force (63.3 percent by 1985).
- more vigorous wage bargaining (wages increase at 11.7 percent per year).
- additional energy investment of 3.1 billion (1971 $) of which 2.3 billion is oil sands.

Policy scenarios:

Six policy instruments are tested individually against the parity-by-1986 solution. The six instruments are later applied and tested in four policy packages. The instruments are:

- tax credit for mortgage interest and property.
- lower rate of growth in the money supply.
- increase in the investment tax credit.
- reduction in corporate tax rate.
- increase in personal taxes.
- decrease in personal taxes.

The policy packages are:

- highly stimulative.
- stimulative.
- stimulative with offset
- restraint

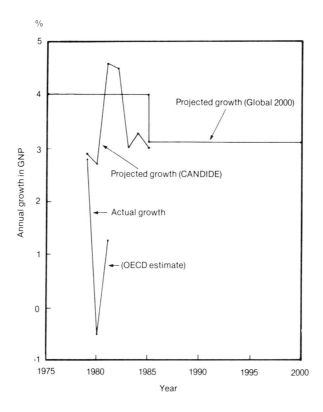

Figure 3-2.   Comparison of the CANDIDE and Global 2000 GNP pro-
jections with actual growth in the Canadian economy. *Sources: Global 2000,*
vol. 2, Washington: Government Printing Office, 1980, pp. 43, 46;
R. S. Preston, et al., *16th Annual Review: Background Simulations and
Policy Alternatives,* Ottawa, Economic Council of Canada, 1979 (scenario
assuming world parity for domestic oil prices by 1986 at $36.41); *OECD
Economic Outlook,* Paris: Organization for Economic Co-operation and
Development, Dec. 1980.

Climate

The climate of the earth has changed significantly in periods of only a few decades,
and further changes are to be expected in the years ahead. Since 1920, the earth has
enjoyed a particularly warm period. Temperatures have been declining, however, since
the early 1940s. Some statistical models of climate suggest a cooling trend in the decades
ahead. Increased emissions from volcanos (e.g., Mount St. Helens in Washington)
could contribute to a decline in temperatures. Other models suggest temperatures will
increase because of increasing concentrations of carbon dioxide in the atmosphere.

The carbon dioxide acts like the glass in a greenhouse, permitting light to enter but limiting the escape of heat. The concentration of carbon dioxide in the atmosphere is increasing steadily each year, and the projected increases in the combustion of fossil fuels (especially coal) together with large losses of tropical forests and soil humus will continue the increases. Virtually all climatological models suggest that the high latitudes will experience larger than average changes in temperature when climate shifts occur. Because of its location in high latitudes, Canada has been and will continue to be influenced significantly by changes in the world's climate.

The climatological analysis in the Global 2000 Report was based on a special study on climate futures undertaken by the National Defense University (NDU), with assistance from the U.S. Department of Agriculture and the National Atmospheric and Oceanic Administration.[19] Because there is as yet no generally agreed upon model of climatic variations, the NDU study developed climatological scenarios based on the subjective judgments of twenty-four expert climatologists — including Dr. C. K. Hare, M. K. Thomas, and G. McKay of Canada — from seven countries. Individual quantitative responses to ten major questions were weighted according to expertise and then averaged, a method of aggregation that preserved the climatologists' collective uncertainty about future climate trends. The aggregated subjective probabilities were used to construct five possible climate scenarios for the year 2000, each having an equal "probability" of occurrence.

The climatologists were nearly evenly divided over the prospects of warming or cooling and most felt that there would probably be no change. Disagreement about causes, effects and trends in climate made for this diversity of opinion.[20]

In the five NDU scenarios — which differ fundamentally in global temperature changes — Canada is mentioned only once, but is implied in all references to high mid-latitudes (40° to 65°) and polar latitudes (65° and higher). A brief summary of each scenario follows, with quotation in depth of the one scenario that mentions Canada specifically.

Large Global Cooling Scenario
    Viewed from the vantage point of the year 2000, an average cooling in the Northern Hemisphere of 0.6°C would have produced the following changes:

> While temperature decreased over the entire globe, the largest decreases occurred in the higher latitudes of the Northern Hemisphere. The north polar latitudes, marked by an expansion of arctic sea ice and snow cover (especially in the north Atlantic sector), had cooled by about 2°C since the early 1970s . . . .
> The northern higher and lower middle latitudes cooled by slightly more than 1°C. The subtropical latitudes in both hemispheres showed a 0.5°C decrease in average temperature, while the remainder of the southern latitudes showed a 1°C decrease. The large global cooling trend was also reflected in a significant decrease in the length of the growing season in the higher middle latitudes and a substantial increase in the variability in the length of the growing season from year to year.
> . . . The higher middle latitudes, particularly Canada, from which the westerlies and their associated storm tracks were displaced, suffered an increased incidence of long-term drought and winter cold.[21]

Moderate Global Cooling Scenario
    0.4°C cooling would result in slightly less precipitation than at present.

Same as Last 30 Years Scenario

By 2000 it could be 0.1°C warmer in Canada if there is no change in the global climate, owing to the greenhouse effect of carbon dioxide accumulations in the atmosphere. There would be no significant change in rainfall.

Moderate Global Warming Scenario

The greenhouse effect of carbon dioxide would cause this warming, which in the higher middle latitudes would increase average temperatures by 0.5°C, and result in slightly more rain and a slightly longer growing season.

Large Global Warming Scenario

The higher mid-latitudes would be 1.4°C warmer, have a longer, rainier growing season, and less variability in precipitation.

In the Global 2000 Study, the five NDU scenarios were reduced to three scenarios of more or less equal probability, as illustrated in Figure 3-3. Unfortunately, only one scenario — no change in climate — could be examined in other aspects of the Global 2000 analysis because none of the other models could accept climate as a variable. As a result, all of the Global 2000 projections assumed a continuation of the climate that prevailed in the 1950s and 1960s, when conditions were quite favorable for agriculture.

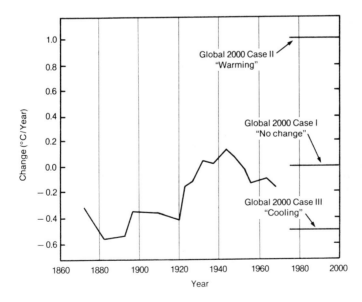

Figure 3-3.   The three Global 2000 Study scenarios compared with the annual mean temperature changes during the past century for the latitude band 0°-80°N. The period 1941-70 is the zero reference base. *Source: Global 2000,* vol. 2, Washington: Government Printing Office, 1980, p. 65.

A change of world climate — either a warming or a cooling — would have many implications for Canada. A global warming would have generally, but not totally, positive effects on Canada. Large expanses of Canada's northern lands would become suited for farming. Throughout the country, growing seasons would be lengthened and precipitation increase. In general, terrestrial ecosystems would become more productive; trees would grow faster. Energy requirements for heating would be reduced. On the other hand, global warming would, over time, melt sea ice and glaciers in volumes that would increase the sea level, flooding coastal lands and cities.

A global cooling trend would likely have adverse effects for Canada. Growing seasons would shorten. Precipitation would decline. Ecosystem productivity generally and tree growth in particular would decline. Ice would increase. Energy needs would increase.

However, between now and the end of the century *weather variability,* rather than long-term climatic change, could become critically important to Canadian farmers, and to food-deficit nations depending on Canadian and U.S. grain production.

Canadian studies of climate changes include three excellent reports which were provided after this text was finalized: G.A. McKay and T. Allsopp, "A Northern Perspective on Climatic Uncertainty," Downsview: Canadian Climate Centre, 1981; G.A. McKay, T.R. Allsopp, and J.B. Maxwell, "Lessons From the Past," Downsview: Canadian Climate Centre, 1981; G.A. McKay and G.D.V. Williams, "Canadian Climate and Food Production," Downsview: Canadian Climate Centre, 1981.

While it was not possible to make any comparison between the Global 2000 climate scenarios and Canadian climatological analysis, the reports identified provide an excellent background from which to begin the incorporation of climatic considerations into Canadian policy analysis.

Technology

The technology chapter of the Global 2000 Report contains no specific reference to individual countries. Its purpose is to state the technological assumptions underlying the projections made in the Global 2000 Study. These assumptions were: (1) general assumptions about technology and public policy, which were considered applicable to all countries, and (2) specific assumptions made for each of the sectoral projections.

On the policy level, the study assumes that all countries are now and will continue implementing programs in the areas of family planning, nuclear power and air pollution control. This in fact is not the case and would require major policy changes by some countries. For example, as pointed out in the chapter on energy, it is quite unlikely that all countries will adopt U.S. new source performance standards.[22]

The technological assumptions underlying each of the sectoral projections were made by the U.S. Government experts preparing the various sectoral projections. There was no attempt to coordinate the assumptions of the different departments and experts.[23] Most of the projections assume rapid technological progress, no setbacks, and no adverse impacts from the use of existing and new technologies. The technological assumptions underlying each of the projections are summarized in Table 3-5.

TABLE 3-5
Technological Assumptions Underlying the
Sectoral Projections of Global 2000 Study

Sector	Assumptions
Population	No major technology breakthroughs or setbacks affecting fertility or mortality rates.
GNP	Significantly increased returns on most LDC gross capital investment.
Climate	No consideration given to deliberate human efforts to modify climate.
Food	Widespread adoption and use of fertilizer and other yield enhancing inputs.
Fisheries	Development of methods for harvesting nontraditional fish species.
Forestry	Development of less wasteful production techniques and of methods for exploiting nontraditional forestry species; intensification with fertilizer and pesticides.
Water	Unknown.
Energy	Widespread deployment of light-water nuclear electric power plants.
Energy Residuals	By 1985, all countries will have adopted U.S. new-source air pollution control standards for carbon monoxide, oxides of sulfur, oxides of nitrogen and particulates, and will have retrofitted all energy facilities to meet these standards.
Fuel Minerals	Continuation of the price-cost relationships and technical trends generally prevailing in years prior to 1974 is assumed in all U.S. oil and gas resource and reserve estimates.
Nonfuel Minerals	Less intensive mineral use in highly industrialized countries, and more intensive mineral use in LDCs.
Environment	Availability of technology to address serious environmental problems; social and institutional factors the primary obstacles to environmental protection.

Source: Global 2000, vol. 2, Washington: Government Printing Office, 1980, pp. 470-75.

Food and Agriculture

The Global 2000 food projections will be of much interest to Canada as the world's second largest food exporter. For the world as a whole, the projections point to a major shift in the food situation. Increasing populations and dietary shifts to more meat consumption will increase rapidly the demand for grain production. At the same time, production increases will be more difficult. Most arable land is already under cultivation and the land that is not will be quite expensive to develop. Increased use of energy-intensive inputs can help increase yields, but at diminishing returns in many exporting countries and at increased production costs everywhere. Opportunities for extensive export are virtually certain, and increased pressure on the agricultural resource base — especially soils — is almost inevitable.

Against this background of world developments, the Global 2000 Study projects Canadian wheat exports to *decrease* by 38 percent over the 1970-2000 period. In most scenarios, Agriculture Canada projects increases in cereal grain exports by 2000, but in at least one scenario, Agriculture Canada also projects decreased exports.

The Global 2000 food projections were prepared by the Economics, Statistics and Cooperative Service of the U.S. Department of Agriculture. A computer-based static-equilibrium model known as the GOL (Grain, Oilseed, Livestock) model was the primary tool used by the Department. The GOL model is made up of approximately 930 econometric equations. The model projects world production, consumption and trade quantities and prices in grains, oilseeds and livestock products, based on exogenous projections of population, GNP, growth in crop yields due to the deployment of more efficient yield-enhancing technology and other variables. Three additional procedures were used to make projections of arable area, total food production and consumption and fertilizer use, but these additional calculations were made without the use of a computer-based model.

There are many policy, technological and environmental assumptions inherent in the Global 2000 food projections. With regard to policy, the projections all assumed that major public and private investment in agricultural land development will be made. With regard to technology, they assumed that widespread deployment and use of fertilizer and other yield-augmenting inputs (together with other factors) will lead to further increased yields comparable to the increases experienced over the past two decades (the period of the Green Revolution). This meant, for example, that annual LDC grain production (in the medium case, over the 1975-2000 period) was projected to increase 125 percent. No environmental considerations (other than land scarcity and weather) are explicitly represented in the model. Similarly, the public and social (that is, not readily quantifiable) costs associated with developing and maintaining the productive capacity required by 2000 are not explicitly represented in the model. The food projections assumed what in retrospect are very low energy prices: constant at $13.00 U.S./bbl from 1975 to 1980, increasing at 5 percent per year thereafter.[24]

Although Canada is one of the eight industrialized countries treated separately in the GOL model, neither Canada nor any of the other industrialized regions is discussed separately in the chapter of the Global 2000. The reason is that while USDA analysts are reasonably confident of the GOL model's results at high levels of aggregation, they are somewhat less confident of the results for individual countries and regions.

In the course of discussing the GOL methodology, some disaggregated figures were presented. These figures (see Table 3-6) include GOL projections for Canadian wheat exports. The projections show Canadian wheat exports increasing 30 percent over the 1970-85 period and declining by 52 percent over the 1985-2000 period. As discussed further below, Canada's own projections suggest further increases in wheat exports over the 1985-2000 period.

Throughout most of the Global 2000 food chapter, Canada is not discussed specifically, but aggregated statistically with Australia and New Zealand in a category termed "Other Developed Exporters." There are, however, a few references to Canada in the general discussion of the projections, excerpts from which follow:

TABLE 3-6
Projected Net Exporters of Wheat (Medium-Growth, Rising Energy Price Case) [a]
(Thousand metric tons)

| | 1970 | | 1985 | | 2000 | | Average Annual Growth Percent | |
	Exports	% Share	Exports	% Share	Exports	% Share	1970-85	1985-2000
United States	17,881	39	48,838	58	58,226	57	7	1
Australia-New Zealand	8,300	18	12,165	15	16,084	16	3	2
Argentina	1,640	4	6,410	8	13,974	14	10	5
Canada	11,750	26	15,288	18	7,311	7	2	-1
South Africa	60	—	839	1	4,108	4	19	11
U.S.S.R.	4,799	11	127	—	1,995	2	-22	20
India	—	—	—	—	166	—	—	—
Euro Six	1,170	3	—	—	—	—	—	—
Total	45,600	101 [b]	83,667	100	101,862	100	4	1

a. These figures are representative of the lowest level of disaggregation within the GOL model and are cited to illuminate the GOL methodology. While Department analysts are reasonably confident of the GOL model's computations at the higher levels of aggregation presented in Chapter 6 of *Global 2000*, vol. 2, they would prefer that these more disaggregated projections not be cited as Global 2000 Study projections.

b. Does not sum to 100 due to rounding.

Source: Global 2000, vol. 2, Washington: Government Printing Office, 1980, p. 557.

Record Growth
   *The world has the capacity, both physical and economic, to produce
enough food to meet substantial increases in demand through 2000.* The projections are compatible in this regard with a number of other studies sug-
gesting a world food potential several times higher than current production
levels. The food growth rates implied in this Study's production and consumption projections are comparable to the record increases reported for the
1950s and the 1960s . . . .[25]

   *Problems of distribution across and within regions . . . detract from the
high world growth rates [projected].* Production and consumption increase at
faster rates in the LDCs than in the industrialized countries. LDC growth,
however, is from a substantially smaller base. Furthermore, the LDC aggregate
and many of the regional totals are somewhat misleading because the difference between individual LDCs — i.e., an Argentina compared with an India,
or an Egypt compared with a Bangladesh — are far wider than the differences
between the industrialized countries total and the LDC total . . . .[26]

Energy Price Impacts
   . . . Even a rough estimate of the impact of higher energy prices on
agricultural production depends on the timing of price increases, long-run
rates of technological change, and short-run input flexibility. The real energy
price increases projected to 2000 in the [Global 2000] energy projections . . .
are so large [$13.00 in 1975 to $35.34 in 2000, constant 1978 $U.S.] as to
suggest that the severity of the impact in the long run depends on the rate at
which energy-conserving technologies replace existing energy-intensive technologies. Little can be done to project the rate or the impact of such long-run
technological change. In the shorter term, however, some estimate of the
impact of higher energy prices can be made on the basis of data on energy
intensity and judgments as to how much flexibility farmers in a particular
country have to change input mixes . . . .[27]

   . . . A variety of cultural practices and management techniques [is] available in the short and medium terms to minimize the effect of energy price
increases. The experience of the [1974-78 period] suggests that food and overall
agricultural production could well adjust in the long run to substantially
higher energy prices, depending on the timing of increases, without the degree
of dislocation implied [by the Global 2000 Study's food projections].

   The model results suggest that, while world production and consumption
levels might not be changed measurably by marked but gradual increases in
energy prices, major shifts within and across sectors and regions would be
likely. The comparative advantage of the resource-endowed LDCs such as
Brazil and Thailand, which use relatively few high energy-intensive inputs,
would improve. Higher energy prices, however, would likely exacerbate
problems of comparative disadvantage in food production common to many
of the industrialized and higher-income LDCs.
   Adjustments in the food-exporting countries would likely be mixed. In
countries such as the United States, higher energy prices could be offset at
least partially by increasing the land resources committed to food production

and by decreasing . . . the use of, or increasing returns to, energy-intensive inputs. The comparative advantage of the traditional food-exporting countries would likely deteriorate relative to the resource-endowed LDCs but improve relative to most of the industrialized countries and several of the resource-tight LDCs. The sizes of these changes in comparative advantage are projected to keep the exporters' sales on the world market at or above the levels projected under a constant petroleum price alternative.[28]

[All of the cases examined in the Global 2000 food projections] suggest that *the agricultural and trade policies of a small number of importers and exporters will play an increasingly dominant role in determining the quantities and prices of food traded on the world market.* The increased importance of policy decisions in the exporting countries would result from their control of scarce excess productive capacity. The experience of the [1973-78 period] suggests that without marked changes in international trading conventions, the role of major but sporadic importers such as the Soviet Union is also likely to increase. Protectionist agricultural and trade policies currently allow large countries or blocs relatively close to self-sufficiency to avoid the costs of adjusting to world production shortfalls. The current structure of the world market also allows them to pass on part, if not all, of the cost of disruptions in their domestic agricultural economies for absorption by the world market. The impact of changes in world supply and demand are consequently likely to be absorbed more and more by countries exporting [regularly] a large proportion of production and countries importing [regularly] a large proportion of [their domestic requirements].[29]

The surplus productive capacity of the traditional exporters — particularly Canada, South Africa, and Australia — is projected to decrease beyond 1985 as a result of growth in domestic demand. Given the added capacity of several emerging developing exporters, however, excess productive capacity is expected to be more than adequate to balance the highest import demand projected in 2000, but at real prices somewhat above 1973-75 levels. The model implies that the major exporters will continue to play a crucial role in balancing world supply and demand by slowing production [whenever world production exceeds demand] in order to avoid the buildup of price-depressing surpluses, and by increasing export availability [whenever world demand exceeds production] to slow down price increases.[30]

All [of the cases examined] suggest that, in addition to population and income growth, shifts in consumption patterns are likely to play a major role in shaping demand, particularly beyond 1985. *Growth in demand and shifts in taste away from calorie-efficient diets based on cereals and starches toward less calorie-efficient, livestock-oriented diets will determine to a large extent the demand price of grains, oilseeds, other high-protein feeds, and possibly food prices in general.*[31]

The environmental consequences of increasing grain production are treated only superficially in the Global 2000 food chapter and the discussion was limited to the impact of fertilizers and pesticides. The basic conclusion is that: "The real food price increases projected for the decades ahead could well make the short-term costs of environmentally positive agriculture seem high and the long-run costs of an environmentally negative agriculture seem small."[32]

Only very limited comparisons are possible between the Global 2000 Study's projections and Canada's own projections. The only quantitative projection in the Global 2000 Study that is specifically about Canada is reported in Table 3-6. This projection shows Canadian *wheat* exports increasing from 11.750 million tonnes in 1970 to 15.288 million tonnes in 1985 (a 30 percent increase) and declining to 7.311 million tonnes by 2000 (a 52 percent decrease over the 1985-2000 period). The text of the Study comments: "The surplus productive capacity of the traditional exporters — particularly Canada, South Africa, and Australia — is projected to decrease beyond 1985 as a result of growth in domestic demand."

Agriculture Canada's study[33] provides projections for 2000 of surplus *cereals* for export, but not *wheat*. A rough estimate of exportable wheat has been derived from the Agriculture Canada work (see box following) showing export figures of 17, 24 and 25 million tonnes for three scenarios. Agriculture Canada's estimates of all-cereal surplus in 2000 ranges from 43.5 million tonnes (high production; domestic consumption reduced by all Canadians eating as recommended by Health and Welfare Canada)

Estimation of Future Canadian Wheat Production and Consumption

Projections of production and consumption of all cereals in Canada to 2000 appear in Volume III of the 1977 Agriculture Canada study, *Orientation of Canadian Agriculture: Social Factors Related to Agriculture and Food.*[34] Unfortunately, these projections lump wheat together with the other cereals, namely barley, oats, corn, rye and mixed grains.

To derive a projection for wheat specifically from the projection of all cereals, it is necessary to know what fraction of cereal production will be wheat. Some idea of this fraction is provided in *A Review of the Canadian Agriculture and Food Complex - The Commodities,* prepared by Agriculture Canada in 1977.[35] In the mid-1970s wheat was planted on slightly over one-half the total area in cereals, or approximately 9.5 million hectares of a total 18.6 million hectares in cereals. Wheat production in the mid-1970s was slightly less than one-half the total cereal production, or roughly 17 million tonnes out of an approximate total of 37 million tonnes, or 45 percent of the total production. For an approximate comparison (and in the absence of wheat-specific projections), it is assumed that wheat production is and will remain approximately one-half of the total cereal production in Canada.

The 1977 Agriculture Canada Study examines several supply and demand scenarios for the year 2000. Three of these scenarios are presented in Table 3-7 along with estimates of exportable wheat and the projected surplus of all grains. Cereal production in the "high productivity supply" scenario, it should be noted, is quite close (within 4 percent) of the "maximum production agriculture" possibility. If the wheat estimates are even approximately correct, most of the grain surplus would be wheat.

TABLE 3-7

Projections of Surplus Cereal Production and Estimates of Exportable Wheat, 2000

Agriculture Canada Projections a			Estimates for Wheat		
Scenario	All Cereals	Total Wheat Production b	Domestic Consumption (@ 200 kg/capita) c	Export-able Wheat	Projected Surplus of all Cereals d
		(million tonnes)			
Potential supply estimated by extrapolating 1960-71 yield trends with crop distribution and areas as reported in the 1971 census.	46.4	23.2	6.0	17.2	18.9
High productivity supply situation, assuming a high level of management on all class 1-3 agricultural soils with crop distribution proportional to 1971 census information.	59.9	30.0	6.0	24.0	32.4
Maximum production agriculture.	62.2	31.1	6.0	25.1	no projection

a. *Source: Orientation of Canadian Agriculture, Vol. III, Economic and Social Factors Related to Agriculture and Food*, Ottawa: Agriculture Canada, 1977, pp. 8, 18.

b. Assumes wheat production equals one-half of all cereals production.

c. Assumes continuation of domestic consumption at per capita rates of the mid-1970s: total domestic consumption for the 1974/75 crop year of 4.6 million tonnes *(Orientation of Canadian Agriculture, Vol. I, A Review of the Canadian Agriculture and Food Complex — The Commodities*, Ottawa: Agriculture Canada, 1977, Table 16.2) divided by Canada's 1975 population of 22.9 million (from U.S. Bureau of the Census computer runs of Oct. 13, 1977) = 201 kg per capita. For a domestic population in 2000 of 30 million people, this per capita consumption amounts to 6 million tonnes.

d. Agriculture Canada, *Orientation of Canadian Agriculture*, vol. III, Table 3, p. 9.

to 8.4 million tonnes.[36] This low Canadian figure *for all cereals* is close to the Global 2000 figure (7.3 million tonnes) *for wheat.*

While the Canadian and U.S. projections are reasonably close, it is not entirely clear whether the assumptions are similar. In the Canadian projection, supply is estimated by extrapolating 1960-71 yield trends with the crop distribution and areas reported in the 1971 census; demand is estimated on per capita consumption levels resulting from maximum economic growth (4.5 percent) and a high elasticity of demand for red meat. The Global 2000 projection assumes a Canadian population growth rate of 2.05 percent (1975-85) and 1.80 percent (1985-2000). Canadian per capita income is assumed to increase annually at 1.95 percent (1975-85) and 1.40 percent (1985-2000). Energy prices are assumed to remain constant from 1975 to 1980 and to increase at 5 percent per year thereafter.

A useful comparison of the Canadian and U.S. food projections would require a more detailed examination of the respective assumptions and models than is possible now because some of the specific assumptions and computer runs are no longer available. To complete the comparison it would also be necessary to know the degree to which the U.S. and Canadian projections result from calculations within the respective models or from exogenous time series input assumptions. In the U.S. GOL model, the final projections are influenced quite strongly and rather directly by time series input assumptions. For example, in the case of the GOL equations related to wheat production,

> . . . roughly 80 percent of the increase in "grain area under cultivation" between 1970 and 1985 is due to an exogenous time trend estimate involving a judgmentally adjusted coefficient. Since roughly 45 percent of the increase in "wheat area under cultivation" over the same period is due to increases in "grain area under cultivation" and roughly 45 percent due to another exogenous time trend, about 80 percent of the increase in "wheat area under cultivation" can be attributed to the influence of exogenous time trends and judgmental adjustments.* Similar reasoning shows that about 85 percent of the projected increase in "domestic wheat production" over the 1970-85 period is attributable to similar exogenous influences (roughly 90 percent for the 1985-2000 period).

> This means that 85-90 percent of the increase in wheat production included in the model's projections is essentially an exogenous input to the model — a premise rather than a conclusion of the modeling exercise. Other "projections" of the model also incorporate significant, directly exogenous components. These are largely based on the judgment of [U.S.] Department analysts regarding future prospects for world grain, oilseed, and livestock products. However, since the endogenous variables are mutually interdependent, this analysis is suggestive only. . . . The importance of exogenous area and production variables varies widely by region, depending on the extent to which the agricultural sector is commercialized and on the extent to which resource availability . . . limits the impact of market factors on future growth.

* U.S. Departmental analysts note that these exogenous trends and adjustments are estimated on the basis of the Department's analysis of regional arable area potential and regional cropping patterns, developed prior to running the GOL model.[37]

While it is impossible to obtain an adequate comparison without much further analysis of the U.S. and Canadian models, a number of questions are raised by even this overall comparison. What fraction of the surplus cereal is likely to be wheat? How is Canadian per capita consumption of grain (including grain consumed indirectly as meat) likely to change? Are the yields projected by Agriculture Canada (based on trends during the 1960-71 period) still realistic? What energy prices or energy subsidies are assumed in the Canadian yield projections? What weather/climate trends are assumed in the Canadian yield projections? Is the assumption that demand will drive production realistic? Is a 4.5 percent per year economic growth to support expanding Canadian demand likely? To what extent would additional cereal production in the Prairies be gained at the expense of accelerated erosion and groundwater depletion and what would be the long-term impact on soils, soil moisture and production?

Fisheries

The short *Global 2000* chapter on fisheries contains only two brief references to Canada. One reference to Canada relates to the income elasticity of demand for food fish in Canada, which is estimated to be such that there would be a 20 percent increase in demand for food fish for every 100 percent increase in income.[38]   The other reference to Canada reports that the 1975 Canadian catch of *living marine resources* totaled 1.0 million metric tons.[39]   This figure is quite close to the 1974 Canadian *marine fish catch* of 830 thousand metric tons given in Table 3-8. (The difference between the U.S. and Canadian figures is probably a difference in definitions: the U.S. figure includes all living marine resources, including crustaceans and molluscs, not just fish.)

Since these are the only references made to Canadian fisheries in the Global 2000 Study, comparisons to Canadian perspectives must be made on more general findings. To make more general comparisons, however, it is necessary to understand how the Global 2000 fishery projections were made.

Although no U.S. Government agency is responsible for making long-term projections of world fish catch, the National Marine Fisheries Service (NMFS) has the best

TABLE 3-8
Canadian Marine Fish Catch

	Atlantic	Pacific	Total
	(million pounds)		*(metric tons)*
1957	1,345.9	491.8	833,802
1961	1,201.1	638.5	834,664
1966	1,913.6	574.8	1,129,038
1971	2,217.3	228.8	1,109,846
1973	1,785.0	338.7	986,252
1974	1,532.5	297.7	830,399

Source: Statistics Canada, *Human Activity and the Environment,* Ottawa: Statistics Canada, 1978, Tables 4.2 and 4.3, p. 64.

data and most qualified experts and the NMFS prepared the Global 2000 fisheries chapter. Given the present state of modeling for the fisheries sector, it was decided that a verbal description would serve better than output from a formal model. Thus, the Global 2000 fisheries projections are based on empirical evidence and on ecological reasons why certain outcomes can or cannot be expected.[40]

In commenting on these two approaches, the Study observes:

> Ecological analysis can provide statements about potential supply but not about demand. In the marine resources forecast, statements of demand were synopsized from FAO sources and from the work of Frederick W. Bell and his colleagues at the National Marine Fisheries Service. Both demand forecasts were based on assumptions about population and income growth and income elasticities of demands for marine products. The Bell analysis also took into account supply constraints and the pressure on prices generated by inelastic supplies.
>
> The concepts, precepts and methodologies of ecology and economics are fundamentally different and stand at odds with one another. This disagreement appears clearly in the fisheries resource forecast. The ecologically derived supply estimates state that it will be reasonable to expect a global catch of around 60 million metric tons in the year 2000 — if environmental degradation does not reduce the basic productivity of the oceans. The economically derived FAO projection states that demand for marine harvests in 1985 will have reached 106.5 million metric tons with the implication that it will probably increase thereafter. The economic estimate by Bell projects that demand in the year 2000 will have reached 83.5 million metric tons.[41]

The two economic estimates of demand (FAO — 106 million metric tons (mmt); Bell — 83.5 mmt) are quite different and both exceed the 60 mmt ecological estimate of potential catch. Even by 1975, Bell's projected demand of 78.9 mmt far exceeded the 69.7 mmt catch in that year of freshwater and marine fish.

For several reasons the marine harvest is not expected to increase on a sustainable basis over its present size. The potential of the north temperate fisheries of the Atlantic and Pacific Oceans is now being fully realized under current fishing effort, leaving only the southern temperate Atlantic and the central Pacific region to be more fully exploited. The Study comments on the more lightly exploited areas:

> The total increased yield from lightly exploited areas has been estimated at 30-50 million tons. The species available strongly influence the development of fisheries. Thus, the estimated increase in potential yield over current yield is made up of hakes in the southwest Atlantic and croakers and small pelagics in the central zones. Some increase in cephalopod yield has also been predicted.[42]

The Antarctic krill resource remains an important, but little known, potential resource:

> Exploration for krill in the Antarctic Ocean (Atlantic sector primarily) is now underway. The potential has been estimated by various authors at 25-100 million metric tons. Doubtless the population is large, but there are many unanswered questions. Do these euphausiids undergo cycles of density and is a

present high what is attracting attention? Will the present turnover rate continue as fishing mortality increases? Will this interfere with recovery of whale populations? The answers are not yet available. The more recent comprehensive fishery-based estimates and the better defined trophodynamic estimates provide a range of potential of 100-150mmt.[43]

At the same time, yields of traditional species are in some cases declining:

The yields of traditional species in the more heavily exploited areas, which are included in the estimates, have not held up in recent years. In many areas, the so-called nontraditional species are already being harvested (e.g., capelin and squid in the north Atlantic) at maximal levels. Thus much of the hypothesized expansion is in fact a replacement yield and is not additional in terms of potential to the present yields. In addition to the ecological constraints on estimates of potential, the more practical constraints of society (economics, technology, management) will surely reduce the ability to utilize what has been estimated as future potential expansion. For example, the most efficient fishing operation at present will average 50 tons per day in good conditions. The same efficiency applied to zooplankton would average much less than half a ton per day.[44]

The section on marine fisheries potential concludes:

These considerations lead to the conclusion that the present world harvest of marine fish of about 60 mmt will not increase on a sustained basis. Furthermore, it will only be maintained with good management of fisheries and protection of the marine environment. The total world harvest of marine renewable resources, based on exploiting natural production, could be increased substantially by the year 2000, perhaps to as much as 100 mmt. To achieve this, however, will require overcoming severe social and economic constraints. Development will have to be carefully planned so that the balance and equilibrium of the marine ecosystem are not radically perturbed. There is not enough information to evaluate the real possibilities of sustained increases in yields, to say nothing of their practicality.[45]

Marine aquaculture could expand considerably, perhaps tenfold, from the 6 mmt level in 1975:

There is cause for reasoned optimism when considering increased food production from aquaculture. Despite institutional, economic, environmental and technological constraints, global yields are increasing. Intensive culture of high-unit-value species — such as pen-rearing of salmon and raceway culture of shrimp — is approaching the point of economic feasibility, and extensive culture of animals that utilize very short food chains — such as oysters, mussels and mullet — has the potential for enormous expansion with existing technology. The 1976 FAO World Conference on Aquaculture concluded that even with existing technology a doubling of world food production from aquaculture will occur within the next decade and that a 5-10 fold increase by the year 2000 is feasible if the necessary scientific, financial and organizational support becomes available.[46]

Canadian fisheries reports provide a similar overall picture, especially for Canada's fisheries in the North Atlantic and North Pacific. These Canadian fisheries are characterized as "seriously depleted" by Statistics Canada.[47] Although no data are available on the catch-to-effort ratio, landings were diminishing in the mid-1970s. The marine catch declined from a peak of 1.129 mmt in 1966 to 0.830 mmt in 1974, the latest year for which statistics were available. On the Atlantic coast, the primary species have been cod, redfish, flounder and herring. Salmon is the principal species caught now on a weight basis in the Pacific; the herring catch has dropped precipitously from 448 million pounds in 1961 to 98 million pounds in 1974.[48]

With domain over the 200 mile coastal strip, Canada now has the opportunity to manage these fisheries carefully. Assuming that Canada reduces the fishing pressures and that the depleted stocks restore themselves, it should be possible to increase Canada's marine landings later in the 1980s. The large unsatisfied world demand for fish and the almost uniquely U.S. phenomenon of large demand for recreational fishing are likely to make Canada a major exporter of its marine catch. It seems likely that the demand for Canadian fish can only intensity in coming years.

Forests

As the world's leading exporter of forest products, Canada is likely to find the Global 2000 Study's analysis of forestry trends of much interest, not so much because of its analysis of Canadian forests (Canada has more detailed studies of its own), but because of the information it provides about world trends. The major contribution of the Global 2000 chapter on forests is that it assembles diverse data on the forests of the less industrialized countries, showing the very rapid rate at which deforestation is occurring there. The analysis suggests that there will be a very rapidly growing demand for Canadian forest products.

For the world as a whole, the Global 2000 Study projects that the growing stock of commercial-sized wood will drop by 47 percent over the 1978-2000 period. (See Table 3-9). In the less developed countries, where most of the deforestation occurs, the projected decline in per capita growing stock is 62 percent. In the industrialized countries, where there is still a relatively large amount of growing stock per capita, there is also a decline, but by only a relatively modest 17 percent. If the demand for forest products increases throughout the world while the supplies available from the less industrialized countries decline rapidly, the value of (and pressures on) remaining forests can be expected to increase rapidly. Canadian forests will be among those in increasing demand.

Canadian and U.S. forest resources are discussed jointly in the Global 2000 Study under the subheading "North America." As shown in Table 3-10, Canada and the

	Canada	North America
Productive forest (ha/capita)	10.3	2.0
Open woodland (ha/capita)	3.2	0.7
Growing stock (cu m / capita)	772.5	179.0

Source: Global 2000, vol. 2, Washington: Government Printing Office, 1980, pp. 21, 120, 123; Canada's population taken to be 22.9 million in 1975.

TABLE 3-9
Estimates of World Forest Resources
1978 and 2000

	Closed Forest (millions of hectares)			Growing Stock of Commercial-Sized Wood in Closed Forests and in Open Woodlands (billions cu m overbark)		
	1978	2000	Percentage Change	1978	2000	Percentage Change
U.S.S.R.	785	775	-1	79	77	-3
Europe	140	150	7	15	77	-13
North America	470	464	-1	58	55	-5
Japan, Australia, New Zealand	69	68	-1	4	4	0
Subtotal	1,464	1,457	-0.5	156	149	-4
Latin America	550	329	-40	94	54	-42
Africa	188	150	-20	39	31	-21
Asian and Pacific LDCs	361	181	-50	38	19	-50
Subtotal (LDCs)	1,099	660	-40	171	104	-39
World	2,563	2,117	-17	327	253	-23
World population (billions)				4.3	6.4	49
Wood per capita (cu m)				76	40	-47

Source: Global 2000, vol. 2, Washington: Government Printing Office, 1980, p. 134.

TABLE 3-10
Global 2000 Estimates of North American Forest Resources, Early 1970s

Resource	Unit	U.S.A. (1970)	Canada (1973)	North America
Stocked commercial forest [a]	Million hectares	194	220	414
Unaccessible productive forest [b]	Million hectares	5	—	5
Reserved forests (parks, etc.) [c]	Million hectares	8	15	24
Total productive forest [d]	Million hectares	207	235	442
Unstocked commercial forest [e]	Million hectares	8	17	26
Open woodlands and other forests of extremely low productivity [f]	Million hectares	103	73	176
Growing stock on commercial forest (underbark volume) [g]	Billion cubic meters	19	19	38
	Cu meters per hectares	93	75	87
Net annual growth on commercial forest land (underbark volume) [h]	Million cubic meters	527	270	797
	Cu meters per hectare	2.6	1.1	1.8
	Percent growing stock	2.9	1.5	2.1
	Cu meters per capita	2.4	11.5	3.3
1974 fellings (underbark volume) [i]	Million cubic meters	402	167	545
1975 fellings (underbark volume)	Million cubic meters	358	147	505
1974 fellings as percentage of net annual growth	Percent	76	62	68

a. *For the U.S.A.*, commercial forest is defined as forest land producing or capable of producing crops of industrial wood in excess of 1.4 cubic meters per hectare per year in natural stands and not withdrawn from timber use. *For Canada*, commercial forest is defined as forest land suitable for regular harvest, capable of producing stands of trees 4 inches diameter or larger on 10 percent or more of the area, excluding agricultural land currently in use.

b. This refers to forest *in Alaska* that meets the production criteria but is too inaccessible to be used commercially.

c. These are forest lands reserved for noncommercial use. Whether all of the 15.5 million hectares reserved in Canada are actually productive forest is not clear from the available sources.

d. This category excludes some woodland that would meet the tree growth criteria, but is not included in forestry statistics because it has been developed for non-forestry commercial use (e.g., residential land).

e. *For Canada*, this is probably an underestimate, as it includes only unstocked federal and provincial lands that have been allocated to wood production.

f. *For the U.S.A.*, this includes stands of pinyon-juniper, woodland-grass, chaparral, subalpine forests, and other woodlands incapable of producing 1.4 cubic meters of industrial wood per hectare per year. *For Canada*, this includes forest land not suitable for regular harvest because of extremely low productivity.

g. *For the U.S.A.*, this is the volume, suitable for industrial wood use, in trees over 5 inches diameter. *For Canada*, the definition is presumably similar. For both, the unstocked commercial forest area is included in the calculation.

h. Net annual growth is total growth less volumes of trees dying annually. Apparently it refers to wood in the parts of trees suitable for industrial wood use, and apparently it does not net out the volume lost to forest fires.

i. Fellings refers to removals plus harvesting losses, apparently only wood of size suitable for industrial wood use is included. This measure is provided to allow comparison of annual fellings to net annual growth. The ratio of fellings to removals was inferred from data provided in U.S. Forest Service (1974), below, and the figures for fellings were calculated by applying that ratio to the removals as reported in FAO (1977).

Source: Global 2000, vol. 2, Washington: Government Printing Office, 1980, p. 123.

United States are about equally endowed with forest resources. Each has over 200 million hectares of productive forest, and about 19 billion cu m of growing industrial-sized wood. On a per capita basis, however, Canada has a substantially greater wealth of forest resources than the United States. (See table, p. 88.)

Canada is experiencing changes in its forest resources that are similar to those occurring in U.S. forests. Although only approximate figures are offered for Canada, the principal changes by 2000 would be in forest age and composition — younger and less diverse forests are projected. The amount of change is expected to be somewhat less in Canada than in the United States, as the following excerpts express:

> The condition of the North American forest environment in the year 2000 will depend to a considerable extent on economic developments that will affect management intensity. *The Outlook for Timber in the United States* forecasts that the U.S. commercial forest area will be 6 million hectares smaller by the year 2000. Similar estimates are not available for the Canadian forest; probably the changes will be less as the smaller population of Canada will be making fewer demands for alternative uses of forest land.
>
> The fact that the annual harvest is less than the net annual growth disguises the low rate of reforestation in North America. The commercial forest area partially or totally harvested plus the area burned have averaged about 4 million hectares per year in the U.S. since 1960. During the same period, the area planted with trees has averaged about 650,000 hectares per year. The remainder, except the relatively small portion dropped from the commercial forest land inventory, is left for natural forest regeneration. If the trend continues, the U.S. forest will be less completely stocked than it is now. This will not significantly affect wood production in the year 2000, but will have a negative effect in the longer term if reforestation programs are not accelerated. The situation in Canada, where the area harvested or burned annually is about 2.5 million hectares, is similar. The pressure for reforestation in Canada is likely to be lower and costs of reforestation there are higher because of the greater problems of accessibility.
>
> In the year 2000, the North American forest is likely to be marginally smaller, be less well stocked, have fewer slow-growing mature trees and more fast-growing young trees, contain larger areas reserved for noncommercial use, and have a lower ecological diversity in the nonreserved areas. The magnitude of these changes will depend partly on exogenous economic factors and partly on the attitude of the public towards forest management.
>
> In recent years, environmental awareness has increased significantly in both Canada and the United States. As a result there has been considerable public resistance to forest management techniques such as clear-cutting, which are economically sound, at least in the short term, but which are aesthetically disagreeable and environmentally dubious. It is likely the management for wood production will be constrained on increasing proportions of the 27 percent of the U.S. commercial forest that is publicly owned and on the 59 percent of the forest that is privately owned by parties other than forest industry companies. It is theoretically possible for the managers of the public forests to increase production of all the types of benefits provided by the forest, but without a greatly expanded environmental education effort, it is unlikely that the public will be well enough informed and motivated by the

year 2000 to demand management programs that will optimize production of all the forest's benefits.[49]

The Global 2000 Study projects a yearly increase of 2 percent in Canadian timber harvests as a result of growing domestic and international demand for forest products:

> Increases in demand for Canadian forest products will depend on the same factors that influence demand in the U.S., except that rising prices of wood relative to other products would dampen demand less for Canada than for the U.S., because Canada would supply a larger proportion of the U.S. demand under that condition. The Canadian wood harvest is expected to increase by about 2 percent per year, to reach 215 million cu m (underbark) in the year 2000. With that increase, the harvest would still be below the net annual growth, which is currently about 270 million cu m (underbark). More significantly, it would be below 240 [million] cu m which is the Canadian Forest Service's estimate of the annual cut allowable for sustained yield conditions on the portion of the Canadian forest that is accessible under current economic and technological conditions.[50]

Canada is projected to continue as a major exporter of forest products. Canada is already the world's largest exporter of forest products, with net exports in 1974 of $4,900 million, principally to markets in the United States, Japan and Europe:

> The interregional linkage provided by international trade in forest products will be stronger in some cases and in others will disappear. Japan and Western Europe will be increasingly dependent on Canada and the U.S.S.R. for pulp supplies and for softwood sawlogs. Japan will no longer be able to import sufficient tropical hardwood sawlogs and veneer logs from Asia, and European importers will be paying much higher prices for sawlogs from Africa. Only northern South America is likely to be exporting more sawlogs in the year 2000 than it does now. The United States will probably remain self-sufficient in pulpwood and may become more nearly self-sufficient in sawlogs as the global supply becomes tighter.[51]

Canada's forest wealth is clearly revealed in the data and projections just presented. The pressures on these resources will grow rapidly, not so much from domestic demand, but from forestry developments and economic conditions around the world:

> Use of land for forests and for agriculture are in approximate equilibrium throughout most of the industrialized nations. Thus the forest area is relatively stable and will be only marginally smaller in the year 2000. The management of commercial forests will become more intensive, and this will lead to lower ecological diversity. The forest area reserved for noncommercial use will increase in North America, and noncommercial factors will become more prominent in forest management decisions in the other industrialized regions. Except in Europe, Japan, and New Zealand, forests in the year 2000 will be less fully stocked than now, as cutting will continue to outpace tree planting and natural regeneration. For the most part, the cutover land will not be allocated to other uses, however, and will be available for reforestation during the 21st century.

If the industrialized nations recover fully from the economic setbacks of the past few years, then consumption of wood will continue to rise and supplies will begin to be tight within the 1978-2000 period. Production costs for softwood exports will rise as more remote areas must be logged in both the U.S.S.R. and Canada, so prices will rise. The already rising demand for imports from the tropical forests of the less developed countries will increase further.

In the more distant future, rising prices for wood products may lead to improved stocking in the northern forests and to heavier reliance by the wood products industry on plantation forestry in southern Europe, in the southern U.S. and in the tropics.[52]

The Global 2000 estimates of Canadian forest resources are based on *Canada's Forests*,[53] prepared by the Canadian Forestry Service in 1974. In 1979 the Canadian Forestry Service issued an updated report, *The Outlook for Timber Utilization in Canada to the Year 2000*.[54] The two sets of data are for the most part not comparable, but a few general comparisons are possible (see Table 3-11).

The older and more recent data provide somewhat different pictures of the productive category of forests in Canada. Direct comparisons are not possible, however,

TABLE 3-11
Comparison of Global 2000
and Recent Canadian Data on Canadian Forest Resources [a]

	Global 2000 [b]	Canadian Forestry Service report of 1979 [c]
Total forest land, km²	no data	3,417,000
Total, non-reserved production forests, km²	no data	3,321,000
Total inventoried, km²		2,934,000
productive	2,350,000	1,984,000
unproductive	730,000	949,000
Wood volume on inventoried, productive, production forests (billion cu m)	19	19.28
Net annual growth, million cu m	270	256
Annual allowable cut, million cu m (1976)	240	256
Timber harvests, million cu m (1976)	no data	140

a. The definitions of the above categories given in the two studies are roughly similar, but sufficiently different to make a precise quantitative comparison questionable.

b. *Source: Canada's Forests*, Ottawa: Canadian Forestry Service, 1974, as reported in *Global 2000*, vol. 2, Washington: Government Printing Office, 1980, pp. 117-35.

c. *Source:* K.L. Aird and J. Ottens, *The Outlook for Timber Utilization in Canada to the Year 2000*, Ottawa: Canadian Forestry Service, 1979.

because the 1979 total is only for the portion of the non-reserved production forests that have been inventoried. For the portion that has been inventoried, 68 percent has been found to be productive. If this percentage holds for all of the non-reserved production forests, the total area of productive forests could amount to 2,246,000 km² which is about 4 percent less than the 1974 estimate of productive forest reported in the Global 2000 Study. The 1979 figures for the volume of wood in productive forests (19.28 billion cu m) is based on an inventory of only 68 percent of nonreserve production forests and thus suggests a significantly higher total than reported in 1974 (19 million cu m). The net annual growth estimate in 1979, however, is less than the earlier estimate, that is, 256 million cu m/yr vs. 270 million cu m/yr. Thus current Canadian estimates suggest that the Canadian forests are slightly larger, but growing slightly more slowly, than reported in the Global 2000 Study.

The more recent analysis suggests other changes affecting Canadian forestry. The expansion in utilization is now expected to proceed more rapidly than expected. In the 1979 report, wood harvests are projected to increase at 2.2 percent per year, resulting in an annual harvest in 2000 of 226 million cu m compared with 215 million cu m projected in the Global 2000 Study.[55] Comparison of the 1974 Canadian data reprinted in the Global 2000 Report to the 1977 Canadian data published by the Canadian Forestry Service[56] shows the value of wood exports rising rapidly. Net exports of Canadian forest products in 1974 were worth $4,921 million ($ Cdn), while in 1977 exports of forest products were worth $14,900 million. In 1977, exported forest products represented 53 percent of the total value of all forest products produced in Canada. The 1979 Canadian report projects an increasingly larger share of Canadian forest products being exported.

Assumptions underlying the forest product trade projections may need further examination. The 1979 projections of future trade are premised on quite rapid growth in the economies of Canada's leading importers, especially the United States, the United Kingdom, Europe and Japan. Direct comparisons with Global 2000 GNP projections are not possible; however, underlying the Canadian projections of 1979 are assumptions about the cost of oil, which are roughly similar to those in the Global 2000 Study and which in retrospect are unrealistically low. From a price of $11.05/bbl in 1976, the Canadian analysis projects an increase of 5 percent per year to 1985 and 4 percent per year from 1985 to 2000, resulting in a cost of $27.50/bbl (1976 $ Cdn) at the turn of the century. These levels and rates are roughly comparable to those in the Global 2000 Study's projections for food and agriculture, and are much too low.

More realistic oil price assumptions and consideration of the inflationary impact of OPEC policies would affect the projections of forest product exports. Increased oil prices and the associated inflation dampen industrial growth in general and housing starts in particular and increase transportation costs. Higher transportation costs, in turn, increase disproportionately the cost of exporting goods such as forest products that have low value per unit. Increased oil prices will also increase the attractiveness of wood as a domestic fuel. A new analysis of the Canadian forestry sector would probably show increased oil prices reducing somewhat the export of forest products. The total demand, however, is likely to continue to grow rapidly.

Management factors affecting growth and supply are discussed only to some extent in the 1979 report. The report does, for example, discuss trends towards more intensive use of trees and use of "weed" species such as lodgepole pine, jackpine, poplars and western hemlock. These trends have long-term implications for growth and supply. More complete cutting of all trees and more complete removal of all tree parts will expose the land to more erosion and accelerate the depletion of soil nutrients, if compensatory measures are not taken. Reforestation is not treated systematically and quantitatively in the 1979 report, but reforestation practices apparently vary considerably among the provinces. In general, the hectares cut seem to be outpacing the hectares replanted.

Water

Although Canada and the United States share several river basins as well as the Great Lakes, the water projections of the Global 2000 Study do not reach this level of detail. Given the local nature of water resources and water use as well as the fact that Canada has an abundance of water, the Global 2000 water projections for Canada itself are of little domestic significance. The projections for the United States and Mexico may be of more interest, however, because the increase in their need for water will create additional pressure on Canadian water resources.

The projections of per capita water availability for North America given in Table 3-12 illustrate a trend. These numbers, in thousands of cu m per capita per year, have the following general meanings: a value of 1.0 or less implies a very low availability; 1.0-5.0 is low; 5.0-10.0 is medium; 10.0 and above is a high availability. Throughout the projection period, all of Canada remains well into the high availability category. All of the U.S. areas listed fall below the high category and the northern states enter the low category. If the southwestern states were listed separately, they would show an even more pronounced water problem. By the end of the century, Mexico falls through most of the low range, approaching the very low category. These figures bring to mind the reasoning behind the North American Water and Power Alliance scheme,

TABLE 3-12
Per Capita Water Availability in North America,
1971 and 2000
(Thousands of cu m per capita per year)

	1971	2000	Percentage Change in Per Capita Water Availability	Percentage Change in Population 1971-2000
Canada	128.0	83.0	- 35	54
Yukon & Northwest Territories	5200.0	3376.6	- 35	54
British Columbia	381.0	247.0	- 35	54
Eastern provinces	87.5	56.8	- 35	54
United States (48)	8.4	6.6	- 21	27
Western states	12.0	9.4	- 22	27
Northern states	5.4	4.3	- 20	27
Southern states	11.6	9.1	- 22	27
Alaska	2033.0	1600.8	- 21	27
Mexico	5.5	1.9	- 69	185

Source: Global 2000, vol. 2, Washington: Government Printing Office, 1980, p. 156.

whereby Canada's great abundance of water in the western provinces would be conveyed to the drier portions of the western United States and to Mexico. In the western states, demands for irrigation and industrial water may increase steeply, prompting further interest in the possibility of interbasin water transfers, including transfers from Canada. The U.S. Census results for 1980 show that U.S. population growth is somewhat more rapid than was assumed in Table 3-12.

The "national accounts" treatment of water resources employed in the Global 2000 Study does not provide a basis for some of the more interesting and meaningful comparisons of water resources data. A more detailed comparison of U.S. and Canadian water resources is presented in Table 3-13. Even this table, however, does not provide sufficient regional disaggregation to illustrate water use patterns within Canada and the United States. The regional level, however, is likely to be the source of water resource management questions for both countries that Canada may have to face. For example, future water deficits in the western United States cannot be examined at this level of aggregation, but could become much more extensive than projected if new demands develop for water use in coal slurry pipelines or in the production of synthetic fuels.

While the analysis of water problems will continue to be largely a localized, river-basin matter, the Global 2000 projections point to some large regional problems developing in the United States and in Mexico. As these problems become more difficult, Canada may expect further interest in large-scale interbasin transfers.

TABLE 3-13
Freshwater Supplies and Uses, Canada and the United States, 1975
(Billion gal /day unless otherwise noted)

	Canada [a]	United States [a]	Use trend in U.S. [b] to year 2000
Percentage of world's renewable water supply	9	8	
Total river flows	2,300	2,150	
Contiguous mainland "reliable" flows (9 out of 10 yrs)	1,470	750	
Average withdrawals mid-1970s	21	338	slight decrease by 2000 after mid-1980s increase
Thermoelectric power plant withdrawals	10	89	declining slightly
Agriculture withdrawals	1.5	157	steady
Consumed in agriculture	no data	86	increasing to 92

a. *Source:* R. Shaffner, et al., "Other Replenishable Resources," in: C.E. Beigie and A.O. Hero, Jr. (eds.) *Natural Resources in U.S.-Canadian Relations, Vol. II Patterns and Trends in Resource Supplies and Policies.* Boulder: Westview Press, 1981, pp. 559-60.

b. *Source:* U.S. Water Resources Council. *The Nation's Water Resources 1975-2000, Vol. I: Summary.* Washington: Government Printing Office, 1978.

Energy

Because of the many uncertainties, it is difficult to make global energy projections for twenty years or more. The primary uncertainty, of course, is the price for crude oil charged by the member countries of the Organization of Petroleum Exporting Countries (OPEC), but even demand is difficult to project because the rapidly increasing price of energy is prompting serious efforts to reduce the amount of energy used to produce a unit of goods and services.

The U.S. Department of Energy (Energy Dept.) had these uncertainties and more to deal with when the Global 2000 energy projections were made in late 1977. At that time the Energy Dept.'s official public position was that the real price for crude oil charged by OPEC would remain constant in real terms at the 1974 level ($U.S. 13.00/bbl) until the year 2000, or longer, and most of the Energy Dept. projections were made assuming no price increase. However, the Energy Dept. did make one projection, at the request of the full team of professionals working on the Global 2000 Study, in which the real price of crude oil was assumed to begin increasing at 5 percent per year starting in 1980. This projection was used as the primary Global 2000 energy projection.

The Energy Dept. world energy model — the International Energy Evaluation System (IEES) — is a family of static-equilibrium supply, demand and production models linked together with a linear programming matrix.[57] The IEES system treats OPEC as a residual supplier, calculating energy production from all other sources and meeting all residual energy demand (at the assumed price) with OPEC oil. The final results are then compared with estimates of OPEC's production capacity. As shown in Figure 3-4, all of the Energy Dept. projections for the Global 2000 Study approach (or exceed) the OPEC production capacity by 1990. As a result the Energy Dept. projections — unlike any of the other projections in the Global 2000 Study — stop at 1990.

The Energy Dept. analysis derives several conclusions from the energy projections made for the Global 2000 Study. These conclusions are summarized as follows:

- Current medium and high economic growth projections appear to lead to situations in which significantly higher prices for petroleum will be required to equilibrate supply and demand by fuel substitution and other means of petroleum demand reduction.

- Petroleum production capability is not increasing as fast as demand. Depending upon economic growth and conservation, a supply-constrained market appears to be a strong possibility for the late 1980s.

- In the long term, the rate of petroleum reserve additions appears to be falling. As a result, engineering considerations indicate that world petroleum production will peak in the 1990-2010 interval at 80-105 million bbl/day, with ultimate resources estimated at 2,100 billion bbl.

- There is a substantial potential for growth in the coal and natural gas supplies beyond the year 2000.

- In the very long term, there appears to be considerable potential for aggressive, conservation-induced reductions in energy consumption.

Since the Global 2000 projections were finalized, the Energy Dept. has prepared revised and updated world energy projections.[58]   The new energy projections still do

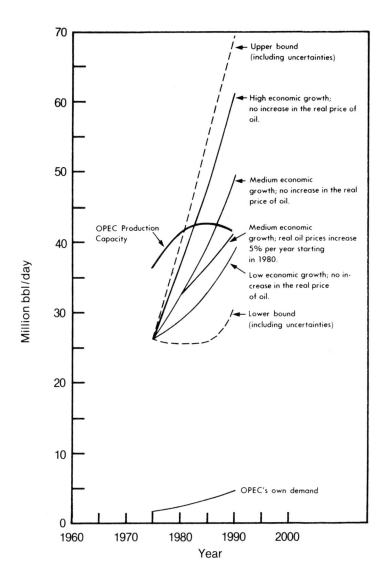

Figure 3-4.   Projected demand (including OPEC's own demand) for OPEC oil, and OPEC's own demand for OPEC oil. *Source: Global 2000,* vol. 2, Washington: Government Printing Office, 1980, p. 169.

not reach 2000, but do extend to 1995. They also include revised estimates of future OPEC prices, revised economic growth projections and revised supply scenarios. The new Energy Dept. oil price assumptions are presented in Table 3-14. For comparison,

TABLE 3-14
New Energy Dept. Oil Price Assumptions

		Price Case	
	High	Mid	Low
		(constant 1979 U.S. $)	
1979	21.53	21.53	21.53
1985	39.00	32.00	27.00
1990	44.00	37.00	27.00
1995	56.00	41.00	27.00

Source: Department of Energy, Energy Information Administration, *Annual Report to Congress, 1979,* vol. 3, Washington: U.S. Government Printing Office, 1980, p. 10.

the oil price assumptions used in the Global 2000 projections were $21.43 for 1985 and $27.52 for 1990 (in 1975 U.S. $).

The Energy Dept.'s new assumptions for economic growth rates are presented in Table 3-15. For comparison, the Global 2000 economic growth rate assumptions for Canada for the 1975-85 period were 4.9 (high), 4.0 (medium), 3.1 (low) and for the 1985-2000 period were 3.7 (high), 3.1 (medium), 2.5 (low). The new supply assumptions include "disruption scenarios," which consist of a cutback in OPEC production of 2 million bbl/day (about 7 percent of 1979 production) in each of the years 1983, 1988, and 1993.

TABLE 3-15
New Energy Dept. Economic Growth Rate Assumptions
(Annual Percentage Rate)

				1977-1995		
				Projection Series		
	1960-1972	1972-1977	World Oil Price Supply Demand	High Low High	Mid Mid Mid	Low High Low
United States	3.9	2.6		2.6	2.7	2.8
Canada	5.4	4.2		3.7	3.4	3.2
OECD Europe	4.7	2.7		2.8	2.5	2.4
Japan	10.6	4.5		4.5		4.3
Australia/ New Zealand	4.9	3.1		3.6	3.4	3.2
Total OECD	4.9	3.0		3.0	2.9	2.8
OPEC		5.0		6.4	5.9	5.8
Other				5.5	5.1	5.1
World		4.1		3.7	3.6	3.5

Source: Department of Energy, Energy Information Administration, *Annual Report to Congress, 1979,* vol. 3, Washington: U.S. Government Printing Office, 1980, p. 9.

The new Energy Dept. assumptions reduce the projected demand for OPEC oil by about 8 million bbl /day in 1990 (roughly a 20 percent decrease) relative to the projection for the Global 2000 Study. The new projections of residual demand for OPEC oil are shown in Figure 3-5. In all three of the cases presented, demand for OPEC oil in 1995 remains below OPEC production capacity, but in the low-price scenario, demand approaches within a few percentage points of OPEC production capacity.

The Energy Dept. projections of oil production and consumption (see Table 3-16)

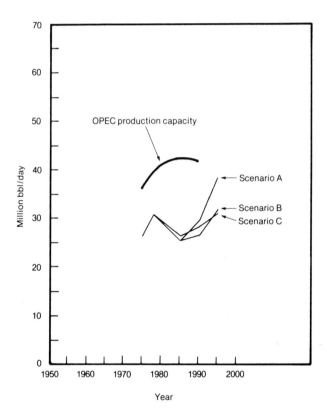

Figure 3-5. Projected demand (including OPEC's own demand) for OPEC's oil. Scenario A: low price ($U.S. 27/bbl in 1995), high supply, low demand; Scenario B: mid price ($41/bbl in 1995), mid supply, mid demand; Scenario C: high price ($56/bbl in 1995); low supply, high demand. *Source:* OPEC production capacity and 1975 production are from *Global 2000,* vol. 2, Government Printing Office, 1980, p. 169; the projections are from Department of Energy, *Annual Report to the Congress, 1979,* vol. 3, Washington: Government Printing Office, 1980, p. 22.

TABLE 3-16

Canadian and U.S. Crude Oil Production, Imports, and Consumption, 1985, 1990, and 1995

(Million bbl/day)

	1978	1985			1990			1995		
World Oil Price ($/bbl)		High 39.00	Mid 32.00	Low 27.00	High 44.00	Mid 37.00	Low 27.00	High 56.00	Mid 41.00	Low 27.00
Supply		Low	Mid	High	Low	Mid	High	Low	Mid	High
Demand		High	Mid	Low	High	Mid	Low	High	Mid	Low
Canada										
Production	1.6	1.5	1.6	1.7	1.6	1.8	1.7	1.7	1.7	1.7
Net imports	0.3	0.1	0.1	0	0.1	-0.1	0.2	0.1	0.2	0.6
Apparent consumption [a]	1.9	1.6	1.7	1.7	1.7	1.7	1.9	1.8	1.9	2.3
United States										
Production	10.3	9.3	9.2	9.1	9.9	9.6	8.9	10.5	9.7	8.1
Net imports	8.0	6.1	6.6	7.6	5.1	6.1	8.7	4.3	6.2	10.7
Apparent consumption [a]	18.3	15.4	15.8	16.7	15.0	15.7	17.6	14.8	15.9	18.8

a. Defined by the Energy Dept. as follows: Domestic production of crude oil and natural gas liquids plus net imports of crude oil and petroleum products. These oil supplies may go to end use consumption or to stocks. Stocks going to end use consumption are not explicitly measured.

Source: Adapted from: Department of Energy, Energy Information Administration, *Annual Report to Congress, 1979,* vol. 3, Washington: U.S. Government Printing Office, 1980, p. 22.

show Canada remaining a small net importer of oil. Typically the projections are for net Canadian imports of a few hundred thousand bbl/day. In the mid-price scenario, the Energy Dept. projects Canada to be a net exporter of oil briefly about 1990. If prices remain low, the Energy Dept. projects Canada to increase its oil imports to about 600,000 bbl/day in 1995. The United States, by contrast, continues to import oil at about 6 million bbl/day in the mid-price scenario.

The costs to Canada, the United States and other countries of the projected oil imports for 1990* are shown in Table 3-17. For Canada, the costs remain less than 1 percent of the gross domestic product (GDP). For the United States, the costs remain about 2.5 percent of GDP.

The Energy Dept. projections for the 1977-1990 period show that energy and oil growth rates will not recover the high levels reached during the pre-embargo days, due to higher energy prices, lower economic growth, lower population growth and conservation programs. Demand for all forms of energy is expected to grow by about 2.1 percent annually, while demand for oil is projected to increase by only 0.1 percent annually. (See Table 3-18).

The Energy Dept. mid price projections show Canada's annual total energy consumption increasing by 50 percent between 1977 and 1995, from 8.6 quads (quadrillion Btus) to 12.9 quads. (See Table 3-19.) The role of oil and coal in meeting energy requirements is expected to decline — in the case of oil, because of higher prices and in the case of coal, because of its "inferior quality as a fuel." Shares of "other" energy sources (presumably nuclear and hydroelectric power) are expected to increase significantly, while consumption of natural gas (expressed as a percentage of total consumption) is projected to remain constant at about 20 percent.

Because of higher prices and conservation efforts, the Department of Energy expects the efficiency of energy use in the Canadian economy to increase. (See Table 3-20.) The ratio of energy use per unit of GDP is projected to decline by 20 percent over the 1973-95 period.

It is difficult to make direct comparisons of the U.S. Department of Energy projections of the Canadian energy future with Canada's own energy projections because the studies are all based on different assumptions and methodologies. It is possible, however, to make some limited comparisons on three topics: (1) projections of total Canadian energy demand in 1990 and the underlying assumptions, (2) projections of future fuel shares, and (3) Canadian production, consumption and imports of crude oil. There are significant differences among the various studies on these points.

Both the U.S. and the Canadian projections[59] show substantial increases in Canadian energy consumption in the decades ahead. (See Table 3-21.) The Canadian conservation strategy implies 10.67 quads of primary energy by 1990; the U.S. projection is for 11.3 quads by 1990. The Canadian Long Term Energy Assessment Program (LEAP) projection for 2000 is 16 quads; no U.S. projections are available for 2000.

Although U.S. and Canadian studies all indicate much further growth in Canadian consumption, the studies generally point to substantially slower growth in consumption in the years ahead than in the years prior to the 1973 oil embargo. The U.S. Department of Energy projection and the Canadian Energy Conservation scenarios have the

---

*   Figures for 1995 are not given in the Energy Dept. report.

TABLE 3-17
Projected World Oil Import Payments 1990
(Billions of 1979 $)

	1978	World Oil Price (1979 $/bbl) Supply Demand	1990 High 44.00 Low High	1990 Mid 37.00 Mid Mid	1990 Low 27.00 High Low
United States					
Import payments	59.4		75.2	75.2	80.6
Percent of GDP [a]	2.6		2.4	2.4	2.5
Canada					
Import payments	2.2		-0.2 [d]	-2.4	1.3
Percent of GDP	1.0		-0.1 [d]	-0.7	0.4
Japan					
Import payments	37.0		100.0	84.1	66.9
Percent of GDP	3.8		6.5	5.6	4.5
OECD Europe					
Import payments	88.1		138.0	119.0	93.1
Percent of GDP	3.0		3.4	3.1	2.4
Australia / New Zealand					
Import payments	2.7 [b]		3.6	2.9	2.8
Percent of GDP	2.0		1.7	1.4	1.4
OECD Total					
Import payments	189.0		317.0	279.0	245.0
Percent of GDP	2.9		3.4	3.1	2.7
Other Non-OPEC					
Import payments	17.8 [b]		18.5	-2.2	-5.7
Percent of GDP	2.2		1.2	-0.2	-0.4
World [c]					
Import payments	207.0		335.0	277.0	239.0
Percent of GDP	2.8		3.1	2.6	2.3

a. Gross domestic product.
b. Estimated.
c. Excludes OPEC and Communist countries.
d. Apparent contradiction with Energy Dept. projection reported in Table 2-16 where the 1990 "high" projection is for Canadian oil imports, not exports as indicated here.

Source: Department of Energy, Energy Information Administration, *Annual Report to Congress, 1979,* vol. 3, Washington: Government Printing Office, 1980, p. 23.

lowest energy growth rates — 2.1 and 2.0 percent, respectively. The other projections range from 2.5 to 5.0 percent annually.

　　Strikingly, all the scenarios (with the exception of the High Growth scenario depicted by the Institute for Research in Public Policy) project energy growth rates that

TABLE 3-18
Canada's Energy and Oil Consumption Growth Rates:
Historical and Energy Dept. Mid Price Projections

	1960-1973	1973-1977	1977-1990
Energy growth rate	5.7	1.6	2.1
Oil growth rate	5.3	0.9	0.1

Source: Derived from Department of Energy, Energy Information Administration, *Annual Report to Congress, 1979,* vol. 3, Washington: Government Printing Office, 1980, p. 29.

TABLE 3-19
Canadian Energy Consumption and Fuel Shares:
Energy Dept. Mid Price Projections for 1985, 1990 and 1995

	Total Energy Consumed	Fuel Share			
		Coal	Oil	Gas	Other
		(Percent)			
1977	8.6	8	45	18	29
1985	10.0	6	38	20	36
1990	11.3	5	35	20	40
1995	12.9	4	34	19	43

Source: Department of Energy, Energy Information Administration, *Annual Report to Congress, 1979,* vol. 3, Washington: Government Printing Office, 1980, pp. 28-29.

are substantially lower than the assumed economic growth rates. These projections are in sharp contrast to historic experience, which has been that economic growth and energy consumption increase in direct proportion to each other. The U.S. projection and IRPP Low Growth Projection are both based on the explicit assumption that an acceptable economic growth rate (3.5 percent) can be maintained while simultaneously reducing the energy growth rate by as much as 50 percent. According to the projections, this disproportionate reduction in energy growth can be accomplished by a combination of strong conservation measures and increased efficiency in energy use. It is also assumed that the increased conservation and energy efficiency can be accomplished without adversely affecting GDP, employment and income.

Rising crude oil prices will, of course, dampen demand and rising prices have been assumed in several of the projections. The Canadian projections for 1990 assume — at least as a goal — that domestic oil prices would be at parity with world oil prices, but world oil prices have risen more quickly and to higher levels than was expected in 1976 and 1977 when these projections were developed. The U.S. Department of Energy's projection assumes that 1 bbl of oil will cost $37 (1979 U.S.$) on the world market in 1990. With the current "oil glut" created by Saudi Arabia, OPEC prices range from $32/bbl to $41/bbl, but the "glut" could disappear quickly if Saudi

TABLE 3-20
Energy Consumption/Gross Domestic Product (GDP) Ratios:
History and Energy Dept. Mid Price Projections

| | 1960 | 1973 | 1977 | 1985 | Mid Price Projection | |
					1990	1995
			Energy/GDP Radios			
			(1,000 Btu/constant 1975 U.S. $)			
United States [a]	47.4	48.1	45.6	39.6	37.0	35.5
Canada	50.5	51.8	48.2	42.6	40.7	39.6
Japan	28.5	30.8	27.4	24.6	25.5	24.6
Western Europe	28.6	31.2	28.9	23.0	22.3	21.5
Australia/New Zealand	25.8	28.3	30.4	25.8	24.1	22.5
Total OECD	37.6	38.4	35.9	30.3	29.2	28.0
Total Non-OECD	36.1	28.3	27.9	28.0	27.8	27.1
OPEC	27.9	23.7	22.7	26.1	26.5	26.8
Other	38.3	29.7	29.8	28.6	28.2	27.2
Total Free World	37.4	36.6	34.4	29.8	28.8	27.8

a. Includes Puerto Rico, Virgin Islands, and purchases for the Strategic Petroleum Reserve.
Source: Department of Energy, Energy Information Administration, *Annual Report to Congress, 1979*, vol. 3, Washington: Government Printing Office, 1980, p. 29.

TABLE 3-21

Comparison of U.S. and Canadian Projections of Canada's Energy Economy, 1990 and 2000

	U.S. Energy Dept. Mid Price Projection [a]	1990		2000		
		Canadian Energy Conservation Scenario [b]	Canadian Energy Strategy Scenario [b]	IRPP High Growth [c]	IRPP Low Growth [c]	LEAP [d]
Annual economic growth rate (percent)	3.4 (1977-1990)	4.2 (1975-1990)	4.2 (1975-1990)	5	3.5 (1975-2000)	3.4 (1975-2000)
Annual energy growth rate (percent)	2.1 (1977-1990)	2.0	3.7	5	2.5	2.8
Population (millions)	no data	27.5	27.5	28.6	28.6	30
World oil price assumptions	$37/bbl (1979 US$)	Goal: Domestic price = World price	Goal: Domestic price = World price	50 percent increase over the 1975 price of $12.70	50 percent increase over the 1975 price of $12.70	Double before 2000
Intentional conservation	yes	yes	no	no	yes	yes
Total primary energy consumption (quadrillion Btu)	11.3	10.67	13.47	26.2	no data	16
Total secondary energy consumption (quadrillion Btu)	no data	6.48	7.96	17.2	8.4	no data

a.　Mid price projections from Department of Energy, Energy Information Administration, *Annual Report to Congress, 1979*, vol. 3, Washington: U.S. Government Printing Office, 1980, pp. 7-34.

b.　Energy, Mines and Resources Canada, *Energy Conservation in Canada: Programs and Perspectives*, Ottawa: Supply and Services Canada, 1978.

c.　R. Clayton, C. Lafkas, G. Kreps and R. Miller, *Canadian Energy: The Next 20 Years and Beyond*, Montreal: The Institute for Research on Public Policy, 1980.

d.　J.E. Gander and F.W. Belaire, *Energy Futures for Canadians: Long-Term Energy Assessment*, Ottawa: Supply and Services Canada, 1978.

Arabia were to cut back its production from its current 10.3 million bbl/day to its normal 8.8 million bbl/day.

Both the U.S. and Canadian projections show a shift in patterns of energy supply and consumption as Canada shifts away from oil to indigenous substitutes — coal, natural gas, uranium and eventually oil from tar sands. Table 3-22 shows the proportionate change in energy supplies for 2000 (Canadian projections) and 1995 (U.S. projections). Since the data in Table 3-22 are for different assumptions and different years, detailed comparisons are not possible, but general comparisons of trends can be made. Both projections show a decline in the contribution of oil to Canada's total energy supply. Both projections show continued reliance on natural gas for about 20 percent of total energy supply. The major discrepancy between the two projections concerns the future of coal. The U.S. projection shows a decline in coal consumption because of "its inferior quality as a fuel,"[60] whereas Canadians project as much as a "fourfold increase by 2000."[61]

As recently as 1975, oil was Canada's major energy source, providing 38 percent of primary and 57 percent of secondary energy.[62] The position of oil will change rapidly, however, in the years ahead, as indicated by both U.S. and Canadian projections. (See Table 3-23.) There are significant differences in the U.S. and Canadian views of Canada's oil future. Both the U.S. and Canadian projections show oil production holding between 1 and 2 million bbl/day, but the U.S. projections of production are constantly 20-30 percent higher than the Canadian projections. On the other

TABLE 3-22
Shifting Patterns of Energy Supply in Canada

	Energy Dept. Projections		Canadian LEAP Projections	
	1977	1995	1975	2000
	(quadrillion Btu)			
Total energy consumed	8.6	12.9	8	16
	(percentage share)			
Oil	45	34	46	30
Gas	18	19	19	20
Coal	8	4	11.5	13.5
Nuclear	29	43	1.7	14.8
Hydro			21.7	15.7
Other (including renewables)	—	—	—	5.9
Total	100	100	99.9*	99.9*

* Does not total correctly because of rounding.

Source: Department of Energy, Energy Information Administration, *Annual Report to Congress, 1979,* vol. 3, Washington: Government Printing Office, 1980, pp. 27-28; and J.E. Gander and F.W. Belaire, *Energy Futures for Canadians: Long Term Energy Assessment Program (LEAP),* Ottawa: Supply and Services Canada, 1978, p. 41.

TABLE 3-23

U.S. and Canadian Projections [a] of Canadian Oil Production,
Consumption and Imports, 1985, 1990 and 1995

	1985		1990		1995	
	Energy Dept.	Canada	Energy Dept.	Canada	Energy Dept.	Canada
	(million bbl / day)					
Production	1.6	1.2	1.8	1.35	1.7	1.4
Consumption	1.7	2.1	1.7	2.2	1.9	2.3
Indicated shortfall	0.1	0.9	- 0.1	0.85	0.2	0.9

a. The Energy Dept. and Canadian projections are both based on similar GDP growth rates of 3.4 percent. The Canadian projections definitely include production from tar sands, but it is unclear whether the Energy Dept. projections include production from tar sands.

Sources: Department of Energy, Energy Information Administration, *Annual Report to Congress, 1979,* Washington: Government Printing Office, 1980, p. 22; R. Clayton, C. Lafkas, G. Kreps, R. Miller, *Canadian Energy: The Next 20 Years and Beyond,* Montreal: The Institute for Research on Public Policy, 1980, p. 21.

hand, Canadian projections of consumption suggest a requirement for more oil con sumption than do the U.S. projections. Herein lies the essence of the Canadian energy problem — the growing gap between estimates of oil production and required oil consumption.

Canada's current policy is to limit its oil imports to one-third of total domestic oil consumption and many Canadians are advocating a policy of zero oil imports by 2000. The Institute for Research on Public Policy has outlined a scenario for achieving zero energy imports by 2000 through development of Canada's indigenous energy resources. (See box.) Whether or not this precise scenario is followed, it seems likely that Canada can keep its oil imports quite small, but that Canada is unlikely ever again to be a significant oil exporter.

Fuel Minerals and Other Energy Sources

No U.S. Government agency is responsible for maintaining estimates of world reserves and resources of fuel minerals. The information presented in the fuel minerals chapter of the Global 2000 Study was compiled by Walter Dupree (then with the Department of Energy) from a variety of sources:

Oil and Gas	Data compiled by M.K. Hubbert for the U.S. Congressional Research Service.
Solid Fuels	Data published by the World Energy Conference (WEC) based on responses to questionnaires sent to countries participating in the WEC.
Uranium	Data published by the WEC, based on responses to questionnaires.
Hydro, Geothermal and Solar	Data obtained from various publications, based usually upon sample measurements rather than on survey data.

Canada's Energy Problem in Brief *

Background

Canada has an open energy economy that permits both imports and exports of energy forms, including oil. Gradually Canada has shifted from being a net exporter of oil to being a net importer. In 1977, for example, Canada imported about 10 percent of its oil consumption. This oil, primarily from Venezuela and the Middle East, is used to supply eastern Canadian refineries, mostly in the Montreal area. Oil import dependence is of increasing concern to Canadians. Current policy limits net imports through 1985 to one-third of consumption or 800,000 bbl/day, whichever is less. While no public policy has been published for the period beyond 1985, there is strong sentiment for reducing net oil imports to zero by 2000. How might this be done?

Projected Energy Need

In 1975 Canada consumed 5.09 quadrillion Btus (quads) of "secondary energy" — energy delivered in a useful form to end-use users in industries, homes, etc. Growth in secondary energy consumption has increased in the past at about the same rate as the nation's gross national product (GNP). Assuming that the GNP increases at 3.5 percent per year and that the consumption of energy per dollar of GNP declines 30 percent by 2000, Canada will need 8.43 quads of secondary energy by 2000, an increase of about 3.3 quads over 1975 consumption. Although this 2 percent rate of energy growth is much slower than the 5 percent growth of the 1958-74 period, it is a growth adequate to continue the lifestyle enjoyed in Canada.

Providing the Energy

The IRPP analysis makes an overall assumption that annual investments in energy development will not exceed 7 percent of GNP because a more rapid investment in the energy sector is thought to have adverse effects on the rest of the economy. In 1975 the investment in energy development was $7.4 billion, or 4.5 percent of GNP. Energy prices are assumed to increase 50 percent over the 1975-2000 period.

Oil: 2.50 Quads

The IRPP analysis assumes that Canadian oil consumption cannot continue to increase and, in fact, in 2000 will be limited to 2.5 quads of secondary energy (3.0 quads of primary energy) compared with 2.9 quads of secondary energy in 1975. This is the equivalent of 1.5 million bbl/day in 2000. This amount of oil would probably be producible from Canadian sources, with about half coming from strip-mined tar sands using currently known and

---

* Based on R. Clayton, C. Lafkas, G. Kreps, R. Miller, *Canadian Energy: The Next 20 Years and Beyond,* Montreal: The Institute for Research on Public Policy, 1980.

(cont'd. on p. 111)

(cont'd. from p. 110)
workable technologies. This development of the tar sands would require an investment of an estimated $20 billion (1975 Cdn $). Other oil development needed would cost about $5 billion. Thus, oil not only can not provide the additional 3.3 quads, but even after a very large investment will provide 0.4 quads less in 2000 than in 1975.

Natural Gas: 1.88 Quads (Secondary)

Canadian natural gas resources (ultimately recoverable) are estimated at about 250 trillion cubic feet (tcf), less 14 tcf committed to export to the United States. If an attempt were made to fill the Canadian energy gap with natural gas alone, more than half of Canada's ultimately recoverable gas would be gone by 2000, and gas production would be declining. To avoid an even larger Canadian energy problem in the twenty-first century, IRPP assumes that natural gas production will be limited to 1.88 quads of secondary energy by 2000, all of which will be used domestically. (For comparison, in 1975 domestic consumption was 1.58 quads and exports to the U.S. totaled 1.12 quads.) The needed 2.6 quad primary production rate (to produce 1.88 quads of secondary energy from gas), could be continued until about 2050, after which Canadian gas production would begin to decline because of depleted resources.

Electricity: 2.19 Quads

To fill the energy gap with electricity would require the development of an installed generating capacity of 271 million kw by 2000. Seventy percent of this energy would be used for residential and other space heating, which would mean that during the summer most of the generating capacity would be unused, unless the electricity were exported to the United States — a distinct possibility. The cost, estimated at $1,200 per kilowatt (1975 Cdn $) would be an astronomical $325 billion, resulting in annual capital carrying charges of $32.5 billion, 8.33 percent of the GNP projected for 2000. This cost exceeds the 7 percent constraint assumed by IRPP.

In an "affordable" electricity supply scenario, 2.19 quads — 25 percent of the secondary energy demand — would be supplied by electricity and used for transportation as well as space heating. Thirty billion kwh per year would be exported to the United States. The cost (in 1975 Cdn $) would be $169 billion, requiring annual carrying charges of about $17 billion in 2000, 4.36 percent of GNP.

Coal: 1.86 Quads

Canadian coal could provide 1.86 quads of secondary energy (including district heating) by 2000 with an annual coal production of 90 million tons, a production rate that could be sustained for a very long time with Canada's coal resource of 228,000 million tons. The cost is estimated at $16 billion (Cdn $) with annual carrying charges of $0.16 billion. Coal combustion, of course, means sulfur oxide production and acid rain, but the IRPP analysts feel that these problems can be overcome through fluidized bed combustion. The increased loading of the atmosphere with carbon dioxide and the land and water effects of the mining are other possible drawbacks to coal.

(cont'd. on p. 111)

(cont'd. from p. 111)

Other Less Feasible Options

Conservation: 1.49 Quads

Conservation could reduce Canadian needs for secondary energy by 1.49 quads, but an estimated cost of 5 percent of GNP for retrofitting old buildings and building new buildings to tighter standards. The IRPP analysis concludes that this 5 percent, combined with other investments in energy, is too high to recommend "super conservation."

Tar Sands: ?? Quads

Tar sands represent a potentially large reserve of petroleum, but they require a very large amount of energy, capital and technology for their development. Rising oil prices could potentially make *in situ* extraction attractive, but production costs will rise rapidly with increasing oil prices because of the large (and somewhat unpredictable) energy requirements for injected steam. Water supply and disposal problems also exist. The technology for large-scale tar sands development is unproven. For all of these reasons the amount of oil likely to be produced from tar sands by 2000 is highly uncertain.

Methanol from Forest Biomass: 1.4 Quads

Although high transportation costs will prevent wood from becoming a major fuel, an estimated 1.4 quads of secondary energy could be produced by methanol from forest biomass. The costs of developing this methanol capacity by 2000 are not estimated, nor is the question of the adequacy of "non-commercial forest products" answered.

Active Solar Heating: 0.5 Quad

Assuming the cost of solar panels systems reduces from approximately $30 (1975 Cdn $) to $10 or $15 per square foot, active solar heating could supply the equivalent of 0.5 quad for space heating.

Conclusions

The projected energy growth summarized in Table 3-24 is much slower than that of the 1958-74 period, but should be adequate to maintain the present Canadian lifestyle and still bring oil imports to zero by 2000. The needed 8.43 quads of secondary energy could be provided as follows: 2.50 quads of oil, 1.88 quads of natural gas, 2.19 quads of electricity, 1.86 quads of coal. The costs are large, but not overwhelming — $225 billion over 25 years with carrying charges of $22.5 billion (5.8 percent of GNP) in 2000. There are, of course, alternatives. One is to allow Canada to become more dependent on imported oil. Another is to reduce the rate of growth in energy consumption still further.

The IRPP analysis considers a case in which GNP grows by 1.75 percent per year as opposed to 3.5 percent per year in the base case. The implications of the slower growth are belt tightening of various kinds and a reduced standard of living. Such slow growth might present political problems and the analysts feel that the 3.5 percent growth can be achieved.

(cont'd. on p. 113)

(cont'd. from p. 112)

TABLE 3-24

Summary of IRPP Analysis of a Canadian Energy Future of 8.43 Quads of Secondary Energy in 2000*

	Secondary Energy		Development Costs		Fraction of GNP in 2000
	1975	2000	Total	Annual	(percent)
	(quadrillion Btus)		(billions of 1975 dollars)		
Most Feasible Set of Options					
Conventional oil (includes 1/2 from strip-mined tar sands by 2000)	2.9	2.5	25	2.5	0.6
Natural gas	1.15	1.88	15	1.5	0.4
"Affordable" electricity (169 million installed Kw)	0.81	2.19	169	16.9	4.3
Coal	0.23	1.86	16	1.6	0.4
Totals	5.09	8.43	$225	$22.5	5.8
Other Less Feasible Options					
Methanol from forest biomass	?	1.4	?	?	?
Solar residential heating	?	0.5	?	?	?
In situ tar sands	?	?	?	?	?

* Assumptions: 3.5 percent annual GNP growth; 30 percent less energy needed per dollar of GNP by 2000; 50 percent real increase in energy prices by 2000; ratio of primary to secondary energy is 1.6:1.0; GNP in 2000 projected to be $390 billion.
Source: R. Clayton, C. Lafkas, G. Kreps, R. Miller, *Canadian Energy: The Next 20 Years and Beyond,* Montreal: The Institute for Research on Public Policy, 1980.

Canada's own estimates have been drawn largely from a report published by the Institute for Research on Public Policy (IRPP), entitled *Canadian Energy: The Next 20 Years and Beyond.*[63] This IRPP report uses data from both government and private sources.

Given the variety of data sources, significant variations in estimates from the United States and Canada are to be expected, but the problems of comparisons of data are complicated even further by the fact that the technical terms used in these two countries to describe resource estimates differ in important ways.

The key technical terms are "reserves" and "resources." The Global 2000 Study used these terms in accordance with the classification system used by the U.S. Geological Survey/Bureau of Mines (see Figure 3-6):

- Reserves: known mineral deposits which can be exploited at a profit at current production costs and mineral prices, and with currently variable technology.

- Resources: mineral deposits which, for economic or technical reasons, cannot be exploited at a profit at this time; plus mineral deposits still to be discovered; plus known reserves.

Canadian definitions of the terms "resources" and "reserves" appear to be identical to those used in the United States, but distinctions within these broad categories (e.g., "measured," "indicated," and "inferred" reserves) and their correlation

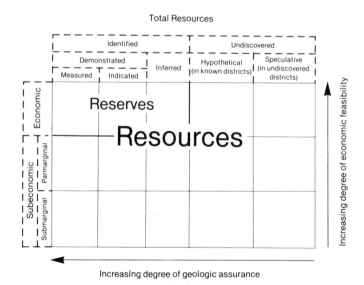

Figure 3-6.   Mineral resources classification system used by the U.S. Geological Survey and Bureau of Mines. *Source: Global 2000,* vol. 2, Washington: Government Printing Office, 1980, p. 188.

with U.S. terms, are not clear; nor is the Canadian use of the term "remaining recoverable reserves," which may be identical to the U.S. term "resources." One interpretation of the correlation between the U.S. and Canadian terms is given in Figure 3-7.

A further caveat: some of the data presented here, while only a few years old, have been outdated by events. "Reserves" are dynamic categories that change with economic conditions and technologies and there have been many changes in both economic conditions and in the technological situation since the 1973 oil embargo. Increased oil prices have stimulated exploratory activity, resulting in additional discoveries as well as better information on "inferred" and "hypothetical" resources. Increased oil prices have changed the economics of mineral exploitation, making it feasible to mine some fuel mineral resources which were previously too expensive. Also, technological innovation, such as the development of *in situ* processing technology for exploiting Athabasca oil sands, increases the potentially exploitable resource base. Such changes are not reflected in all of the resource data currently available.

The Global 2000 Study's chapter on fuel minerals addresses world resources and reserves of fuel minerals (petroleum, natural gas, coal, nuclear fuels, oil shale and tar sands), and provides estimates for other energy sources (hydraulic, geothermal and solar energy). Canada is specifically mentioned in the sections on petroleum, natural gas, hydraulic resources and tar sands. For coal, uranium and oil shale, only regional figures are available, Canada being included in "North America."

Crude Oil

The Global 2000 Study provides the following estimates of Canadian crude oil resources (not including tar sands): ultimate total production of 34 billion bbl; cumulative production to 1976 of 7.2 billion bbl; crude oil remaining of 77 billion bbl. The crude oil remaining has an energy content of 446 quads and represents 92 percent of Canada's ultimate total production. (By comparison, the United States has 48 percent of its crude oil remaining.) Canada is estimated to have had 6.0 billion bbl of proven reserves in 1978 and to have produced 0.5 billion bbl in 1977. This gives a reserve-to-production ratio of 12.0. (This ratio for the United States is 9.8.)[64]

Canadian estimates of their petroleum reserves — 10.65 billion bbl — are about 75 percent higher than the Global 2000 figure:

IRRP		Global 2000	
	(billion bbl)		
Remaining recoverable reserves (1978)[a]	10.65	Estimated Reserves (1978)	6
Resources	no data	Remaining Resources (1976)	77

a. The Canadian figure includes light and heavy crude from established reserves as well as new discoveries. It is unclear whether the Global 2000 figures include heavy crude.

Sources: R. Clayton, C. Lafkas, G. Kreps, and R. Miller, *Canadian Energy: The Next 20 Years and Beyond,* Montreal: The Institute for Research on Public Policy, 1980, p. 133; and *Global 2000,* vol. 2, Washington: Government Printing Office, 1980, pp. 190-191.

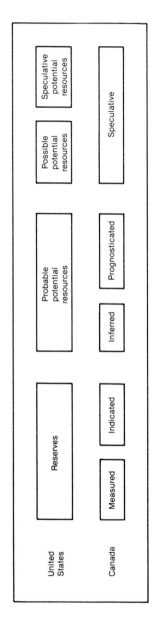

Figure 3-7. Approximate correlations of terms used in different resource classification systems. *Source:* T. Greenwood, "Uranium", in C.E. Beigie and A.O. Hero, Jr., *Natural Resources in U.S.-Canadian Relations*, vol. 2, Boulder: Westview Press, 1980, p. 330.

Natural Gas

The Global 2000 estimates of Canadian natural gas resources are ultimate total production of 663 tcf; cumulative production to 1976 of 26 tcf; remaining resources of 637 tcf. The remaining resources have an energy content of 650 quads and represent 96 percent of Canada's ultimate total production. (By comparison, the United States has 60 percent of its natural gas resource remaining.) Canada is estimated to have had proven resources of 58 tcf in 1978, compared with 210 tcf in the United States.[65]

Canadian estimates of proven natural gas reserves in established areas are close to 30 percent higher than the Global 2000 figures. It is unclear, however, if the Global 2000 figures include the "new area" reserves. If they do not, the U.S. and Canadian estimates are essentially identical. Uncertainty about Canadian "ultimately recoverable reserves" is reflected in the wide difference in U.S. and Canadian estimates:

	IRPP	Global 2000
	Proven Reserves	Estimated Reserves
	(tcf)	
Established areas	59 (1975)	
New areas [a]	15.6 (1977)	
Total	74.6	58 (1978)[b]
	Ultimately Recoverable Reserves [c]	Remaining Resource
Total	250	663

a. MacKenzie Delta-Beaufort Sea, Arctic islands and Deep Basin.
b. It is unclear if this figure includes the "new area" reserves.
c. "Ultimately Recoverable Reserves" includes proven and all expected future discoveries.
Sources: R. Clayton, C. Lafkas, G. Kreps, and R. Miller, *Canadian Energy: The Next 20 Years and Beyond,* Montreal: The Institute for Research on Public Policy, 1980, pp. 47-48; and *Global 2000,* vol. 2, Washington: Government Printing Office, 1980, p. 192.

Hydro

Canada's large hydroelectric power potential is an important resource that was not discussed in the Global 2000 Study. On the basis of average annual streamflow, Canada's present hydropower generating capacity is 94,500 megawatts, capable of generating 535,000 gigawatt hours per year.[66]

Hydropower projects do, however, produce large adverse as well as beneficial impacts and, over time, social and political resistance to the negative impacts can be expected to grow and come into conflict with the economic and political pressures for hydroelectric power developments.

Hydraulic Energy Resources

According to the Study, the Canadian Government is investigating the feasibility of constructing tidal power plants at three sites, which would have a combined electric power output of 4,900 megawatts and an annual energy output of 15,643 gigawatt hours. There are apparently only 100 sites around the world where the conversion of tital energy is practicable.[67]

Coal

No specific figures are given for Canada in the Global 2000 Study, although the Study states that the Western nations (the United States, Canada and Western Europe) have 56 percent of world solid fuel resources based on Btu content.

The Study also presents an aggregate figure for North American coal reserves and resources, but again no breakdown on a country-by-country basis:

IRPP Canada's Coal Resources		Global 2000 North America's Coal Resources	
(billions of short tons)			
Measured	31.9	Reserves	229
Indicated	14.6		
Inferred	182.0		
Total	228.0	Total resources	3,978

Sources: R. Clayton, C. Lafkas, G. Kreps and R. Miller, *Canadian Energy: The Next 20 Years and Beyond,* Montreal: The Institute for Research on Public Policy, p. 105; and *Global 2000,* vol. 2, Washington: Government Printing Office, 1980, p. 193.

The U.S. Department of Energy published in 1980 an estimate of "recoverable reserves" of coal for Canada totaling 6.1 billion short tons.[68] This figure is much lower than the IRPP figure of 31.9 billion short tons.

Biomass

Information in the Global 2000 Study on Canada's biomass potential is based on a report issued by the Canadian Department of Energy, Mines and Resources entitled "Tree Power, An Assessment of the Energy Potential of Forestry Biomass in Canada." Canada is currently harvesting about 51×10^6 ODt (oven-dried metric tons) of wood, mostly for commercial purposes. This figure is about one-eighth of Canada's estimated annual forest productivity. Over the long term (between now and 2025) methanol derived from noncommercial forest products and biomass waste could provide a significant portion of Canada's carbon-based fuel requirements. Prerequisites to exploiting this potential energy source include the adoption of different management practices and harvesting techniques. There are also some environmental dangers of intensive forest exploitation to be considered.[69]

Geothermal

The Study indicates that only three countries (Canada not being one) have made estimates and published data on geothermal energy resources. However, the Study assumes that the amount of lowgrade geothermal energy in Canada is very large.[70]

Oil Shale

The Global 2000 estimates place most of the world's identified shale oil reserves in North America. However, oil shale deposits many times as large as those already identified are thought to exist. No specific data are given for Canada.

Tar Sands

According to the Study, the bulk of the world's known tar sands resources are in Canada, concentrated in the Athabasca field in Alberta. Oil in place in Canadian tar sands is estimated to total 731 billion bbl.* Not all of this total is recoverable, however. Using only surface mining and aboveground processing, an estimated 26.5-85.0 bbl might be recovered. If the use of *in situ* processing technology (not yet developed) is included, recovery might increase to 250-285 billion bbl.[71]

The Study notes that Canada is the only country commercially producing oil from tar sands and comments extensively on the Athabasca field:

> The Athabasca field in Alberta, Canada, is one of the largest deposits of oil in the world, extending over 21,000 square miles. It is estimated to contain 626 billion barrels of bitumen in-place, with 74 billion barrels lying beneath less than 150 feet of overburden and 552 billion barrels beneath overburden ranging in depths from 150 to 2,000 feet. Estimates of oil in-place in other deposits in the Athabasca region total 105 billion barrels. Thus, the total in-place estimate for the Athabasca region is 731 billion barrels. This does not include the heavy oil in the Canadian Cold Lake area, which is estimated at 164 billion barrels in-place.
>
> One estimate of the oil-generating potential of the Athabasca field is 285 billion barrels, with 85 billion barrels currently possible by open pit mining of near-surface deposits, which are often 200 feet thick. The other 200 billion barrels would have to be recovered by *in situ* techniques. Another estimate places the total recoverable resource at 250 billion barrels, with 26.5 billion barrels recoverable using established open pit mining and established aboveground recoverable techniques.
>
> Great Canadian Oil Sands, Ltd. has been producing oil from the Athabasca deposit since September 1967. Its plant is the only commercial tar sands facility in operation. Another plant (Syncrude Canada, Ltd.) has been built and is expected to begin operating in the near future. There are no significant extraction plans for any other area of the world.[72]

When the Global 2000 Study was written, the technology for *in situ* processing of tar sands was apparently still regarded as undeveloped. As of 1977, according to the IRPP, this technology has been technically proven in the Cold Lake area and was at an early pilot stage in Athabasca.[73]

The tar sands are an important resource for Canada, as they are expected to supplement declining reserves of conventional oil. According to one Canadian study, "Oil production by 2000 and from then to 2025 is assumed to come mainly from the oil sands and heavy oil deposits of western Canada (with additional supplies from the conventional areas or frontiers as these become available.)"[74] The IRPP describes the Athabasca tar sands as Canada's "ace in the hole," making it possible for Canada to remain an oil economy for quite some time *if* it becomes technically and economically feasible to exploit the entire amount of reserves. As of this writing, the IRPP estimated that only 22 billion bbl are recoverable from near surface deposits using existing commercial technology apparently including *in situ* processing.[75]

---

* The estimates of Canada's total tar-sand resources may be conservative. According to a *Science* editorial about the Global 2000 Study, resources of oil in-place are 1,300-2,400 billion bbl. (Editorial, "The Global 2000 Report," *Science,* vol. 209, August 15, 1980.)

Canada's present production from tar sands is about 125,000 bbl/day. Production costs are about $20 (Cdn)/bbl, and the selling price is about $30/bbl.[76] Exxon Resources Canada hopes to construct a plant in the Cold Lake area at an estimated cost of $7 billion, which would produce 140,000 bbl/day. The projected impact on the balance of payments is an annual savings of $1.5 billion (1980 Cdn $).[77]

	IRPP	Global 2000
	(billions of bbl)	
Estimated oil (bitumen) in place		
Cold Lake	165	164[a]
Athabasca	715	731
Total	880	895
Estimated recoverable oil (bitumen)[b]		
Using *in situ* technology	22-55	250-285
Using only surface mining and above ground processing	51[c]	26.5-85

a. The Cold Lake reserves were excluded from the official Global 2000 estimates, but were mentioned in a footnote and are included here for comparison.
b. Recoverable bitumen. Recoverable up-graded oil is given by IRPP as 55-170 bbl, using *in situ* technology.
c. Recoverable bitumen. Recoverable up-graded oil is given by IRPP as 27 bbl.
Sources: R. Clayton, C. Lafkas, G. Kreps, and R. Miller, *Canadian Energy: The Next 20 Years and Beyond,* Montreal: The Institute for Research on Public Policy, 1980, p. 187; and *Global 2000,* vol. 2, Washington: Government Printing Office, 1980, p. 200.

Solar Energy

The Study makes no specific mention of Canada with regard to solar energy and notes that there is currently no systematic collection of data on solar energy resources or use in the world. However, regional and world estimates of solar energy potential based on biomass and wind are of interest.

Estimates on the solar energy potential can be obtained from the annual production of biomass. Energy from biomass can be obtained directly by burning waste products, or produced from oil-producing plants and marine kelp. It has been estimated that the world produces 150×10^9 tons per year of biomass, with an estimated energy content of between 1,500 and 2,400 quadrillion Btu annually.[78]

Wind Energy

Estimates of total wind energy are given in the Study. The total wind energy dissipation rate overland in the Northern Hemisphere in winter is estimated to be about 167×10^9 watts; in the Southern Hemisphere it is about 24×10^9 watts.

The total wind energy generated overland is therefore about 0.19×10^{12} kilowatts, or $1,660 \times 10^{12}$ kWh (kilowatt hours) per year. It is estimated that placement of wind turbines 175 feet in diameter, spaced 16 to the square mile over the entire land area and operating an average of 2,000 hr/yr would yield about 120×10^{12} kWh/yr. Scaling this down to cover 2.5 percent of the area of the U.S., or an area about the size of Utah, would provide about 190×10^9 kWh/yr or about 10 percent of U.S. electrical energy consumed in 1972.[79]

Uranium

North America, according to the Study, has about 98 percent of estimated total world uranium resources, but no specific figures are given for Canada. Detailed Canadian estimates were also not available.* Estimates of Canadian resources presented here are from a chapter by Ted Greenwood and Alvin Streeter, appearing in *Natural Resources in U.S.-Canadian Relations,* edited by Beigie and Hero:

Canada Beigie and Hero [a]		North America Global 2000 [b]	
(Thousand short tons)			
Reasonably assured		Quantity recoverable	
$80/kg	189	$10-$35/lb	770
Estimated additional		Additional [c]	
$80/kg	445	resources	2,740
$80-$130/kg	424		

a. The economic classification systems used by the United States and Canada differ. According to Greenwood and Streeter, "The U.S. uses projected forward-cost categories that do not include sunk costs. Canada uses price categories. As a practical matter, U.S. cost categories and Canadian price categories approximately one-third higher are usually treated as equivalent." (C.E. Beigie and A.O. Hero, Jr., *Natural Resources in U.S.-Canadian Relations,* vol. 2, Boulder: Westview Press, 1980, p. 331.)

b. The Global 2000 estimates are from the World Energy Conference, 1976.

c. Includes all indicated and inferred reserves in addition to quantity recoverable.

According to the Beigie and Hero publication, Canada has a large share of the world's uranium resources: 10 percent of the world's total for reasonably assured resources at $80 U.S./kg; 28 percent of estimated additional resources at $80/kg, and 49 percent of estimated additional resources at $80-$130/kg.[80]

Nonfuel Minerals

The U.S. Government does not have the capability to develop regionally disaggregated world projections of nonfuel mineral supplies and demands. What information that could be pieced together for the Global 2000 Study came from a variety of sources including analysis carried out at the Department of the Interior and by Wilfred Malenbaum at the University of Pennsylvania.

Nowhere in the nonfuel mineral supply and demand projections is Canada treated individually. In the demand projections,[81] Canada is aggregated with Australia, Israel, New Zealand and South Africa in a category termed "Other Industrialized Nations." In the supply projections, Canada is included, along with Mexico and the United States, in a category termed "North America, Western Europe, Australia and Japan."

---

* The IRPP report contains some general figures not tied to any particular price of uranium: "Measured and indicated reserves of uranium are 19,000 tonnes while additional probable reserves are 320,000 tonnes." Clayton, et al., *Canadian Energy,* p. 161.

The inclusion of Canada with such diverse nations as Israel, Australia, New Zealand and South Africa is a consequence of the particular method used to project future demand for nonfuel minerals. This method, "intensity-of-use" (IOU), projects future mineral demand on the basis of past trends in per capita GNP. The trends differ widely from country to country, but the originator of this analysis, Wilfred Malenbaum from the University of Pennsylvania, found sufficient similarities among nations to group them into ten subdivisions. More specifically, Malenbaum found sufficiently similar patterns of general economic development, economic growth rates, and per capita GDP for Canada, Israel, Australia, New Zealand and South Africa to project their use of minerals collectively as a group. Malenbaum's projections are based on a theoretical IOU curve which assumes a decline in the per capita use of minerals in the more advanced stages of industrialization. This assumption conflicts with the assumption underlying the World Bank's projections of GDP. The World Bank's GDP projections, which were used in the Global 2000 Study, assume that the industrialized nations will import volumes of LDC metals at rates *greater* than their economic growth, i.e., will consume *more,* not less, nonfuel minerals as their industrialization advances. The World Bank assumption, of course, leads to relatively optimistic projections of LDC minerals exports and economic growth. Historical statistics support both higher and lower consumption according to the mineral being analyzed.[82]

Although regionally disaggregated world projections of nonfuel mineral supplies and demands are not available from U.S. Government sources, some nonfuel minerals data specific to Canada is found in the periodically updated "Mineral Commodity Profiles," which is to be published by the Bureau of Mines in a revised edition of *Mineral Facts and Problems.*[83] However, due to the differences in definition of terms used by the U.S. and Canadian governments, useful comparisons cannot be derived, as illustrated in Table 3-25. Resources in Canada and the United States are discussed in Beigie and Hero's recent study, *Natural Resources in U.S.-Canadian Relations,*[84] which may be consulted for further reference.

Environment

Canada is mentioned explicitly in only a few instances in the environmental chapter of the Global 2000 Study: with respect to climatic change,[85] acid rain,[86] air pollution,[87] the environmental implications of energy development,[88] and the impacts of acid rain on Canadian forestry.[89] In addition, the environmental chapter mentions several other changes or impacts — land deterioration, polar ice melt, water shortages in the western United States and international migration — that have significant implications for Canada. In general, however, the import of these changes and impacts for Canada is not fully discussed in the Study. Also, several environmental topics of potential concern to Canada — pollution control in and management of the Great Lakes and the St. Lawrence River, management of other shared river basins and marine pollution hazards associated with the transport of Alaskan oil by ship from Port Valdez to the lower forty-eight states — are not mentioned at all.

In the pages that follow, the various explicit environmental Global 2000 references to Canadian environmental problems are considered first. These are followed by environmental topics that are important to Canada which are discussed in the Global 2000 Study but without explicit reference to Canada. Additional and confirmational

TABLE 3-25
Comparison of U.S. and Canadian Estimates of
Reserves of Selected Nonfuel Minerals in Canada

	Canadian Estimates	U.S. Estimates
Copper (million metric tons)	15.8	32 to 35
Lead (million metric tons)	8.9	12
Zinc (million metric tons)	26.4	26
Nickel (million metric tons)	7.1	7.8 to 8.7
Molydenum (thousand metric tons)	461.6	500
Silver (metric tons)	29,100	22,081
Gold (kilograms)	410,000	1,400,000
Potash (million metric tons)	no data	9,074

Source: R.T. Williams, "Canadian Reserves of Seven Metals," *Canadian Mining Journal,* Feb. 1980; Bureau of Mines, U.S. Department of Interior, *Mineral Industries of Canada, Australia and Oceania,* Washington: Government Printing Office, 1979.

information from Canadian sources[90] is also presented to provide perspective on these issues.

Climate

The Global 2000 Study presents three climate scenarios for the remainder of the century: no change, global warming, and global cooling. Since global warming or cooling would affect high latitude and polar regions of the earth more than equatorial and adjacent latitudes, Canada would be strongly affected if there were cooling or warming, as the following passages note.

The Case II (Warming) scenario . . . leads to an increase of 1°C in global temperatures, with most of the warming in the polar regions and the higher middle latitudes. Precipitation increases are predicted for the higher middle latitudes with little change elsewhere. Fewer extremely cold winters might be expected, but the chance that the interior of the U.S. would experience hot summers and widespread drought conditions resembling those of the mid-1930s is likely to increase. The warming would be substantially beneficial to Canadian and Soviet wheat production; it would be moderately detrimental to wheat in Argentina, Australia and India and marginally unfavorable to corn (maize) in Argentina and the U.S. . . . The effects on energy usage, while not calculated, are probably negligible. Deforestation would probably increase in the higher middle latitudes as more of the land became arable. Pressures on forests elsewhere would depend on population growth and concomitant needs for food, fuelwood, building materials and other forest products.

The Case III (Cooling) scenario leads to a global temperature decrease of 0.5°C, with 1°C cooling in the higher and middle latitudes and smaller changes near the equator. Precipitation amounts decrease, and month to month and year to year variability increases. Storm tracks shift equatorward, bringing precipitation to the higher latitudes of deserts, but causing equatorward expansion of these deserts. Monsoon failures would become more frequent and

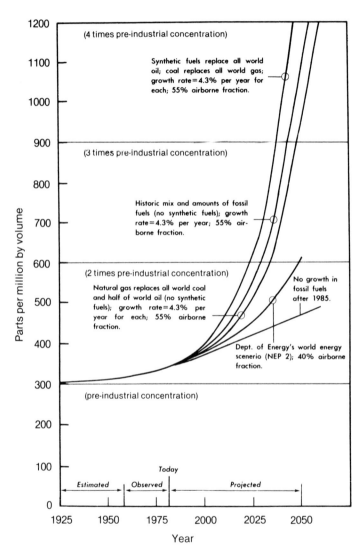

Figure 3-8. Carbon dioxide concentrations implied by various energy scenarios. Synthetic fuels derived from coal are assumed to release 3.4 x 10[15] grams of carbon in CO_2 per 100 quads of energy. Airborne fraction is the percentage of emitted CO_2 that remains in the atmosphere. *Source: Global 2000,* vol. 2, Washington: Government Printing Office, 1980, p. 262.

severe in India, and the Sahel would experience more frequent, severe droughts. Wheat yields in Canada and the Soviet Union would be reduced, but other key crops would not be severely affected . . . . The demand for energy would increase, particularly in the middle and higher latitudes, where increasing amounts of energy would be needed for heating. Also, greater variability of climate might call for higher levels of heating-fuel reserves. Additional demands for energy might also result from attempts to relieve drought effects in densely populated areas by producing water in massive desalinization programs. Forested areas at higher latitudes of the Northern hemisphere would become less accessible and grow more slowly.[91]

The Study found that most climatologists anticipate global warming rather than cooling, as a consequence of the "greenhouse" effect of increasing concentrations of carbon dioxide (CO_2) in the atmosphere. Figure 3-8 shows the Department of Energy's projection of CO_2 loading, which under several scenarios would cause a 2-3°C warming as early as 2050. The full consequences of global warming for Canada could be very great, since in addition to more rain and warmer temperatures, there would in time be melting of the polar ice caps, which would raise sea levels worldwide by approximately 5 meters.[92]

Acid Rain

Also brought about by energy production, acid rain is already causing damage in Canada. The following passage from the *Global 2000 Study* mentions Canada specifically:

The immediate consequence of both [sulfur oxide] SO_x and [nitrogen oxide] NO_x emissions is the acidification of precipitation. These gaseous compounds react in the atmosphere to form sulfuric acid and nitric acid, which, in turn, precipitate out of the atmosphere in both rain and snow. The acidified precipitation falls anywhere from a few hundred to a few thousand miles away from the source, depending on the strength of the prevailing winds . . . . As a result, the pH of rainfall is known to have fallen from a normal value of 5.7 to 4.5-4.2 (high acidic values) over large areas of southern Sweden, southern Norway, and the eastern U.S. . . . In the most extreme case yet recorded, a storm in Scotland in 1974, the rain was the acidic equivalent of vinegar (pH 2.4). . . . Equivalent changes have almost certainly occurred elsewhere, for example, downwind of the German, Eastern European and Soviet industrial regions. Effects of acid rain are only beginning to be understood but have now been observed in lakes, rivers and forests, in agricultural crops, in nitrogen-fixing bacteria, and in soils.

The clearest ill effects of acid rainfall observed to date are on lake fisheries. A survey of over 1,500 lakes in southwestern Norway, which has acid rainfall problems similar to those of southern Sweden, showed that over 70 percent of the lakes with a pH below 4.3 contained no fish. This was true for less than 10 percent of the lakes in the normal pH range of 5.5-6.0. . . . Similar effects have been found in lakes in the Adirondack mountains of New York . . . and in some areas of Canada.[93]

In addition to damage to fish life, detrimental effects on plant life are also being recorded:

Effects of acid rain on forest growth are only beginning to be understood. The effects on tree-seed germination are mixed. . . . Reductions in natural forest growth have been observed in both New England and Sweden. . . . One study tentatively attributed a 4 percent decline in annual forest growth in southern Sweden to acid rain. . . . Other observers feel that a decline in Scandinavian forest growth has not been conclusively demonstrated but suspect that the even more acidic rainfall expected in the future will cause slower growth.[94]

. . . [Acid rain] may reduce forest growth in some areas, especially in northern Europe, the northeastern U.S., southern Canada, and parts of the U.S.S.R. Acidification of soil may also occur over a period of years. The acid rain phenomena will probably reduce rates of growth and increase the difficulty of reforestation efforts.[95]

Effects on crops and soil are also noted:

The effects of acid rain on nonforest agricultural crops are under study and are beginning to be reported. Shoot and root growth of kidney bean and soybean plants have been found to be markedly reduced as a result of simulated acid rain of pH 3.2. . . . Similarly, nodulation by nitrogen-fixing bacteria on legumes is significantly reduced by simulated acid rain. . . . The growth of radish roots has been observed to decline by about 50 percent as the pH of rain falls from 5.7 to 3.0.

The sensitivity of soils to acidification by acid rain varies widely from area to area, depending largely on the amount of calcium in the soil. Calcium buffers the soil against acidification, but is leached out by acid rain; this leaching of calcium and soil nutrients has been found to increase with decreasing pH, and the pH of soils has been observed to decline more rapidly with more acidic rains. . . . The acidic soils that can result from acid rain could be expected to significantly reduce crop production in the affected areas unless large amounts of lime were applied.[96]

. . . The extent to which acid rain will adversely affect food production is still unknown, but over the next 20 years it will probably have much more effect than is assumed in the [Global 2000 Study's] food and agriculture projections. [The food projections assume no effect.][97]

If the Study's projected energy growth and pollution emissions are realized in the coming years, Canada can expect more damage from acid rain stemming from U.S. industrial and energy activities in the northeast:

The [projected] 13 percent increase in [U.S.] coal combustion by 1990 implies that large areas in and near industrial areas will continue to receive highly acidic rainfall. The rainfall in these areas is likely to become increasingly acidic as SO_x and NO_x emissions increase. The areas affected are likely to extend hundreds of thousands of miles downwind from the sources, a total geographic area large enough to include many lakes, watersheds and farmlands. The combined adverse effects in these areas on water quality (and indirectly on soil quality and plant growth) are likely to become increasingly severe.[102]

Analysis* performed for the Department of Energy shows that New York and New England would *increase* their emissions of sulfur oxides, assuming continuation of and compliance with U.S. air quality regulations and assuming a continuation of energy policies that were in existence prior to the deregulation of U.S. domestic oil and gas.

The reports of acid rain damage in Canada are extensive. For example, Lydia Dotto, writing in *Canadian Geographic,* makes these points:

• As of late 1979, 140 Ontario lakes had been acidic for a sufficient period of time to become, in effect, "dead." As many as 50,000 Ontario lakes are becoming increasingly acid, and by 2000 will have had time to have completed the death process. The best game fish (e.g., the aurora trout) are usually the first to die.

• Canada receives about 4 million metric tons (mmt) of sulfur dioxide (SO_2) each year from the United States. Canada emits about 5.5 mmt of SO_2 annually, of which 1 - 1.5 mmt cross into the United States.

• Air pollution from Ontario contributes to acid rain in Quebec and the Maritime Provinces (and possibly Greenland and Scandinavia). Quebec produces a significant amount of pollution, but most of the acid rain from this pollution falls in the Maritimes. Sulfur dioxide-laden air masses reaching north-central Saskatchewan have been discovered to be coming from the Alberta tar sands region, where two sands plants release 600 tons of sulfur per day of operation.

• The impacts on forests are difficult to assess due to masking effects of other factors such as climate and insects.

• Ontario undertook a $1.5 million program of acid rain impact surveys and related baseline studies in 1980.[99]

Canada has an extensive number of studies and reports on acid rain[100] and the analysis now available demonstrates quite conclusively that emissions in both the United States and in Canada are involved in causing the acid rain in both countries.

In recognition of this fact, the United States and Canada signed a Memorandum of Intent on Transboundary Air Pollution on August 5, 1980. This memorandum establishes a program of research and policy attention which should lead to substantial improvements in the acid rain problems being experienced by both countries. An impact assessment group and a research consultation group have been established and have submitted progress reports.[101] At this point one must assume that both nations will continue steps toward progress, as agreed in the 1980 Memorandum of Intent.

Other Environmental Effects of Energy Development

Further increases in atmospheric concentrations of carbon dioxide (and the associated consequences for global climate) and the acid rain resulting from air pollutants produced during the combustion of fossil fuels are probably the two implications of energy development most important for the Canadian environment. Two other environ-

---

* Canadians concerned with acid rain would be well advised to examine this analysis carefully. Richard J. Kalagher et al., *National Environmental Impact Projection No. 1,* McLean, Va.: MITRE Corp., Dec. 1978.

mental implications of energy development, however, should be kept in mind: the effects of oil and gas exploitation in previously untouched areas and nuclear hazards.

An increase in oil and gas exploitation in previously untouched arctic areas and coastal zones will result in significant disturbance of these areas, pollution from well blowouts and transportation accidents and from chronic, low-volume spills. The special vulnerability of the Arctic areas is mentioned in the Global 2000 Study:

> As the search for oil and gas intensifies, exploitation and extraction will take place in areas previously untouched. The marine environment in parts of the Arctic is now vulnerable to conditions accompanying the exploitation of fossil fuel resources. The construction of artificial drilling islands dredged up from bay bottoms, will have locally adverse effects on Arctic sea life, as will low level losses of oil incurred during routine production and transportation. Accidental large volume spills or well blowouts would pose serious problems, for the very nature of the far northern environment would make cleanup efforts and ultimate ecosystem especially difficult.[102]

The Global 2000 and other projections suggest a significant expansion of the Canadian nuclear power industry between now and 2000. This prospective expansion raises several environmental and societal problems, notably nuclear waste disposal, reactor safety and nuclear weapons proliferation. These issues are discussed briefly in the Global 2000 Study.[103]

Intensification of Silviculture

The Global 2000 Study suggests that demand for Canadian forest products will increase for export, for all of the traditional domestic uses and for use as biofuels. Together these prospects for growing demands on Canadian forests suggest that an intensification of silvicultural practices is likely. This intensification has numerous environmental implications:

> To date, experience with intensive silviculture is limited to a very small number of complete planting-to-harvest cycles. Furthermore, intensive silviculture is being practiced at present on a regional scale only in Europe, although significant local developments are taking place in Japan, North America, the People's Republic of China, Brazil, South Korea and New Zealand.[104]

While experience is limited, there are several concerns about the environmental consequences of intensified forest production patterned after Green Revolution agriculture:

> There are other reasons for environmental concern about increased silvicultural intensity: (1) In both the industrialized nations and the LDCs, the ability of many forest soils to sustain short-rotation tree cropping is doubtful. Recent U.S. research indicates that even in quickly recovering temperate-zone forests, the loss of soil nutrients following a clear-cutting operation is significant. (2) There is some evidence that plantations of uniformly aged trees do not stabilize watersheds as well as the natural forests that preceded them. (3) Applications of pesticides and fertilizers are likely to affect eco-system elements other than the trees they are intended for, reducing the diversity of both flora and fauna and threatening the health of forest lakes

and streams. (4) In some places intensively managed forests may even become sources of pollution (from fertilizers and other applied chemicals), where they once functioned as filters of air and water.[105]

Little empirical data concerning the environmental consequences of silviculture could be gleaned from Canadian environmental reports. Environment Canada's *Fourth-Quarter Century Trends in Canada* does list a number of generic issues having potential environmental implications: use of chemicals (herbicides, insecticides); thinning of stands, road building and logging, reforestation with monocultures; and disposal of waste products.[106] Actual experience with these matters was not reported. Air and water pollution from the pulp and paper industry, however, is noted to be a major problem. Environment Canada notes that during 1971-1980 it was estimated that $681 million (1970 Cdn$) would have to be spent by the pulp and paper industry to meet "current (environmental) standards."[107] Statistics Canada reports that during 1969-75, water pollution control expenditures for pulp and paper mills represented the greater part of total water pollution control expenditures in the Atlantic provinces (96 percent), Quebec (68 percent) and British Columbia (87.8 percent).[108]

Land Deterioration
Intensification of cereal and other food crop production is contributing to erosion and loss of organic matter in the United States and elsewhere in the world. U.S. concerns are expressed in the following passages, which might also apply to Canada:

The U.S. Soil Conservation Service considers soil losses of 1 ton per acre for shallow soils and 5 tons per acre for deep soils to be the maximum that can be sustained annually without harming productivity. Although difficult to estimate, the extent to which soil losses exceed this figure appears to be great. For example, a survey of 283 U.S. farms in the Midwest, Great Plains, and Pacific Northwest recently conducted by the General Accounting Office (GAO) found that 84 percent had annual soil losses in excess of 5 tons per acre. . . . In Iowa and Illinois, the two corn-dominated states covered by the GAO study, half the farms surveyed lost between 10 and 20 short tons per acre per year. These findings are consistent with those of other studies.[109]

The Canadian problem of land deterioration was recently summarized by Roy Vontobel in a *Canadian Geographic* article, "Our Precious Topsoil is Wasting Away." Vontobel reports that:

- *Alkalinization* with sodium and magnesium salts has affected 3 million acres of cereal-growing farmlands in Saskatchewan, and additional acreage in Alberta. The land being damaged or lost is the best cropland. The loss is thought to be caused in part by what is called "summer fallowing," a technique which enhances the downward percolation of rainwater which later re-emerges on the soil surface (especially topographic depressions) loaded with soluble salts.

- Soil compaction is a serious problem in Quebec and southern Ontario (where corn monoculture has increased in recent years), as well as in New Brunswick (where it has diminished the traditional potato crop).

- Erosion is adversely affecting soils in all provinces.

• Loss of organic matter in the wheat farms of Saskatchewan (where 45 percent of all Canadian farmlands are located) has lowered their productivity and accelerated the process of alkalinization.[110]

Official documents in Canada do not seem to reflect the apparent seriousness of land deterioration problems being voiced by soil scientists, especially Dr. Donald A. Rennie, of the University of Saskatchewan.

Loss of Farmland to Urbanization

The Global 2000 Study includes the following discussion of the loss of farmland to urbanization:

. . . A recent study by the Organization for Economic Cooperation and Development (OECD) indicates that in the OECD (industrialized) countries urban land area has been growing about twice as fast as the population. . . . This trend is due in part to sprawling residential patterns. In 1972 each additional U.S. suburbanite required 0.15 hectares of land (0.09 hectares of which was taken out of cultivation) for development purposes. This loss is nearly half the average agricultural land per capita (0.19 hectares) projected for the LDCs by the year 2000. . . . On a percentage basis, even higher loss rates are being experienced in some industrialized nations [see Table 3-26]. Surveys in developing countries show lower per capita land losses to development, but the high rates of population growth and the limited amounts of prime farmlands are likely to make such losses equally important in the LDCs.

In the face of rising energy costs, it is unclear whether the trend toward urban, suburban, and industrial sprawl will continue or reverse. Energy concerns will gradually encourage both greater compactness (for the efficiency needed by large centralized energy facilities) and more decentralization (for the more diffused, land-intensive, and self-sufficient settlement patterns that efficiently use solar and other small-scale renewable sources of energy, such as windmills, biogas plants and biomass). However these forces eventually balance out, it seems likely that significant amounts of land will be removed from cultivation or potential cultivation between now and 2000. The OECD countries again provide an example. Should 1960-70 rates of land loss continue, the OECD countries will have lost an average of 2.5 percent of their agricultural lands by 2000, as shown in the table. A substantial portion of the higher cost of food production projected for 2000 . . . is a direct result of the costs of expanding arable area to compensate for development losses.[111]

The Science Council of Canada and Agriculture Canada have both expressed concern about the loss of Canadian agricultural land to urbanization. Canada now has 69 million acres in farms. An additional 50 million acres have agricultural potential, but half are in poor climatic zones and remote from markets. Farmland lost in southern central Canada is irreplaceable, being three to six times more productive than new land brought into agricultural use.[112]

Canada's major urban areas are located almost exactly where Canada's best farmlands are, namely land capability classes 1 to 3. Loss of farms to urban sprawl is particularly rapid in Ontario, where average values of farmland are 4 to 8 times the values in other provinces. Agriculture Canada estimates that by the year 2000 urban

TABLE 3-26
Loss of Agricultural Lands, 1960-2000, Selected
Industrialized Countries [a]

	Average Annual Rate of Loss 1960-70	Projected Cumulative Loss 1978-2000
	(percent)	
Austria	0.18	5
Belgium	1.23[b]	24
Denmark	0.30	6
Finland	0.28[c]	6
France	0.18	4
West Germany	0.25	5
Japan	0.73[d]	15
Netherlands	0.48[e]	10
New Zealand	0.05	1
Norway	0.15	3
Sweden	0.33	7
Turkey	0.04	1
United Kingdom	0.18	4
United States (excluding Alaska)	0.08	2
Weighted total		2.5

a. It is unclear why the *Interfutures* study did not include Canada in this table, but losses in Canada may be similar (or less than) those in the United States: about 0.18 percent per year or a 5 percent loss by 2000.

b. 1959-70.

c. 1959-69.

d. 1965-75.

e. 1966-72.

Source: 1960-70 data from Organization for Economic Cooperation and Development, *Interfutures,* Ch. 13, "Physical Environment," Paris, May 16, 1977 (draft) p. 22; as reprinted in *Global 2000,* vol. 2, Washington: Government Printing Office, 1980, p. 282.

development in Quebec and Ontario will have taken 300,000 and 500,000 hectares, respectively, out of farmland.[113]

Great concern is expressed by the Science Council for the urbanization of the Niagara fruit belt, the "most important area in the country for soft fruit" which if lost will mean that "Canada will have no hope for self-sufficiency in soft fruit production."[114]

Impacts of Metallurgical Industries

The Global 2000 Study cites an article from the *Canadian Forestry Chronicle* which records the damage to vegetation caused by pollution from the smelters in the Sudbury district of Ontario.[115] These smelters are reported to emit 2.7 million tons of sulfur oxides annually "causing losses of timber with a value of $117,000 per year in a 720 square mile zone of severe damage."[116]

No confirmation of this impact was contained in various reports seen from Canada. However, much attention continues to focus on INCO's Copper Cliff Smelter, whose 1,250-foot high stack is the largest single source of sulfur dioxide pollution in North America. Inaugurated in 1974, this giant smelter was allowed to emit up to 3,600 tons per day of SO_x under a 1978 control order, although actual emissions were averaging 2,500 tons per day in 1980. In 1983 emissions will have to be reduced to 1,950 tons per day.[117]

References

1. For example, i) The Latin American World Model; ii) The World 2 and 3 Models; iii) The World Integrated Model (WIM); iv) The United Nations Model; and v) The Model of International Relations in Agriculture (MOIRA).

2. See: *The Global 2000 Report to the President*, vol. 2, Washington: Government Printing Office, 1980, pp. 7-38, and 501-20; and U.S. Bureau of the Census, *Illustrative Projections of World Populations to the 21st Century*, Washington: Government Printing Office, 1979, pp. 109-10.

3. Informetrica, Ltd., "Total Population and Household Formation, projections of June 12, 1980."

4. The U.S. Census derivation of base-year population for the Canadian projections is described in the U.S. Bureau of the Census report, *Illustrative Projections of World Populations to the 21st Century*, pp. 109-10:

   The base population data were taken from the official 1975 midyear population estimate of Canada (including Bermuda, Greenland, and St. Pierre and Miquelon) published by the United Nations Statistical Office in 1977. Total population estimates for Bermuda, Greenland, and St. Pierre and Miquelon for midyear 1975 (U.S. Bureau of the Census current estimates) were added to the 1975 total for Canada. Total population estimates, midyear 1975, are as follows:

Country or area	Population
Canada	22,799,600
Bermuda	59,719
Greenland	50,047
St. Pierre and Miquelon	5,983

   The total populations of these three areas were distributed by age and sex in the same proportions as the age-sex distribution of Canada.

5. Ibid.

6. Ibid.

7. Ibid.

8. *Global 2000*, vol. 2, p. 31.

9. Ibid., p. 33.

10. Workshop on Alternative Energy Strategies, *Energy: Global Prospects, 1985-2000*, New York: McGraw-Hill, 1977.

11. Ibid.

12. *Global 2000*, vol. 2, pp. 521-34, and vol. 3, chap. 3.

13. A brief description of SIMLINK and other models used in the Global 2000 Study is contained in *Global 2000*, vol. 3, chap. 3.

14. The economic projections used for Canada are contained in R.S. Preston, et al., *16th Annual Review: Background Simulations and Policy Alternatives,* Ottawa: Economic Council of Canada, Oct. 1979.
15. Ibid.
16. The assumptions about the U.S. economy appear to have been taken from the Wharton econometric model at the University of Pennsylvania. See R.S. Preston, et al., *16th Annual Review: Background Simulations and Policy Alternatives,* Ottawa: Economic Council of Canada, Oct. 1979, Table 4-1.
17. Not all of the inflation and economic problems in the industrialized nations are due to the increasing price of petroleum. For an interesting discussion of the Kondratieff cycle and other factors see: Jay W. Forrester, "Changing Economic Patterns," *Technology Review,* Aug./Sept., 1978.
18. *OECD Economic Outlook,* Paris: Organization for Economic Cooperation and Development, Dec. 1980.
19. *Climate Change to the Year 2000: A Survey of Expert Opinion,* Washington: National Defense University, Feb. 1978.
20. Ibid.
21. *Global 2000,* vol. 2, p. 52.
22. Ibid., p. 180.
23. Ibid., p. 470.
24. Ibid., pp. 490-91.
25. Ibid., p. 77.
26. Ibid., p. 79.
27. Ibid., p. 85.
28. Ibid.
29. Ibid., p. 89.
30. Ibid., p. 95.
31. Ibid., p. 89.
32. Ibid., p. 104.
33. *Orientation of Canadian Agriculture,* vols. I-III, Ottawa: Agriculture Canada, 1977.
34. *Orientation of Canadian Agriculture,* vol. III.
35. *Orientation of Canadian Agriculture,* vol. I, Ottawa: Agriculture Canada, 1977.
36. *Orientation of Canadian Agriculture,* vol. III, p. 9.
37. *Global 2000,* vol. 2, p. 552.
38. *Global 2000,* vol. 2, p. 113.
39. Ibid., p. 108.
40. Ibid., pp. 564-65.
41. Ibid., p. 565.
42. Ibid., p. 111.
43. Ibid.
44. Ibid.
45. Ibid.
46. Ibid., p. 112.
47. *Human Activity and the Environment,* Ottawa: Statistics Canada, 1978, p. 62.
48. Ibid.
49. *Global 2000,* vol. 2, p. 124.

50. Ibid., p. 124.
51. Ibid., p. 133.
52. Ibid., p. 125.
53. *Canada's Forests,* Ottawa: Canadian Forestry Service, 1974.
54. *Outlook for Timber Utilization in Canada to the Year 2000,* Ottawa: Canadian Forestry Service, 1979.
55. *Global 2000,* vol. 2, p. 124.
56. *Outlook for Timber Utilization in Canada to the Year 2000,* Ottawa: Canadian Forestry Service, 1979, p. 91.
57. *Global 2000,* vol. 2, pp. 439-96 and chap. 20, and vol. 3, chap. 6. Also see: M.L. Shaw and M.J. Hutzler, *The International Energy Evaluation System,* vol. 1 and 2, Springfield, Va.: National Technical Information Service, 1979.
58. Department of Energy, Energy Information Administration, "International Energy Assessment," in Department of Energy, *Annual Report to Congress, 1979,* vol. 3, Washington: Government Printing Office, 1980, pp. 7-34.
59. Data from three Canadian publications are used for these comparisons. *Energy Conservation in Canada: Programs and Perspectives* prepared by Energy Mines and Resources Canada in 1978 (Ottawa: Supply and Services Canada, 1978), presents two scenarios for energy demand in 1990. The first scenario, referred to as the "Energy Strategy Scenario," is a government projection of a high price-low economic growth situation, published initially in a major energy policy report entitled *An Energy Strategy for Canada: Policies for Self-Reliance.* The second scenario, the "Energy Conservation Scenario," uses the *Energy Strategy Scenario* as a point of departure and investigates the impact on demand of intentional conservation measures. *Canadian Energy: The Next 20 Years and Beyond* was prepared for the the Institute for Research on Public Policy (IRPP) (Montreal: Institute for Research in Public Policy, 1980). This IRPP report presents two scenarios for the year 2000. The IRPP "High Growth" scenario assumes a continuation of historical rates of economic growth and energy demand. The IRPP "Low Growth" scenario assumes lower economic and energy growth rates. *Energy Futures for Canadians: Long Term Energy Assessment Program (LEAP)* is a study prepared for Energy, Mines and Resources Canada in 1978 (Ottawa: Supply and Services Canada, 1978). The LEAP report assesses the world and Canadian energy picture to 2025 and outlines a program of action.
60. Department of Energy, Energy Information Administration, *Annual Report to Congress, 1979,* vol. 3, p. 24.
61. J.E. Gander and F.W. Belaire, *Energy Futures for Canadians: Long-Term Energy Assessment Program (LEAP),* Ottawa: Supply and Services Canada, 1978, p. 33.
62. R. Clayton, C. Lafkas, G. Kreps and R. Miller, *Canadian Energy: The Next 20 Years and Beyond,* Montreal: The Institute for Research on Public Policy, 1980, p. 19.
63. Ibid.
64. *Global 2000,* vol. 2, pp. 190-91.
65. Ibid., p. 192.
66. U.S. National Committee for the World Energy Conference, *World Energy Conference, 1974,* New York: World Energy Conference, 1974.
67. *Global 2000,* vol. 2, pp. 195-96.

68. Department of Energy, Energy Information Administration, *Annual Report to Congress, 1979*, vol. 2, p. 129.
69. Ibid., p. 367.
70. Ibid., p. 197.
71. *Global 2000*, vol. 2, pp. 199-200.
72. Ibid., p. 199.
73. Clayton et al., *Canadian Energy*, p. 187.
74. Gander and Belaire, *Energy Futures for Canada: Long-Term Energy Assessment Program (LEAP)*, p. 32.
75. Clayton et al., *Canadian Energy*, p. 19.
76. Walter DuPree, U.S. Bureau of Mines, personal communication, 1981.
77. *Oil and Gas Journal*, Dec. 29, 1980, p. 000.
78. *Global 2000*, vol. 2.
79. Ibid.
80. C.E. Beigie and A.O. Hero, Jr., *Natural Resources in U.S.-Canadian Relations*, vol. 2, Boulder: Westview Press, 1980, p. 331.
81. Ibid., pp. 206-07.
82. Ibid., pp. 453-99.
83. U.S. Bureau of Mines, *Mineral Facts and Problems*, Washington: Government Printing Office, 1975.
84. Beigie and Hero, Jr., *Natural Resources*, vol. 2.
85. *Global 2000*, vol. 2, p. 259.
86. Ibid., p. 336.
87. Ibid., p. 351.
88. Ibid., p. 367.
89. Ibid., p. 411.
90. The three sources used here probably represent only a small sampling of what is undoubtedly a large technical literature on environmental problems in Canada: Environment Canada, *Fourth-Quarter Century Trends in Canada*, Ottawa: Supply and Services Canada, 1975; Statistics Canada, *Human Activity and the Environment*, 1978; Science Council of Canada, *Canadian Food and Agriculture Sustainability and Self Reliance: A Discussion Paper*, Ottawa: Supply and Services Canada, 1979.
91. *Global 2000*, vol. 2, p. 259.
92. Ibid., p. 404.
93. Ibid., p. 336.
94. Ibid.
95. Ibid., p. 411.
96. Ibid., p. 337.
97. Ibid., p. 418.
98. Ibid., p. 337.
99. Lydia Dotto, "What Acid Rain Does to Our Land and Water," *Canadian Geographic*, Dec. 1979/Jan. 1980, pp. 34-41.
100. See, for example: "How Many More Lakes Have to Die?," *Canada Today*, February 1981; Environment Canada, *Downwind: The Acid Rain Story*, Ottawa: Supply and Services Canada, 1981; NRC Associate Committee on Scientific Criteria for Environmental Quality, *Sulfur and its Inorganic Derivatives in the Canadian Environment*, Ottawa: National Research Council of Canada, 1977; and

The Province of Ontario, *A Submission to the United States Environmental Protection Agency Opposing Relaxation of SO₂ Emission Limits in State Implementation Plans and Urging Enforcement,* Toronto: Ministry of the Environment, March 12, 1981.

101. Impact Assessment Work Group, *Impact Assessment: Interim Report,* Ottawa and Washington: Canada/United States Coordinating Committee on the United States-Canada Memorandum of Intent on Transboundary Air Pollution, February 1981; United States-Canada Research Consultation Group on the Long Range Transport of Air Pollutants (LRTAP), *The LRTAP Problem in North America: A Preliminary Overview,* Downsview, Ont.: LRTAP Scientific Program Office, Environment Canada, 1979; United States - Canada Research Consultation Group on the Long-Range Transport of Air Pollutants, *Second Report,* Downsview, Ont.: LRTAP Scientific Program Office, Environment Canada, 1980.

102. *Global 2000,* vol. 2, p. 311.

103. Ibid., p. 356.

104. Ibid., p. 326.

105. Ibid.

106. Environment Canada, *Fourth-Quarter Century Trends in Canada,* 1975.

107. Ibid., p. 54.

108. Statistics Canada, *Human Activity and the Environment,* 1978, p. 115.

109. *Global 2000,* vol. 2, p. 281.

110. R. Vontobel, "Our Precious Topsoil is Wasting Away," *Canadian Geographic,* April/May 1980, pp. 50-59.

111. *Global 2000,* p. 282.

112. Science Council of Canada, *Canadian Food and Agriculture Sustainability and Self-Reliance,* May 1979, p. 52.

113. Agriculture Canada, *Orientation of Canadian Agriculture, vol. 1, 1977,* p. 42.

114. Science Council of Canada, *Canadian Food and Agriculture,* p. 31.

115. S.N. Linson, "Effects of Sulfur Oxides on Vegetation," *Canadian Forestry Chronicle,* vol. 48, no. 4, 1972, pp. 1-5.

116. *Global 2000,* vol. 2, p. 387.

117. "Ontario Cabinet Orders Inco to Cut Stack Emissions," *Globe and Mail,* September 3, 1980, p. 1.

Appendices

Appendix A
A Bibliography of
Canadian Futures Studies

A preliminary investigation of Canadian studies of the future produced two studies of world futures and several studies of the Canadian future. A variety of Canadian sectoral studies were also identified (see Table A-1). The Canadian studies of the world are considered first.

Canadian Studies of World Futures

W. Baker (ed.), *Shaping the Future: Canada in a Global Society,* Centre for Policy and Management Studies, Ottawa, 1979.

This large volume contains papers and proceedings of a conference on "Shaping the Future: Canada in a Global Society," held in Ottawa in 1978. The papers presented in this conference cover a wide range of Canadian issues in a global context relating to science and technology, business and labor, including industrial relations, economic growth, policy making and socio-cultural responses. Slater's paper, "The Canadian Economy in a Global Perspective," provides some well-reasoned speculations relating to prospects for growth in productivity, foreign trade, exploitation of natural resources and issues relating to inflation and unemployment, but is not based on extensive quantitative analysis.

H.H. Postner, "Canadian Implications of the United Nations World Input-Output Model," paper presented at Twelfth Annual Meeting of the Canadian Economics Association, University of Western Ontario, London, Ont., May 1978.

This study begins with the U.N. World Development Model developed by W. Leontief, et al. *(The Future of the World Economy,* New York: Oxford University Press, 1977). The U.N. World Development Model aggregates Canada and the United States into a North American Region (NAR), one of 15 regions in the U.N. model. The Postner study disaggregates Canada from the NAR using a 46-sector Canadian long-term model, which includes 10 nonrenewable resource sectors. This model is linked to NAR in the world system through estimates of Canada's shares of NAR nonresource exports and resource production. Four different Canadian gross domestic product targets are set for the year 2000 in the context of four different global model scenarios. The Canadian model then provides detailed pictures of production, investment and foreign trade for Canada in 2000. Postner's 1979 report provides an analysis of input-output relationships in the Canadian economy within a global context and a discussion of how these relationships are likely to change in the future.

TABLE A-1
Canadian Sectoral Studies

	Canadian re. Canada	Canadian re. World
Technological projections	*16th Annual Review: Background Simulations and Policy Alternatives*	*16th Annual Review: Background Simulations and Policy Alternatives*
Forestry projections	*The Outlook for Timber Utilization in Canada to the Year 2000*	
Water projections	*Water for Energy Development*	"Draft Report on Long-term Perspectives for Water Use and Supply"; ECE
Energy projections	*Energy Supply-Demand Integrations to the Year 2000*	*Energy Supply-Demand Integrations to the Year 2000*
	Energy and Industry	
	The Energy Squeeze	
	Canadian Energy: The Next 20 Years and Beyond	
Environment projections	*The Selective Conserver Society*	
	Canadians in Conversation About the Future.	

H.H. Postner, "Canada and the Future of the International Economy: A Global Modeling Analysis," Economic Council of Canada, Discussion Paper No. 129, March 1979.

Canadian Studies of Canada's Future

B.L. Erydon and B. Cain, "Simulations with CANDIDE to the Year 2000," Economic Council of Canada, Discussion Paper No. 89, May 1977.

The objective of this study is to examine the feasibility of using the CANDIDE model as a tool in long-term analysis. The study analyzes the consequences of recent demographic trends in the country, probable and selected energy-related investments and the adaptation of Canadian industrial sectors to increased foreign competition. This analysis is done by developing a reference scenario and examining deviations that could occur from the reference case. The study provides projected indicators of economic activity, foreign trade, population growth and energy development to the year 2000.

Statistics Canada, *Population Projections for Canada and the Provinces, 1976-2001,* Feb. 1979, Cat. No. 91-520.

Demographic projections for Canada to the year 2001 are contained in this report from Statistics Canada. [6] These projections (and earlier unpublished versions) have been used in many projective studies including the studies by Postner and by Erydon and Cain (see above).

G. W. Davies, "Macroeconomic Effects of Immigration: Evidence from CANDIDE, TRACE and RDX2," Report to the Department of Manpower and Immigration, 1976.

This study examines the macroeconomic effects of immigration on the Canadian economy with reference to the unemployment rate and inflation. Three models are employed. While the analysis stops in 1980, the study is of importance for its methodological contribution.

Science Council of Canada, *Canada as a Conserver Society: Resource Uncertainties and the Need for New Technologies,* Report No. 27, Sept. 1977; and
K. Valaskakis, P.S. Sindell, and J.G. Smith, *The Selective Conserver Society,* McGill University.

These two books make the case for Canada becoming a conserver society. The analysis is quantitative in part, but no formal economic model is used. These books have been widely read in the United States and elsewhere. In 1978 the Science Council presented the Conserver Society work in Washington at the request of the Executive Office of the President.

C.E. Beigie and A.O. Hero, Jr., *Natural Resources in U.S.-Canadian Relations,* vol. 1-3, Boulder: Westview Press, 1980.

Canada's future is tied in many ways to its relations with the United States and issues relating to natural resources will become an increasingly important factor in Canadian-U.S. relations. This massive, well documented, thoughtful report is a milestone in contemporary work on U.S. and Canadian relations. This work, supported by the C.D. Howe Research Institute and by the World Peace Foundation, will be essential reading for years to come for everyone concerned professionally with Canada's future.

Other Reports of Interest

A.P. Carter and P.A. Petri, "Factors Affecting Long-Term Prospects of Developing Regions," Economic Council of Canada, Discussion Paper No. 117, June 1978.
Economic Council of Canada, *A Climate of Uncertainty: Seventeenth Annual Review,* Ottawa: Supply and Services Canada, 1980.
D.M. Paproski, *Environmental Management in a Canadian Context,* Discussion Paper No. 73, Ottawa: Economic Council of Canada, January 1977.
D.M. Paproski, *Weighing Conflicting Concerns in The Context of Frontier Development,* Discussion Paper No. 96, Ottawa: Economic Council of Canada, Sept. 1977.
R.S. Preston et al., *Canada: The Medium Term Performance and Issues,* Ottawa: Economic Council of Canada, Nov. 1980.
Energy, Mines and Resources, *The National Energy Program 1980,* Ottawa: Supply and Services Canada, 1980.
The Medium-Term Prospects for the Canadian Economy, 1980-1985, Ottawa:

Department of Finance, Oct. 1980.

A Structural Analysis of the Canadian Economy to 1990, Ottawa: Industry, Trade and Commerce, May 1978.

Users Guide to Statistics Canada Structural Economic Models, Ottawa: Statistics Canada, Sept. 1980.

G.A. McKay and T. Allsopp, *Climatic Change and Energy Use: A Northern Perspective on Climatic Uncertainty,* Downsview, Ont.: Canadian Climate Centre, 1981.

G.A. McKay, T.R. Allsopp, and J.B. Maxwell, *Lessons from the Past,* Downsview: Canadian Climate Centre, 1981.

G.A. McKay and G.D.V. Williams, *Canadian Climate and Food Production,* Downsview, Ont.: Canadian Climate Centre, 1981.

N.K. Choudry, et al., *The Trace Econometric Model of the Canadian Economy,* University of Toronto Press, 1972.

R.G. Bodkin and S.M. Tanny, eds., *CANDIDE Model 1.1,* vol. 1 and 2, Economic Council of Canada, 1975.

Dept. of Industry, Trade and Commerce, "A Structural Analysis of the Canadian Economy to 1990," Discussion Paper, Ottawa, 1978.

Economic Council of Canada, "For a Common Future," Ottawa, 1978.

Economic Council of Canada, "A Time for Reason," Ottawa, 1978.

Cathy Starrs, *Canadians in Conversation About the Future,* Ottawa: Environment Canada, 1976.

National Energy Board, *Canadian Oil: Supply and Requirements,* September 1975.

National Energy Board, *Canadian National Gas: Supply and Requirements,* April 1975.

General

For a Common Future: A Study of Canada's Relations with Developing Countries, Economic Council of Canada, 1978.

Report of Parliamentary Task Force on North/South Relations, Preliminary Report, August 1980; Final Report, December 1980.

Strengthening Canada Abroad, prepared by Export Promotion Review Committee, Roger Hatch, Chairman, Department of Industry, Trade and Commerce, November 1979.

Canada's S&T Contribution to World Food Supply, a series of recent reports available from the Science Council of Canada.

Agriculture

Orientation of Canadian Agriculture, (4 vol.), Agriculture Canada Task Force, 1977.

Future Agricultural Research Mission: 1975/85, Research Branch, Agriculture Canada, August 1975.

L.A. Christie, *Agricultural Research In Canada: Priorities Funding & Manpower,* Library of Parliament, April 1980.

D.G. Hamilton, *Evaluation of R&D in Agriculture and Food in Canada,* Report to Canadian Agricultural Research Council, January 1980.

Proceedings of Canada & World Food Conference, Royal Society of Canada and Agricultural Institute of Canada, Ottawa, 1977.

Policy

A Food Strategy For Canada, released by Minister of Agriculture & CCA, 1977.

Appendix B
An Overview of Canadian Long-Term Policy Models*

Long-range policy models for government analysis and planning are conveniently divided into global models and national models. The Canadian models will be taken up under these two topics.

Global Models

Very few national governments have developed global models and while Canada does not have a global model of its own, the Economic Council of Canada (ECC) had adopted the U.N. World Development Model (UNWDM) for analysis of Canadian relations with third world countries. An adaptation was necessary because the U.N. World Model lumps Canada and the United States together into a single North American Region (NAR), one of 15 regions considered in the UNWDM.

The objective of the Canadian work was to disaggregate Canada from NAR without formally restructuring the UNWDM into sixteen regions. The Canadian works begins with the 1977 version of the UNWDM[1] (which is based on 1970 data) and with a revised UNWDM scenario developed for the ECC by the Brandeis University team that helped construct the UNWDM originally.

As a next step, a simple 46-sector, long-term model of the Canadian Economy (including 10 nonrenewable sectors) was constructed. This model is linked to the NAR in the UNWDM through estimates of Canada's shares of NAR nonresource exports and resource productions. Four different Canadian gross domestic product (GDP) targets are set for the year 2000 in the context of four different global model scenarios. The Canadian model then yields detailed pictures of production, investment and international trade for Canada in 2000. Business investments in fixed capital stocks and inventories are endogenous, as are all imports and resource exports. Endogenous variables are solved through a stepwise solution procedure; the fixed GDP targets are achieved by iteration involving scalar adjustments of personal consumption expenditures. Special calculations reveal Canadian balance-of-trade, terms-of-trade and sectoral comparative advantage under alternative scenarios in the year 2000.

The Canadian use of the UNWDM and its national implications are still at an exploratory level. The work done to date[2] provides a methodology for exploring the Canadian impacts of global economic developments. Such analysis permits comparisons

---

* This appendix has been prepared on the basis of information provided by Statistics Canada, Industry, Trade and Commerce, and the Department of Employment and Immigration.

143

of the Canadian economy in the year 2000 with that of other regions in the global system using a consistent and interdependent framework.

National Models

There are a number of Canadian national models — i.e., models of Canada — some of which are considered briefly here with respect to their potential usefulness for analyzing the range of issues raised in the Global 2000 Study in a strictly Canadian context. These models are primarily quarterly and annual macroeconometric models. Two of the models do not belong to these categories and are discussed separately.

Canada's quarterly macroeconomic models include the Bank of Canada's RDX2 model, the Conference Board's AERIC model, the University of Toronto's quarterly version of the TRACE model, the Data Resources Inc. (DRI) quarterly model, and Statistics Canada's SCQUEM model. In general these models are used for 8 quarter macroeconomic forecasts and for analysis of economic stabilization policies. Although these models attempt to examine the dynamic properties of the Canadian economy for periods of 8 quarters or so, they are not suitable for analyzing the issues raised in the Global 2000 Study for periods of 2 or more decades.

Canada also has several annual macroeconomic models, including the Economic Council version of CANDIDE (see box following), the University of Toronto's TRACE (see box following) model, and Informetrica Ltd.'s TIM model. These models have medium-term time horizons of up to approximately ten years. They generally include more industrial detail than the quarterly models discussed above. Like their quarterly counterparts, these models are intended to address macroeconomic neo-Keynesian issues of stabilization policy. They usually incorporate an input-output transformation to bridge demand formation and factor incomes. They include demographic blocks so that the population-GNP linkage is made. Both TRACE and CANDIDE are used in conjunction with the Wharton annual model. While these models can be used for some types of analysis extending out about ten years, they are of only limited use for issues extending over several decades.

Summary Description of the CANDIDE 2.0 Model

Developer and contact person: Dr. Ross Preston, Economic Council of Canada, Ottawa.

Objectives and applications: Analysis of short-term dynamics and fiscal policies; medium to long-term structural projections.

Time span: Annual iterations up to approximately one decade.

Method of modeling: Keynesian medium-term model in which the level of economic activity and prices are determined by interaction of demand and supply functions within the context of past activity levels, external influences and monetary and fiscal settings. Uses a three-step procedure in-

(cont'd. on p. 145)

(cont'd. from p. 144)	volving input-output methods. Forecasts of U.S. variables from Wharton Annual and Industry Model used as exogenous input.
Disaggregation:	Level of disaggregation differs by type of variable. 170 final demand categories. 65 sectors for real outputs. Employment, wages, unit labor costs calculated on basis of 12 sectors.
Experience of use:	See "Dynamic Properties of Four Canadian Macroeconomic Models: A Collaborative Research Project," Institute for Policy Analysis, University of Toronto, 1979.
Advantages:	Extensive disaggregation enables detailed impact studies to be made. Overall design focuses on longer run. Few exogenous assumptions needed: activity variables for Canada's trading partners, tax rates, exchange rate.

Summary Description of the TRACE
(Toronto Annual Canadian Econometric Model)

Developers and contact person:	David K. Foot and John A. Sawyer, Institute for Policy Analysis, University of Toronto.
Area of application:	Policy Analysis.
Time span:	Annual iterations up to approximately one decade.
Method of modeling:	Keynesian model in which output is determined each period by interaction of a final demand schedule for domestically produced goods with an aggregate supply schedule.
Restrictions:	Money supply is exogenous. Production and employment in agriculture are exogenous. Government and personal sectors are exogenous.
Experiences of use:	See: "Dynamic Properties of Four Canadian Macroeconomic Models: A Collaborative Research Project," Institute for Policy Analysis, University of Toronto, 1979.

Version one of the Canadian EXPLOR model, developed by the Department of Industry, Trade and Commerce has been running since 1978. It has a time horizon of 15-20 years. EXPLOR (see box following) is an input-output model incorporating a demographic sector, econometrically estimated demand equations, price formation, and inverted production functions. The model is addressed primarily to international trade. The input-output coefficients are projected exogenously. The model has a five-year, static-equilibrium projection-interval.

The Long-Term Simulation Model (LTSM) being developed by Statistics Canada consists of a set of submodels that analyze the flows of materials and energy from the resource base through the various transformation processes in the economy.[3] The submodels project stocks, flows and processes in terms of physical quantity that can be described in economic terms using current prices. The model does not represent decision-making processes and institutions in detail, and handles policies exogenously. The residential energy submodel has been developed in detail and is used as an independent model.

Summary Description of the Canadian EXPLOR Model

Developer and contact person:	W. Johnson, Department of Industry, Trade and Commerce, TSA (20) 235 Queen Street, Ottawa, Ontario K1A 0H5.
Objectives and applications:	Medium to long-term economic analysis; policy simulation.
Time span:	5-year static-equilibrium solution intervals.
Method of modeling:	Comparative static input-output model.
Applications:	Tariff effects of the multilateral trade negotiations, impact of the construction of the northern pipeline.
Disaggregation:	Production, trade, consumption, price and other data for 68 sectors.
Restrictions:	No detailed income side; limited number of policy variables; no cyclical dynamics.
Input data needed:	Macro-variables for construction of base case; impact variables, as required.
Programming language:	SIMSYS (Informetrica Ltd.), Fortran-based.
Experiences of use:	See: "A Structural Analysis of the Canadian Economy to 1990," Department of Industry, Trade and Commerce, Mar. 1978.
Advantages:	Shows intersectoral flows and dependencies; consistent sectoral disaggregation; can be adapted to wide range of scenarios.
Further developments:	New version of model in development stage, with expansion to 140 sectors.

In the LTSM, emphasis is placed on the modeling of the flows of materials and energy that are required to meet human needs. The model explicitly represents flows of resources and energy that are transformed by the economy into finished products ready for human use or consumption. The model represents: the economic transformation processes which generate flows of waste materials and thermal waste into the environment; the processes of consumption, which result in a flow of discarded goods and wastes into the environment; naturally occurring processes in the environment which react in various ways to human activity and the waste flows that emanate from it.

No attempt is made in LTSM to represent the institutional decision making processes that control economic activity, nor is any attempt made to "value" stocks or flows, or even future scenarios.

To the greatest extent possible, material and energy flows and stocks are measured in physical quantity units. Transformations are represented as relationships between input and output flows. Mass and energy balances principles are maintained and as a result the model must be disaggregatged with regard to both commodities and economic activities.

A concept of tension provides for disequilibrium between supplies and requirements for resources, energy and labor. Where discrepancies between supplies and requirements exist, the LTSM user may simulate alternative ways making supplies and requirements compatible. The model assures internal consistency and compatibility with physical, chemical and thermal laws. Materials and energy shortages can be made up through importation across national boundaries, provided that materials and energy in excess supply are exchanged for them. Accordingly, terms of trade must be handled explicitly.

The LTSM model is most usefully thought of as a set of loosely connected — but, in total, comprehensive — submodels. The disequilibrium aspects of the overall model permit block recursive solutions, which in turn make possible a development strategy that elaborates each block independently, provided that the boundaries of each block are defined at the outset.

The model is long-term in outlook, spanning a fifty-year time-horizon, but is not intended to make *predictions* over fifty years. Its analytic focus is much shorter term: decisions made in the next few years, which involve investment in facilities that have an expected life of thirty or forty years are analyzed over the life of the assets.

A first version (LTSM Version 1) was designed and implemented in the period 1974-1976. This version is operational[4] and currently consists of three major blocks: a demographic block, a demand block and a production block.

The demographic block calculates population by age and sex given immigration, emigration, fertility and mortality. Household formation is modeled using headship rates. Labor force is calculated by applying age-sex specific participation rates to the population.

The demand block consists of a number of independent submodels covering consumer expenditures, residential construction, the government's current and capital expenditures, business investment expenditures and exports. The approach is "bottom up." Categories of consumer and government expenditures are related to population, households, or relevant segments of the population. Stock/flow models of residential dwellings, automobiles and other consumer durables relate stocks to population variables using penetration rates. New production maintains required stocks after allowing for discards. Operating expenditures are related to stocks. Exogenous business investment is accumulated into stocks. Exports and the commodity composition of exports are exogenous.

The production block uses an input-output model to transform demands for goods and services from the demand block into industry activity levels and imports. Employment, capital stock and energy requirements are then related to industrial activity levels using projected employment / output, capital / output and energy / output ratios. Import share coefficients are adjusted to maintain balanced trade, given terms of trade. The concept of tension was used in two places: between labor supply (calculated in the demographic block) and labor demand; and between supplies of capital (accumulated from investment in the demand block) and requirements for capital stock (which are related to industrial activity levels in the production block.)

In spite of the fact that a number of components of the model are under-developed or not implemented (resource flows and stocks, waste flows) the model has been used to support a number of studies. Three important sets of conclusions have emerged from these studies:

(1) There is a growing imbalance between labor supply and labor demand (excess supply). Four factors contribute to this result: saturation of consumer durables, increases in labor productivity, increased female participation and the age structure of the population.

(2) Employment is invariant to the level and composition of foreign trade (assuming no change in the terms of trade.)

(3) Growth rates of energy requirements are significantly lower than those observed in the decades of sixties and seventies and are not proportional to economic growth.

The residential energy block (REM) keeps track of the stock of residential dwellings by kind of unit (single, double, row, apartments), by period of construction, by kind of heating equipment and fuel and by thermal characteristics (insulation in ceilings, walls and basements and air infiltration). REM calculates the requirements for space heat from data on type of house, thermal characteristics, external temperature, amount of sun and internal thermostat setting. The conversion of fuel to space heat is represented separately. The model keeps track of appliance stocks and energy requirements for appliances and hot water.[5] The REM model may be used in a stand-alone mode or in conjunction with the demographic model. REM is suitable for examining energy savings from changes in building standards for new houses, thermal retrofitting of existing houses, new space heating systems and efficiency improvements in space heating equipment and appliances.[6]

Plans have been made to implement a second version (LTM Version 2) of the long-term model with work started in January 1981. It is expected that the second version will be operational by the end of 1981. A number of improvements will be made, particularly with respect to the treatment of energy and energy supply.

The present model has a weakness in the input-output coefficients used to represent technological processes in the production block. A data base of industrial process descriptions is being compiled to strengthen the representation of technology. Sample data for about 250 processes have been completed.

Statistics Canada is also attempting to develop an integrated approach for documenting the impact of human activity on the environment. The work is being conducted under the "Stress Response Evaluation Statistical System (STRESS)" program. Analysis of environmental impacts has traditionally been focused on air, water, and land, with emphasis on pollution. The STRESS program focuses more on carrying capacity considerations.[7]

Forestry is a very important aspect of the Canadian economy and Canadians have developed an extensive array of models to assist in the management of Canadian forestry resources. The following material provides summary descriptions of fourteen Canadian forestry models. The models concerned are:

Roundwood consumption and timber harvest model
  Canadian Forestry Service.

A linear programming model of the Canadian forest industry
  L. Copithorne, Economic Council of Canada.

New Brunswick budworm management model
  C.S. Holling et al., IIASA.

PAPRISIM II
  Pulp and Paper Research Institute of Canada.

Modèles d'allocation et de simulation (MODAS)
  Ministère de l'Energie et des Ressources du Québec.

SIMPULP — Canadian pulp and paper simulation model
  R.A. Muller, McMaster University.

Nova Scotia forest resource model
  Nova Scotia Department of Lands and Forests.

I-O model of Ontario forest based industries
  H.C. Raizada and J.C. Nautiyal, University of Toronto.

Ontario wood supply and forest productivity model (OWOSFOP)
  Ontario Ministry of Natural Resources.

Computer assisted resources planning project (CARP)
  D.H. Williams et al., University of British Columbia and British Columbia Forest Service.

Forest estate model
  British Columbia Forest Service

Production forecast method
  British Columbia Forest Service

FORSIM
  Data Resources Inc.

Data Resources pulp and paper model
  Data Resources Inc.

Summary Description of "Budworm"

Developers and contact persons: C.S. Holling, Bill Clark, Dixon Jones and Gordon Baskerville

Area of application: Forest & Pest Management

Objectives: Testing of alternative methods, generation of alternative policies

Time span: 100-200 years.

(cont'd. on p. 150)

(cont'd. from p. 149)

Method of modeling:	(1) simulation; (2) optimization; (3) differential equations; (4) catastrophic manifolds.
Examples of real applications:	Changed forest inventory methods; basis of a task force report by Cabinet; now in process of establishing budworm control policies under Baskerville's direction.
Disaggregation:	Four hundred 6 x 9 mile grids.
Restrictions:	None.
Interrelations to other sectors:	None.
Input data needed:	Depends on which model. For field simulation model, initial tree age distribution, proportion of host trees, and the weather trace are needed.
Programming language:	FORTRAN.
Computer needs:	For full model a very large computer is needed, but various simplified versions are available.
Experiences of use:	Expensive.
Advantages:	It is robust; there are alternative models; it has been vigorously validated; it is useable at a number of levels.
Applicability to different circumstances:	The simpler versions have been successfully applied to 22 other forest pest systems.

Summary Description of
the Roundwood Consumption and Timber Harvest Model

Developer and contact person:	Keith L. Aird and Hans Ottens, Canadian Forestry Service, Ottawa, Ontario K1A 1G5.
Objectives and applications:	National timber supply/demand analysis; simulation and forecasting of varying impacts on national timber harvest levels, industrial and other roundwood consumption wood costs, forest product production and price levels.
Time span:	Annual.
Method of modeling:	Econometrics, simulation.
Applications:	See: Canadian Forest Service, Forestry Technical Report No. 29.
Restrictions:	None: The model is in the public domain.
Interrelations to other sectors:	Exogenously linked to end use industrial activity; prices and other macroeconomic

(cont'd. on p. 151)

(cont'd. from p. 150)	variables in the Wharton Annual Model of the U.S. economy and the CANDIDE model of the Canadian economy.
Input data needed:	End use industrial output, export and substitutable materials prices, forest product production cost, interest rates and other economic data on domestic and international forest product and related industries.
Programming language:	APL/Fortran-based econometric software package.
Computer needs:	Computer large enough to support software package for large-scale econometric models.
Advantages:	Allows the conduct of national assessments of impacts of policies or economic conditions on production of forest products and/or timber harvests.
Applicability to different circumstances:	Can be exogenously linked to any set of macro-econometric models of Canadian or other national economies with a similar level of industrial detail.
Further developments:	Anticipated additions include submodels to analyze the impact on wood processing costs of various inputs and to simulate timber inventory and forest growth impacts of harvesting and other practices.

**Summary Description of
"A Linear Programming Model of the Canadian Forest Industry"**

Developer and contact person:	Lawrence W. Copithorne and José Quiroga; Economic Council of Canada, P.O. Box 527, Ottawa K1P 5V6.
Objectives and applications:	Regional economic analysis, policy simulation and measurement of economic rents; finds harvesting and processing activities that maximize the industry's contribution to gross domestic product.
Time span:	One year, 1973. Dynamic extension is possible, but expensive.
Method of modeling:	Linear programming.
Applications:	Analysis of policy alternative in British Columbia. See Chapter 7 of: Lawrence

(cont'd. on p. 152)

(cont'd. from p. 151)

Copithorne, *Natural Resources and Regional Disparities,* Ottawa: Economic Council of Canada, 1979.

Disaggregation:

Sixty-five forestry zones; over 100 logging activities; over 100 sawmilling activities; co-products taken into account; 9 kinds of lumber; 10 markets for each type of lumber.

Restrictions:

Currently a static model. Currently demands fixed price and upper limit quantities. The model as it stands is now out of date.

Interrelations to other sectors:

Monitors inputs among 5 Canadian regions; integrated logging and sawmilling industry.

Input data needed:

Total allowable cut by region; processing costs; labor supplies; product prices; market demands by region.

Programming language:

MPSX (Mathematical Programming System Extended) of IBM.

Computer needs:

Any machine that can handle the IBM Standard linear programming package.

Experiences of use:

See Lawrence Copithorne, *Natural Resources and Regional Disparities,* Ottawa: Economic Council of Canada, 1979.

Advantages:

Measures natural resource rents and opportunity costs; takes into account transportation network flows and processing and marketing options.

Applicability to different circumstances:

The method is extremely valuable and flexible.

Further developments:

None planned.

Summary Description of Modèle D'Allocation et de Simulation (MODAS)

Developer and contact person: Ministère de l'Energie et des Resources du Québec; Service de l'Informatique du M.E.R.

Area of application: Conçu pour faciliter la préparation des documents "Profils biophysiques" et "Plans de gestion" pour les 44 unités de gestion qui divisent la province de Québec.

Objectives: Déterminer le niveau de coupe maximum sans rupture de stock que peut supporter un

(cont'd. on p. 153)

(cont'd. from p. 152)

territoire pendant un nombre d'années dé-
termine.

Déterminer la dimension du territoire requis
pour soutenir un niveau de coupe fixé à
l'avance.

Estimer les coûts reliés à la récolte de la
matière ligneuse. Les trois éléments peuvent
être considérés dans une perspective plus large
visant à faciliter les prises de décision con-
cernant l'aménagement d'un territoire.

Time span: Variable en fonction du but de la simulation
et du type de forêt que supporte le territoire
visé: 10-20 ans dans le cas d'une liquidation
pour un territoire, 120-150 ans dans le cas du
calcul d'un rendement soutenu.

Applications: 1979 Unité de gestion "Baie des Chaleurs
(12)": Evaluation des niveaux de couple sous
rendement soutenu sur un horizon de 120 ans
suivant que l'on envisage ou non un programme de reboisement.

1979 Unité de gestion "Rivière Rouge (61)"
et "Assomption-Mattawin (62)": Evaluation
de la Baisse de possibilité causée par la mise en
place future du Parc Mont-Tremblant, suivant
plusieurs tracés susceptibles d'être retenus.

1978 Unité de gestion "Quévillon (87)":
Calcul de la variation de la proportion sciage
du volume récolté en fonction du diamètre
fin bout requis pour les billes de sciage.

1978 Unité de gestion "Chibougameau (26)":
Détermination d'un rayon économique autour
d'un point de transformation en fonction
d'un coût maximum fixe pour le bois livré à
l'usine.

Restrictions: Le modèle utilise comme donnée de base les
résultats compilés par le service de l'Inven-
taire forestier et qui sont gardés sur fichier
informatique. Le territoire qu'on désire analy-
ser doit donc avoir été l'objet d'un inventaire.

De plus le modèle est soumis à la précision de
cet inventaire ce qui signifie que pour la grande
majorité des travaux fait à ce jour, le terri-

(cont'd. on p. 154)

(cont'd. from p. 153)

toire doit au moins couvrir un bassin-secon-
daire ce qui est un minimum pour l'utilisation
des résultats de l'inventaire décennal.

Enfin le facteur limitatif le plus important est
sans doute le manque de données de base,
permettant de bien décrire le dynamisme de la
forêt. En fait, dans son état actuel le modèle
permet de simuler l'aménagement intensif,
faisant intervenïr de l'éclaircie précommerciale, de l'éclaircie commerciale et de la
fertilisation, mais les données permettant d'ex-
primer l'effet de tels traitements sur l'évolution des strates sont à ce jour trop peu nom-
breuses ce qui diminue considérablement la
valeur des résultats qu'on pourrait obtenir
grâce au modèle.

Les données décrivant le scénario d'aménagement envisagé: le programme de traitement
appliqué à chaque strate et qui comprend ou
non de l'éclaircie précommerciale, de l'éclaircie commerciale et de la fertilisation, et qui se
termine toujours par une coupe finale, suivie
ou non par du reboisement artificiel.

Les données décrivant les coûts de la coupe
finale, du changement, du transport, de la
construction et de l'entretien des routes, etc.

Experiences of use: Utilization très intensives depuis 5 années et
des milliers de simulations nécessaires à la
confection des documents "Plan de gestion"
et "Profil biophysique" des 44 unités de gestion, et pour répondre à quantité de demandes
spécifiques en dehors de ce mandat original.

Advantages: L'emploi d'un modèle informatique permet
évidemment de manipuler rapidement et de
façon sure, les données existantes et de com-
piler de l'information sur l'état actuel de la
forêt, ce qui est déjà un net avantage. Mais
l'aspect le plus intéressant est qu'il nous est
permis de simuler, c'est-à-dire de prévoir, dans
une certaine mesure, l'évolution probable de
la forêt. Les nouvelles données facilitent
grandement les prises de décision en aménagement forestier.

(cont'd. on p. 155)

(cont'd. from p. 154)

Further Developments:	Amélioration au niveau des données de base grâce au remesurage des parcelles-échantillon permanentes.
	Des modifications sont en cours afin de rendre possible l'introduction de données relatives aux pertes dues à la tordeuse des bourgeons de l'épinette.
	Des modifications sont prévues afin de pouvoir obtenir de meilleures données en terme de biomasse.
Disaggregation:	Unités de gestion (44 pour la province de Québec). Unités d'aménagement (de 1 à 4 par U.G., 69 pour le Québec). Parcelles (300 à 400 par U.A.).
Programming language:	Assembler, COBOL, FORTRAN.
Computer needs:	IBM 3033, MVS 3.8, 700K Vs.

Summary Description of
the Canadian Pulp and Paper Simulation Model (SIMPULP)

Developer and contact person:	Dr. R.A. Muller, Department of Economics, McMaster University, Hamilton, Ontario.
Application and objectives:	Canadian Pulp and Paper Industry, model response of output and employment to change in cost of production.
Time span:	Estimated for 1947-1969.
Method of modeling:	An econometric industry model containing 14 stochastic equations estimated econometrically together with a number of identities.
Applications:	Estimated impact of pollution control requirements on levels of employment and output.
Disaggregation:	Output disaggregated to newsprint, woodpulp, other paper and board.
Restrictions:	The model would need to be re-estimated for application to a different time period.
Interrelations to other sectors:	No explicit connections.
Input data needed:	Selected macroeconomic variable including exchange rate, U.S. newsprint circulation, Canadian and U.S. GNP.
Programming language:	FORTRAN.

(cont'd. on p. 156)

(cont'd. from p. 155)

Computer needs:	Minimal.
Experiences of use:	Output and employment show low response to cost changes.
Advantages:	Consistency with economic theory. Parameters are estimated from historical data.
Applicability to different circumstances:	The structure is dependent on features of the Canadian industry.
Further developments:	An alternative approach to econometric modeling of production in the industry has been developed by the author. This new approach could be incorporated in a revised model.

Summary Description of the Nova Scotia Forest Resource Model

Developer:	For Nova Scotia Department of Lands and Forests, N.S. Research Foundation Corp. and Woods Gordon & Co.
Contact persons:	G. Peter MacQuarrie (N.S.L.&F.) or K. Runyon (C.F.S., Fred. N.B.)
Area of application:	Province of Nova Scotia.
Objectives:	A generalized model for policy evaluation of provincial and regional effects of developmental programs.
Time span:	One year periods; base data 1974; maximum 20 years.
Method of modeling:	Repetitive simulation, supply solution via 2 step, allocation algorithm.
Example of real applications:	None available.
Disaggregation:	167 supply zones; 3 ownerships; 10 products; 55 mill locations; 3 covertypes.
Interrelations to other sectors:	Primary and secondary forestry sectors only. Assume derived demand selling in an elastic market.
Input data needed:	Extensive.
Programming language:	FORTRAN IV & PL1, UCANDU Utility
Computer needs:	IBM 360 or 370 (OS or VS), 700 K, 1/2 Pack File Storage (3330 Drive), two 9-track tape drives.
Experiences of use:	Model is still in the prototype stage.
Further developments:	None proposed at present.

**Summary Description of
an Input-Output Model of Ontario Forest-Based Industries**

Developer and contact persons: H.C. Raizada and J.C. Nautiyal, Faculty of
Forestry, University of Toronto.

Area of application: Inter-forest industry relationships in Ontario.

Objectives: To get some idea of the inter-connectedness
of forest industries.

Time span: 1969.

Method of modeling: Regular input-output model construction.

Applications: Used at the time of the preparation of "The
Forest Industry in the Economy of Ontario"
by the Ontario Ministry of Natural Resources.

Disaggregation: All forest industries were disaggregated into
18 industries.

Restrictions: Restricted to forest industry.

Interrelations to other sectors: Not related to other sectors.

Input data needed: Input and output figures for various industries.

Programming language: FORTRAN IV.

Computer needs: Modest.

Experiences of use: See "Applications," above.

Advantages: Simple to understand.

Applicability to different
circumstances: Cannot be used in other provinces, but gives
reasonable idea about the inter-industry con-
nections in the late 1960s and early 1970s.

Further developments: Mr. Raizada made another model for Ontario
Ministry of Natural Resources.

**Summary Description of the
Ontario Wood Supply and Forest Productivity Model (OWOSFOP)**

Developer and contact persons: Dr. Frank Raymond, Dr. John Osborn

Area of application: Forest Inventory changes over time

Objectives: Determination of allowable cut and illustration
of impacts of cutting/regeneration strategies
on forest.

Time span: Variable, currently at 120 years in 5 year
intervals.

Method of modeling: Simulation.

(cont'd. on p. 158)

(cont'd. from p. 157)

Applications:	Direct use for determination of calculated allowable cut. Shows possible state of forest over time for specific management strategies.
Disaggregation:	Forest data by working group (cover type), site class, and acres and volumes by age classes.
Restrictions:	Needs inventory data on acres and volumes by age classes in regular divisions, i.e., 20 years.
Interrelations to other sectors:	None.
Input data needed:	Acres and volumes by age class.
Programming language:	FORTRAN IV.
Computer needs:	Run on PDP 10. Versions require 16-60K. Used interactively, not batch.
Experiences of use:	Used by field forester to determine allowable cuts and effects of management on allowable cuts.
Advantages:	Faster and more versatile than existing system; permits analysis of previously unanswered questions.
Applicability to different circumstances:	Can use any forest inventory data (if available) as stated above in Restrictions/Input data needed.
Further developments:	Improve calibration, partition volume into species.
Other comments:	This model is still in a very primitive form and contains some very large biological assumptions.

Summary Description of
the Computer Assisted Resource Planning Model (CARP)

Developers:	D.H. Williams, G.G. Young, S.M. Smith, J.C. McPhalen, and M.M. Yamada
Contact person:	D.H. Williams
Area of application:	Timber supply estimation
Objectives:	To determine harvest rates for sustained yield units in British Columbia.
Time span:	1 - 2 rotations (up to 200 years).
Method of modeling:	Linear programming.

(cont'd. on p. 159)

(cont'd. from p. 158)

Applications:	British Columbia Ministry of Forests Timber Supply Area (TSA) analysis.
Disaggregation:	Not applicable.
Restrictions:	None; model is in the public domain.
Interrelations to other sectors:	None.
Input data needed:	Inventory data; volume age curves.
Programming language:	FORTRAN, IBM MPSX
Computer needs:	Large mainframe, e.g., IBM 370-168, IBM 3033, Ahmdahl
Applicability to different circumstances:	Specific to British Columbia crown land management.
Other comments:	The CARP project ceased in 1976, and metamorphosized into the British Columbia MOF Production Forecast Method used in their TSA analyses. The initial installation work was accomplished by Dr. Steven Smith, and is now maintained by Mr. Darrell Erico of the BC MOF Planning Division.

Summary Description of the Forest Estate Model

Developer and contact person:	Dr. S.M. Smith, Strategic Studies Branch, B.C.F.S., Victoria, B.C.
Application and objectives:	Timber supply analysis; to allow strategic analyses of wood supplies and to simulate the forest dynamics of harvested forest stocks.
Time span:	Up to 150 years.
Method of modeling:	Simulation model of the inventory projection type.
Applications:	Forest and Range Resource Analysis and Five-Year Program, B.C.F.S., March 1980.
Disaggregation:	Any forest estate.
Restrictions:	None.
Interrelations to other sectors:	Through Land Base and Harvesting Rules.
Input data needed:	Area summaries; yield equations; land base and harvesting rules; required levels of harvest.
Programming language:	FORTRAN IV
Computer needs:	IBM 148, or larger.

(cont'd. on p. 160)

(cont'd. from p. 159)

Experiences of use:	Analysis of wood supplies in British Columbia, and silvicultural program development.
Advantages:	Very flexible; simple data requirements; easily understood output; relates industrial expectations to biological capability.
Applicability to different circumstances:	Wide possibilities.
Further developments:	Simple links to large scale economics are being developed.
Other comments:	This model has proved to be extremely successful in analyzing wood supplies under a wide range of conditions. Results and output have been directly useful in developing basic and intensive programs of forest management.

Summary Description of the "Production Forecast Method"

Developers:	Dr. S.M. Smith, later modified by D.W. Ormerod and D. Errico, all of the B.C. Forest Service
Contact persons:	D. Errico, Planning Branch, B.C.F.S., Victoria, B.C.: Dr. S.M. Smith, Strategic Studies Branch, B.C.F.S., Victoria, B.C.
Application and objectives:	Timber supply analysis; to develop allowable cuts for Timber Supply Areas.
Time span:	Up to 350 years.
Method of modeling:	Linear programming.
Applications:	Fort Nelson Timber Supply Area Allowable Cut
Disaggregation:	Timber supply area.
Restrictions:	Those of Timber Ram and harvesting rules.
Interrelations to other sectors:	Through land base and harvesting rules.
Input data needed:	Area summaries; yield equations; land base; and harvesting rules.
Programming language:	FORTRAN IV and PL1
Computer needs:	IBM 370
Experiences of use:	Several timber supply areas.
Advantages:	Recognizes log supply patterns and transportation facilities within the timber supply area;

(cont'd. on p. 161)

(cont'd. from p. 160)

has the advantage of linear programming techniques.

Applicability to different circumstances:

Fairly good possibilities.

Other comments:

See: S.M. Smith 1978 "A Two Phase Method for Timber Supply Analysis" published in the Proceedings of "Operational Forest Management Planning Methods," Pacific Southwest Forest and Range Experiment Station, U.S.D.A., General Technical Report PSM-32.

Summary Description of the "FORSIM" Forest Sector Models

Developers:

Johan Veltkamp, Bernard Fuller, Data Resources Inc. (DRI)

Contact persons:

Salley Foskett, Bernard Fuller

Area of application:

U.S. and Canada; softwood and hardwood lumber; softwood plywood; particleboard; hardboard; waferboard and oriented strandboard.

Objectives:

Forecast demand, supply and prices for above product areas; forecast stumpage availability and prices.

Time span:

Quarterly and monthly model, forecast horizons from one month to 20 years.

Method of modeling:

Econometrics.

Examples of real applications:

Regular quarterly and monthly forecasts for forest products companies and other clients; special products to analyze policy impacts on the forest products industry, and investment alternatives.

Disaggregation:

Data and forecasts disaggregated to regional level in the United States for both demand and supply; for supply only in Canada. 50 grade/dimension items are modeled.

Restrictions:

Ongoing development to simulate feedbacks into model; e.g., product prices help determine stumpage prices which in turn determine relative regional costs and market shares and in turn feed back into demand, supply and product price.

(cont'd. on p. 162)

(cont'd. from p. 161)

Interrelations to other sectors:	Models are derived from macroeconomic indicators combined with use factors. Little direct feedback into macromodels from industry models, but interrelation between each of the industry sectors is available.
Input data needed:	Macroeconomic variables; remainder is endogenous.
Programming language:	DRI package.
Computer needs:	Burroughs mainframe
Experiences of use:	Model has been in use in early form since 1970; additions and new developments lead to a constant upgrading and improvement of the model.
Advantages:	Provides a dynamic overview of the solid-wood products industry allowing sensitivity analyses.
Applicability to different circumstances:	Very flexible tool for short and long-term planning. Model enables user to use own assumptions on many levels.
Further developments:	Development is ongoing — additional product areas, more regional breakouts, and further integration into macro and industry models.
Other comments:	The FORSIM Model has been utilized by up to 40 clients over a 10 year period.

Summary Description of the "Pulp and Paper" Models

Developers:	Johan Veltkamp and Rodney Young, Pulp and Paper Group, Data Resources Inc. (DRI).
Contact persons:	Sally Foskett, Rodney Young
Area of application:	Demand and supply model for pulpwood, pulp, and paper in the United States, Canada, Scandinavia, Western Europe and Japan.
Objectives:	Forecast demand, supply, trade and prices for pulpwood, pulp and paper in the regions covered. Ability to simulate the model.
Time span:	Continuing development work, modeling was begun in 1977.
Method of modeling:	Econometrics
Applications:	Quarterly forecasts used in DRI Pulp and

(cont'd. on p. 163)

(cont'd. from p. 162)

	Paper Reviews; numerous special projects done for clients.
Disaggregation:	The model is very detailed, especially for North America. The U.S. sector includes modeling of 50 paper and board grades, 9 pulp grades, and regional pulpwood and wastepaper markets. Five major paper and board groups and the major chemical pulps are modeled on an international basis.
Restrictions:	The major restrictions are that the submodels are not completely integrated and the size of the model makes it costly to run.
Interrelations to other sectors:	The Pulp and Paper Model is closely tied to other sectors of the economy through indicators of demand for paper and board products and through production costs such as energy, chemical, capital, etc.
Input data needed:	Input requirements are mainly information on the general economy and other industrial sectors.
Programming language:	Data Resources internal language.
Computer needs:	The size of the model makes computer needs extensive.
Experiences of use:	The experiences of using the model have been mainly favorable. The size and complexity of the model are both its major advantages and disadvantages. A substantial amount of knowledge about the model and computer resources is necessary to solve the model.
Advantages:	The advantages of the model are its accurate representation of the functioning of the pulp and paper industry, the integrated nature of the model, and its large scope.
Applicability to different circumstances:	One of the major objectives in building the model was to create a simulation tool. The model has many entry points to enhance the incorporation of different scenarios. The model gives consistent, integrated output for each alternative.
Further developments:	Development work is continually in process. Present development work is on world wood markets, LDC pulp and paper demand, and interrelationships between different printing and writing grades in the United States.

References

1. W. Leontief et al., *The Future of the World Economy,* New York: Oxford University Press, 1977.
2. For further details on the work done to date, see H.S. Postner, "Canada and the Future of the International Economy: A Global Modeling Analysis," Discussion Paper No. 129, Ottawa: Economic Council of Canada, March 1979.
3. R.B. Hoffman, "Users Guide to the Statistics Canada Long Term Simulation Model," Ottawa: Structural Analysis Division, Statistics Canada, February 1977; "Structural Analysis Division Document Index," Ottawa: Statistics Canada, February 1981.
4. "Structural Analysis Division," Ottawa: Statistics Canada.
5. S.F. Gribble, "Appliance Model: Reference Manual and Illustrations," Working Paper No. 80/07/31, Ottawa: Structural Analysis Division, Statistics Canada.
6. S.F. Gribble and K.E. Hamilton, "Energy Futures: Scenarios and Perturbations," Working Paper 77/11/01, Ottawa: Structural Analysis Division, Statistics Canada; R.H.H. Moll, K.H. Dickinson, and R.B. Hoffman, "Alternative Off Oil Scenarios for Ontario: Results Obtained from Statistics Canada Housing Model," Ottawa: Structural Analysis Division, Statistics Canada, January, 1981.
7. A. Friend, "Conceptual Framework and a Unified Approach to Environmental Statistics," invited paper for the 42nd Session of the International Statistical Institute, Manila, Phillipines, Dec. 4-14, 1979.

Appendix C
U.S. Global Models of Potential Interest to Canada

There are four global models that have been developed in the United States and that are of potential interest to Canada. These are the U.S. Government's global model (used in the Global 2000 Study), the World 2 and World 3 models, the World Integrated Model, and the U.N. World Model. Each of these models is described briefly in the following paragraphs.[1]

The U.S. Government's Global Model

The third volume of the Global 2000 Study[2] presents basic documentation on the long-term sectoral models used by the U.S. Government to project global trends in population, resources and the environment. These models were the basis of the projections developed for the Global 2000 Study.

Each of the sectoral models described in volume 3 of the Global 2000 Study is a Government developed or Government endorsed model. Most of the models were developed directly by Government agencies. Three of the models — the GNP model, the nonfuel minerals demand model, and one of the population models — were developed by non-Governmental organizations, but have been applied or recommended by one or more Government agencies as being the best models available for the particular types of projections they provide.

Collectively, the sectoral models are referred to throughout the Global 2000 Study as the Government's "global model." This term is more than a convenient means of reference. Collectively the sectoral models described here provide the U.S. Government with the same type of projections that other global models provide their users — projections of population, GNP, food, energy, minerals, water, environment, etc.

The Government's global model is different from other global models in several ways. First, the sectors of the Government's global model do not reside in a single computer but are located around Washington (and in other cities) in the computers of different departments and agencies, and non-Governmental organizations. The location of the sectors, however, is only a matter of convenience. All of the sectors — including those that are now only computational procedures performed with a calculator or adding machine — could be placed in a single computer without altering in any way their functioning.

An important way in which the Government's global model differs from other global models is that there are only very limited interactions among the sectors of the Government's global model. In most global models, the various sectors (food, population, energy, water, etc.) interact extensively. In the Government's global model intersectoral interactions are severely limited. Prior to the Global 2000 Study the primary

165

mode of interaction among the sectoral models was not via a data channel or magnetic tape, but via the Government Printing Office (GPO). The departments and agencies made projections with their sectors of the Government's global model, and sent the results to GPO. Subsequently, GPO published a report. Other agencies then purchased the report and transferred the new sectoral projection into other sectors of the Government's global model.

It is important to recognize that when the Government departments and agencies designed or adopted the various sectors of the Government's global model, the sectors were not designed to be used as a well integrated, collective whole. Instead, it was assumed — implicitly or explicitly — that each sector (and department) acted more or less independently of the other sectors (and departments), and that the glacial interaction of the sectors through GPO was sufficient to insure the degree of internal consistency needed for the Government's global policy analysis. In recent years this assumption has come increasingly into question. Few knowledgeable analysts now believe it acceptable, for example, to assume each and every sector will have access to all of the land, energy, water, and capital that it may need, which is an assumption inherent in essentially every sector of the Government's global model, an assumption that follows directly from the lack of integration.

The Global 2000 Study was able to increase slightly the degree of integration in the Government's global model by accelerating and expanding somewhat the interactions among some of the sectors. This process first involved bringing people together. Prior to this study, not one of the persons ultimately responsible for the long-term global projections in any of the participating agencies knew anyone with a similar responsibility in any other agency. The Global 2000 Study identified these people, brought them together, and found ways to improve and increase the interactions among the sectors of the Government's global model. The results achieved — described in volume 2 of the Study,[3] especially in Chapters 1 and 14 — still fall far short of the interlinkages achieved in many other global models.

In spite of the discipline established by the Global 2000 Study to ensure consistency, a number of internal contradictions were inherent in the analysis and, unavoidably, they remain. To put it simply, the analysis reported in volume 2 of the Study (Chapter 14) shows that the executive agencies of the U.S. Government are not now capable of presenting the President with internally consistent projections of world trends in population, resources, and the environment for the next two decades.

These contradictions do not completely invalidate the overall results of the Study — in fact, the Study's projections are the most consistent such set the government has ever produced — but they do suggest that the results of the projections understate the severity of potential future problems. The analysis also points to ways in which the quality of the government's long-term analytic tools can be improved.

One of the most important findings of the Study is that the sectoral trends interact with each other in the real world in ways that are not represented in the U.S. Government's global model — essentially because of the institutional context in which the elements of the model were developed and are being used. This context emphasizes sectoral concerns at the expense of interactions among sectors and leads to distorted and mutually inconsistent projections. Important decisions — involving billion dollar federal programs and even the national security — are partially based on these projections. For these reasons, the Global 2000 Study specifically recommended that efforts be made to improve significantly the quality of the U.S. Government's analytical tools.

The World 2 and World 3 Models

The World models were developed for the Club of Rome's[4] project on The Predicament of Mankind. World 2 was developed by Jay W. Forrester and published in his book, *World Dynamics.*[5] World 3 was developed by Dennis Meadows et al., and is the basis for the first report to the Club of Rome, *The Limits to Growth.*[6]

The World models are based on the System Dynamics methodology. This methodology was developed by Jay W. Forrester at the Massachusetts Institute of Technology. System Dynamics is a specific philosophy or approach to the development of dynamic simulation models. The resulting models represent reality in terms of sets of coupled, nonlinear differential equations — a technique of long-standing success in engineering and economics.

The World models are relatively simple global models and have been highly controversial.[7] Critics and admirers alike generally agree that these models stimulated much useful rethinking of population, resource, environmental and developmental issues. These models also demonstrated how highly interrelated these considerations have become.

The World Integrated Model

The World Integrated Model (WIM) was developed by M. Mesarovic of Case Western Reserve University and E. Pestel of the University of Hannover as the basis for the second report to the Club of Rome. The results of the analysts were published in 1974 in a book entitled *Mankind at the Turning Point,*[8] which reaches conclusions that are only somewhat less frightening than those of *The Limits to Growth.*

The WIM model, however, is much more elaborate than the original World models. A disadvantage to the model, however, is that the published documentation[9] is far less detailed than that available for the World models. At least three U.S. Government agencies[10] are now attempting to understand the WIM model and evaluate its potential for policy analysis.

The U.N. World Model

In response to the controversy produced by the reports to the Club of Rome, the United Nations contracted with W. Leontief to analyze the prospects for world development. The resulting report was published in *The Future of the World Economy.*[11]

The U.N. World model uses the input-output methodology developed by Leontief. The equations for the model are published as an appendix to *The Future of The World Economy.*

The Economic Council of Canada (ECC) has shown interest in the U.N. World Model. This model treats the United States and Canada as a single North American Region (NAR), one of fifteen regions in the U.N. Model. The ECC has attempted to separate Canada out of the NAR without going to the full effort of disaggregating the model into sixteen regions.

References

1. Additional information on these and other global models can be found in *The Global 2000 Report to the President,* vol. 2, *The Technical Report,* Washington:

Government Printing Office, 1980, pp. 453-681.

2. *The Global 2000 Report to the President,* vol. 3, *Documentation on the Government's Global Sectoral Models: The Government's "Global Model,"* Washington: Government Printing Office, 1981. (The discussion in this appendix of the U.S. Government's global model is drawn largely from the preface to volume 3 of the Global 2000 Study.)

3. *Global 2000,* vol. 2.

4. For information on the Club of Rome, see: A. Peccei, *The Human Quality,* Oxford: Pergamon Press, 1977.

5. J.W. Forrester, *World Dynamics,* Cambridge, Mass.: The M.I.T. Press, 1971.

6. Reports on the Club of Rome's project on The Predicament of Mankind: D.H. Meadows, D.L. Meadows, J. Randers, and W.W. Behrens III, *The Limits to Growth,* New York: Universe Books, 1972; D.L. Meadows et al., *Dynamics of Growth in a Finite World,* Cambridge, Mass.: The M.I.T. Press, 1974; D.L. Meadows and D.H. Meadows, *Toward Global Equilibrium: Collected Papers,* Cambridge, Mass.: The M.I.T. Press, 1973.

7. See, for example: H.S.D. Cole, *Models of Doom,* New York: Universe Books, 1973; W.L. Oltmans, *On Growth: The Debate of the Century,* New York: G.P. Putnam, 1974; W.L. Oltmans, *On Growth II: The Debate of the Century,* New York, G.P. Putnam, 1975.

8. M. Mesarovic and E. Pestel, *Mankind at the Turning Point,* New York: Reader's Digest Press, 1974.

9. B.B. Hughes, *World Modeling,* Lexington: Lexington Books, 1980.

10. Wassily Leontief et al., *The Future of The World Economy,* New York: Oxford University Press, 1977.

Index